Sociolinguistics in Wa

Mercedes Durham • Jonathan Morris
Editors

Sociolinguistics in Wales

palgrave
macmillan

Editors
Mercedes Durham
Cardiff University
Cardiff, United Kingdom

Jonathan Morris
Cardiff University
Cardiff, United Kingdom

ISBN 978-1-137-52896-4   ISBN 978-1-137-52897-1   (eBook)
DOI 10.1057/978-1-137-52897-1

Library of Congress Control Number: 2016956499

Cover image © ilolab - Fotolia

Printed on acid-free paper

This Palgrave Macmillan imprint is published by Springer Nature
The registered company is Macmillan Publishers Ltd.
The registered company address is: The Campus, 4 Crinan Street, London, N1 9XW, United Kingdom

Contents

Author Bios

Patrick Carlin is a Research Associate at the School of Welsh, Cardiff University. His research interests focus on the relationship between language policy, political communities and territory. He is the co-author of *The Welsh Language Commissioner in Context: Roles, Methods and Relationships* (2016) and has written articles in *Regional and Federal Studies* and *The International Journal of the Sociology of Language* on language and identity in a number of regions of Europe from a comparative perspective.

Daniel Cunliffe is a Reader in the School of Computing and Mathematics at the University of South Wales. His research explores the relationship between technology and minority language maintenance and revitalisation. He is currently researching language behaviour in social media and the role of technology in language behaviour change. He has published in a number of journals including *Journal of Computer-Mediated Communication, Journal of Multilingual and Multicultural Development* and *Sociolinguistic Studies*.

Peredur Davies is a Senior Lecturer in Welsh Linguistics at the School of Linguistics and English Language at Bangor University, Wales, where he teaches primarily through the medium of Welsh. His Ph.D. was earned at Bangor (2010) and investigated word-order convergence in Welsh, including a focus on code-switching. His current research interests also include the sociolinguistics of Welsh, Welsh–English bilingualism and morphosyntactic change in Welsh.

Margaret Deuchar is Emeritus Professor in Linguistics at Bangor University and Affiliated Lecturer in the Department of Theoretical and Applied Linguistics,

University of Cambridge. Her research is on bilingualism, especially corpus-based approaches to code-switching. She has collected and analysed data on Welsh–English, Welsh-Spanish and Spanish-English. She is especially interested in the role of linguistic and extra-linguistic factors in influencing code-switching patterns, and in what we can learn from interdisciplinary approaches.

Kevin Donnelly has worked on a number of under-resourced languages (most recently Welsh, Māori, Swahili and Gàidhlig) with the aim of producing new language-related materials such as corpora, taggers and writing systems (kevin-donnelly.org.uk). He has a particular interest in using free and open-source software to construct these resources.

Mercedes Durham is a Senior Lecturer in Sociolinguistics at Cardiff University. She does research on language variation and change, focusing particularly on dialects of English, the acquisition of variation and attitudes. She has written a monograph on *The Acquisition of Sociolinguistic Competence in a Lingua Franca Context* and published in a wide range of journals including *Journal of Sociolinguistics, English Language and Linguistics, English World-Wide, Journal of English Linguistics* and *Language Variation and Change.*

Jeremy Evas is a Lecturer at the School of Welsh, Cardiff University, following a career as freelance translator, and as Director of Policy and Terminology at the Welsh Language Board, and Director of Strategy at the inception of the Welsh Language Commissioner. His main research and teaching interest is language planning, for Welsh and other languages. His work centres on language technology, software localisation, translation software, language policy and language behaviour change.

Amal Hallak is a Research Fellow at Cardiff University, working with Dr. Frances Rock as part of the team on the AHRC-funded project: Translation and Translanguaging: investigating linguistic and Cultural Transformations in Superdiverse Wards in Four UK Cities. Together they research how people use Arabic alongside in English in everyday life in the Cathays area of Cardiff. Amal is finishing her Ph.D. in Critical and Cultural studies at the Centre for Critical and Cultural Theory, Cardiff University. Her research interests are in sociolinguistic and cultural studies, translation, literary theory and fashion. In particular, she is fascinated by the linguistic and cultural constructions of identity in both migrant and indigenous communities.

Diarmait Mac Giolla Chríost is a Professor in the School of Welsh at Cardiff University. He has written widely on various aspects of language planning and policy and the sociology of language. His books include *Language, Identity and Conflict; Language and the City; Jailtacht. The Irish Language, Symbolic Power and Political Violence in Northern Ireland* (nominated for the Orwell Prize); and *The Welsh Language Commissioner in Context.*

Robert Mayr is a Senior Lecturer in Linguistics at the Centre for Speech and Language Therapy and Hearing Science, Cardiff Metropolitan University, and a Research Associate at the Centre for Research on Bilingualism, Bangor University. His research is interested in understanding speech development in bilinguals and multilinguals across the lifespan, with a focus on the phonetic and phonological aspects of first and second language acquisition, first language attrition, language contact and atypical development.

Ineke Mennen is a Professor of English Applied Linguistics at the Department of English Studies, University of Graz. She is interested in understanding along which dimensions speech, and in particular prosody, differs across languages or language varieties, and how such differences are generated in speech production, evaluated in speech perception, acquired in first or second language acquisition, and lost or broken down in conditions of attrition or speech impairment.

Chris Montgomery is a Lecturer in Dialectology at the University of Sheffield. His research concerns Perceptual Dialectology, with a specific interest in methodological approaches to the study of non-linguists' perceptions. Chris has published articles in the *Journal of Sociolinguistics,* the *Journal of Linguistic Geography,* and *Studies in Variation, Contacts and Change in English.* He was the editor (alongside Jennifer Cramer) of *Cityscapes and Perceptual Dialectology: Global Perspectives on Non-linguists' Knowledge of the Dialect Landscape* (Mouton de Gruyter), and with Karen Corrigan of a special issue of *English Language and Linguistics* on the role of place in historical linguistics. In addition, he has published numerous book chapters in other edited collections.

Jonathan Morris is a *Coleg Cymraeg Cenedlaethol* Lecturer in Linguistics and Applied Linguistics at the School of Welsh, Cardiff University. His research focuses on sociolinguistic aspects of bilingualism and second language acquisition. In particular, he is interested in phonetic and phonological variation in Welsh–English bilinguals' speech and completed his Ph.D. on this subject in 2013 (University of Manchester). He has recently published on attitudes towards Welsh in the *International Journal of the Sociology of Language* and on phonetics and Welsh–English bilingualism in the *International Journal of Bilingualism.*

Heli Paulasto is a Senior Lecturer in English Linguistics at the University of Eastern Finland. She specialises in dialectology, sociolinguistics and contact linguistics, with a focus on the morphosyntax of Welsh, Celtic and other contact-induced varieties of English as well as learner Englishes. She is the author of *Welsh English Syntax: Contact and Variation* (2006) and co-author of *English and Celtic in Contact* (2008, with Markku Filppula and Juhani Klemola) and the forthcoming book *Welsh English* (with Rob Penhallurick).

Caroline Piercy works in Text-to-Speech internationalisation in the Speech team at Google. Her interests are in the field of Language Variation and Change. She completed BA Linguistics at the University of Sussex and MA and Ph.D. Linguistics at the University of Essex. Following that she was a research assistant at Stanford University and was a Mellon Career Development Fellow at Oxford University. Her Ph.D. examined phonetic and phonological change in the BATH vowel in Dorset in the southwest of England.

Frances Rock is a Reader in the Centre for Language and Communication Research at Cardiff University. Her work investigates the mediation of experiences in social worlds through language and other means. Frances' research has focussed on the examination of language and communication in policing contexts and workplaces. Frances' publications include the monograph "Communicating Rights: the language of arrest and detention" (2007) and the co-edited collection "Legal-Lay Communication: Textual Travels in the Law" (2013). She is an Editor of the *International Journal of Speech, Language and the Law*. She is currently working on the AHRC-funded research project entitled: Translation and Translanguaging: Investigating Linguistic and Cultural Transformations in Superdiverse Wards in Four UK Cities.

List of Figures

List of Tables

Part 1

Introduction

1

An Overview of Sociolinguistics in Wales

Mercedes Durham and Jonathan Morris

Nod y bennod gyntaf yw rhoi trosolwg o sosioieithyddiaeth yng Nghymru a chyflwyno'r ymchwil sydd yn ymddangos yn y gyfrol. Yn gyntaf, rydym yn ystyried y sefyllfa ieithyddol yng Nghymru ac yn crynhoi hanes cyffyrddiad rhwng y Gymraeg a'r Saesneg. Yn ail, rydym yn cyflwyno adolygiad o waith blaenorol ar sosioieithyddiaeth yng Nghymru. Yn drydydd, trafodir y penodau eraill yn y gyfrol ac, i gloi, rydym yn pwyso a mesur cyfeiriadau posibl ar gyfer ymchwil yn y dyfodol.

Introduction

If you ask someone about language in Wales, the fact that it is a bilingual country inevitably comes up. On the surface, this is accurate, as both Welsh and English have official status and there are many Welsh–English bilingual speakers. In practice, the level of bilingualism varies between communities and there are differences in the way Welsh is acquired, with some learning at home and some through school.

M. Durham (✉) • J. Morris
Cardiff University, Cardiff, UK

© The Author(s) 2016   **3**
M. Durham, J. Morris (eds.), *Sociolinguistics in Wales*,
DOI 10.1057/978-1-137-52897-1_1

A long history of campaigning for increased rights (Williams 2008: Chapter 8) has led to recent legislation which aims to ensure that Welsh is not treated any less favourably than English in Wales (Welsh Language Measure 2011). The Welsh Language Measure not only establishes Welsh as an official language in Wales, but also places responsibility on a number of official and non-official organisations to provide services in Welsh. The Measure and other legislation are seen as vital to not only guarantee parity between the languages, but also to ensure that Welsh remains a living language. As we will discuss below, the situation of contact between Welsh and English has been fraught at times and the increase of the English language in Wales has been the result of a number of societal changes. The twentieth century has seen English become the most widely spoken language in Wales because of language shift in some areas and widespread bilingualism among Welsh speakers.

The situation of Welsh and English in Wales makes it interesting for linguistics generally, and sociolinguistics especially, not least because it is distinctive compared to the rest of the UK. This volume aims to showcase some of the research recently conducted on Wales and to underline how valuable insight from the country is to understand broader sociolinguistic questions.

This chapter acts as an introduction to the volume as a whole, outlining the current linguistic situation of Wales and the history of Welsh and English in the country. We then provide an overview of earlier sociolinguistic research on Wales, before briefly introducing the chapters in the volume. The chapter will close with a discussion of what kinds of future research might be valuable to understand the language situation in Wales in the context of ongoing societal changes.

Languages Spoken in Wales Today

The most up-to-date source of information about language use in Wales is found in the 2011 National Census (Office for National Statistics 2012). There are two sets of questions which are relevant to our discussion: one question which asks respondents about their main language and a set which focuses on Welsh-language ability.

The first question, as it was phrased in Wales, asked whether the respondents' main language was English or Welsh and, if it was neither, what language it was.[1] This means that this question cannot tell us what the distribution of English and Welsh is, and it cannot help us gauge how many speakers consider Welsh their main language or how many might feel they use them equally. It can, however, give us a partial idea of what other languages are spoken in Wales, although it is likely some respondents who choose English or Welsh as their main language might have been fluent in other languages as well.

The second set of questions asked whether respondents could speak, read and/or write in Welsh. This grants us greater insight into Welsh and/or English-language use, although, as noted, it does not reveal how many consider Welsh their main language. The value should not be taken to come solely from those who had English or Welsh as their main language, as speakers who did not select English/Welsh as their main language may also have had some Welsh ability.

Taken together, these sets of questions can provide a broad idea of language use in Wales. Table 1.1 below, presents the raw numbers and the percentages for the relevant answers to these two sets of questions (taken from the census website).[2]

Table 1.1 Raw numbers and percentages for language-related questions on the National Census 2011 (Wales only)

Overall number of respondents	2,955,841	
Q: What is your main language?	Number of respondents	%
English or Welsh	2,871,405	97
European languages (inc. French, Spanish, Portuguese and Polish)	40,538	1.37
Arabic	6800	0.23
West/Central Asian language	3241	0.11
South Asian language (inc. Punjabi, Urdu and Bengali)	15,665	0.53
East Asian (inc. Chinese)	13,816	0.47
African languages	3485	0.12
Other	891	0.03
Q: Can you understand, speak, read or write Welsh?	Number of respondents	%
Welsh ability	562,016	19

---

[1] For those who responded neither, there was another question asking more specifically about their ability in English (or Welsh). We will not be focusing on this question here.

[2] In order to present the results as clearly as possible, language families are not broken down and only languages that were reported over 1000 times are named within the families.

The table makes it clear that English and Welsh are the main languages spoken in Wales and they represent the main languages of nearly all the population (ONS 2012). Languages with at least 5000 speakers in Wales are the following: Polish (17,001 speakers), Arabic (6800 speakers), Chinese (8103 speakers), and Bengali (including Sylheti and Chatgaya) (5207 speakers). Although most respondents in Wales have English or Welsh as their main language, the various other languages reflect migration patterns to the country (see Evans 2015; Markaki 2016).

Moving to Welsh use, Table 1.1 shows that 19% of the population use Welsh in some way (the census shows that around 15% can read and write it as well as speak it). While this represents around a fifth of the population, it highlights that many people in Wales may have little contact with Welsh. To understand the current situation of Welsh, it is important to show how it has come to be and what historical, political, and social changes have led to this situation.

History of Welsh and English Language Contact

Findings from the 1901 census indicate that 49.9% (n = 929,824) of the Welsh population were able to speak Welsh and that 15.1% (n = 280, 905) of these were monolinguals (Great Britain Historical GIS Project 2004). The current levels of Welsh use, discussed above, represent a substantial shift away from this. The twentieth century has seen the end of Welsh monolingualism and the contraction of the language to Western heartland areas (H.M. Jones 2012: 13).[3] This is reflected in the geographical profile of the language today, as the areas with the highest proportion of Welsh speakers are in the Western counties: Gwynedd (65.4%), Isle of Anglesey (57.2%), Ceredigion (47.3%), and Carmarthenshire (43.9%, see StatsWales 2012).

---

[3] Because of the numerous authors with the last names Jones and Thomas in this chapter, we have decided for clarity to include their first name (or initial) when discussing their work.

Despite substantial changes to the sociolinguistic profile of Wales during the twentieth century, contact between Welsh and English and the history of language shift had started much earlier. The following sections chart this shift beginning with the early development of Welsh.

Old Welsh, a Celtic language, related to Irish, Scottish Gaelic, Manx, Cornish and Breton, developed from Brythonic during the sixth century. The Western advance of the Kingdom of Wessex during the late sixth century isolated the Brythonic-speaking Celts of Wales from those of South-West Britain, which led to the separate evolutions of Welsh and Cornish (Filppula et al. 2008: 8–9). In this period, Wales was largely monolingual and contact with the Anglo-Saxons was restricted to some areas near the English border (Beverley-Smith 1997: 16) and to a few isolated Flemish and Saxon communities in the South-West (Toorians 2000).

This early period is marked by a growing sense of Welsh identity and attempts to politically unify Wales (Davies 1990: 78). In 1282, however, with the defeat of the last native prince of Wales and the resulting ceding Wales to the English crown, Wales lost its independence. On the one hand, the effect of this on the language was not completely straightforward and to a certain extent the position of the language was strengthened rather than weakened (e.g. Welsh law continued to be practised and 'the domains of the language were considerably extended,', R.O. Jones (1993: 537)). On the other hand, contact between the English and Welsh gentry had already led to an increase in prestige for the English language and the beginning of a gradual top-down process of Anglicisation.

The process of Anglicisation intensified following the Acts of Union in 1536 and 1543. The English legal system replaced the Welsh one and sections of Welsh land were annexed to the English crown. English became the sole language of official business and those who held any position of authority in Wales were therefore required to be bilingual (Abalain 1989: 131). This would have been limiting for the majority of the Welsh population as they were not English speakers. Williams (2009: 204) underlines, however, that this should not be taken to mean that there was 'forced bilingualism for the mass of the population'. Instead, the domains in which Welsh was spoken were increasingly restricted and it became increasingly seen as having a lower status to English (Williams 2009: 205).

As might be expected, the shift to English from Welsh was strongest among the gentry, who saw English as a prestige variety (Beverley-Smith 1997: 36) and who chose to send their children to English grammar schools or to one of the few (English-medium) Tudor grammar schools established in Wales.

This period is also marked by a resurgence of Welsh in religion due to the Protestant Reformation. Welsh became increasingly visible as a language of religion and culture and, crucially, as a printed language. William Morgan's 1588 translation of the Bible provided a model of Standard Welsh for future generations (R.O. Jones 1997b: 148, 159).

The next period to have influenced language use is the Industrial Revolution, which came to Wales in the late eighteenth century, and which was, initially, largely concentrated in the East. It led to migration within the country, but also immigration from outside Wales because of increased demand for skilled workers. The presence of a large community of English-speakers in the East, and the use of English as the commercial language (Mathias 1973: 51), coupled with the low prestige Welsh had been seen to have since the Middle Ages, meant that immigrants did not learn Welsh. In fact, R.O. Jones (1993: 546) notes that not only did the English incomers not learn Welsh, 'but bilingualism amongst the speakers of Welsh led to an intergenerational language switch to English in these mixed language areas'.

The migration patterns during the Industrial Revolution meant that the Western counties remained largely monolingual (Welsh), whereas there was a division between bilingual and monolingual (English) areas in the East (Löffler 1997: 69). However, it should be noted that Western areas were not unaffected by Anglicisation, and it is not the case that Welsh became completely extinct in the East.

In 1870, education in Wales became systematised and was delivered entirely through the medium of English (Williams 1973: 94).[4] Welsh was actively suppressed by the education system in this period, exemplified by

---

[4] Many Welsh speakers learned to write in Welsh through Sunday Schools (Williams 2003: 6).

the 'Welsh Not' (R.O. Jones 1993: 548).[5] Together, these intensified the link in people's minds between English and prosperity.

Welsh, at the turn of the twentieth century, was in a situation of language shift. However, the last century and the twenty-first century have been marked by conscious attempts to reverse language shift and there has been an increase of Welsh in domains such as education, law, and media.

The revitalisation measures have been helped by the introduction of 'large-scale immersion schooling' (M.C. Jones 1998: 17) with a view to ensuring that more of the population had some competency in Welsh. It is worth noting that the movement for Welsh-medium provision had already started in the late 1800s (Williams 1973: 97) with the passing of the Intermediate Education Act (Ministry of Education 1949: 3). The aim at that point, however, was to introduce Welsh schooling to facilitate the learning of English amongst pupils. From the twentieth century onwards, the aim shifted towards teaching Welsh. By 1946, 40% of pupils in secondary grammar schools took Welsh as a subject (Ministry of Education 1949: 8).

The introduction of Welsh schooling began in earnest with the establishment of the first Welsh-medium primary school in 1947 and a secondary school in 1956 (Aitchison and Carter 1994: 44). This marked a period of increased concern for the vitality of the language and the recognition of its importance in education as well as 'a matter of national concern' (Ministry of Education 1953: 1).

In other areas, mobilisation on the part of activists led to the Welsh Courts Act of 1942, which allowed for the use of Welsh in the court (Lewis 1973: 197). Following the Second World War, this mobilisation on the part of campaigners intensified. The foundation of *Cymdeithas yr Iaith Gymraeg* (the Welsh Language Society) in 1962 is an example of such a movement, which, in particular, campaigned throughout the latter half of the twentieth century for equality between Welsh and English

---

[5] The 'Welsh Not' refers to a system used in Welsh schools during this period in order to discourage the use of the Welsh language. A pupil who was overheard speaking the language would be forced to wear a piece of wood with the initials W.N. attached to a piece of string. When another pupil was overheard speaking Welsh, the wood would be passed to them. At the end of the day, the pupil wearing the Welsh Not would be punished physically.

(Davies 1973: 261). Welsh was fortunate in these revitalisation efforts, compared to many other minority language situations, because the efforts 'got underway when family transmission of the language was still not uncommon and when there was a reasonably large constituency of younger native speakers' (Ferguson 2006: 107).

It is generally agreed that the campaigns undertaken by the *Cymdeithas Yr Iaith Gymraeg* directly led to the installation of bilingual road signs in Wales and the establishment of a Welsh-language television channel (B. Jones 1997a: 57). The demand for Welsh-medium television grew during the 1970s and became a reality in 1982 with the launch of *Sianel Pedwar Cymru* (S4C; Channel Four Wales).

In terms of the legal position of the language, Coupland and Aldridge (2009: 6) note that 'the 1993 Welsh Language Act required public sector agencies to deal with their clients in the language of their choice, and therefore effectively imposed at least a bilingual façade on public services'. In order to oversee the Act, the Welsh Language Board was established and continued to work until 2011 with the aim of promoting the language and implementing bilingual practice.

The period towards the end of the twentieth century is one in which Welsh had grown in visibility and was marketed as a symbol of Welsh national identity across the nation, not just in the Welsh-speaking heartland. The language currently enjoys more explicit official legal status than at any point in its history and the efforts of organisations such as *Cymdeithas yr Iaith Gymraeg* have ensured that the language is now visible across more domains than ever before. There are networks of Welsh-medium schools all over the country and it is possible for a child to go from nursery to postgraduate education in Welsh. The provision of Welsh in Higher Education has recently been strengthened with the establishment of the *Coleg Cymraeg Cenedlaethol*, which funds and promotes Welsh-medium Higher Education courses and facilitates the training of Welsh-medium lecturers at Welsh universities. Moreover, language planning initiatives continue to form part of government policies which aim to 'see the Welsh language thriving in Wales' (Welsh Government 2012: 14).

There still remains, however, cause for concern over the vitality of the language. There has been much work on the use of Welsh in various contexts such as the home (e.g. Gathercole 2007; K. Jones and Morris 2009), at school and by young people more widely (e.g. Musk 2006; Hodges 2009; Morris 2010; Morris 2014; Selleck 2015), in the community (e.g. McAllister et al. 2013), and online (e.g. Cunliffe et al. 2013).

The transmission of Welsh appears to largely depend on the linguistic background and perceived linguistic ability (Gathercole 2007), although some research has found that other factors such as the proportion of Welsh-speaking population in the community and socioeconomic background play a role (H.M. Jones 2013). K. Jones and Morris (2009) found that parents with more positive attitudes towards the language created more opportunities for children to use Welsh. In mixed-language households, this thesis was also confirmed, although they conclude that children whose mothers spoke Welsh had significantly more exposure to the language because mothers often were the primary caregivers (K. Jones and Morris 2009: 128).

Surveys of language use and ethnographic studies both highlight the relationship between use of Welsh and both community language and first language acquired (e.g. H.M. Jones 2008). Recent research suggests that the number of fluent Welsh speakers has been relatively stable in the past decade and is 11% of the population. Most fluent speakers live in the areas with the highest proportion of all Welsh speakers (Gwynedd, Isle of Anglesey, Ceredigion and Carmarthenshire) and are more likely to speak Welsh daily than non-fluent speakers (Welsh Government and Welsh Language Commissioner 2015).

The link between language acquisition and language use is seen in studies of young people. Coupland et al. (2005: 18–19) found that young people see Welsh in complex functional terms and 'prioritise symbol over use'. Musk (2006) used a conversation analytic (CA) framework to look at attitudes towards bilingualism amongst school children, and his findings lead him to distinguish between three categories: Welsh-dominant bilinguals, 'floaters', and English-dominant bilinguals. Morris (2014) found that home language was a defining characteristic of peer-group membership in a Welsh-dominant area: there was little engagement with Welsh amongst those from the English-speaking peer group, and in the English-dominant area studied, English was the language of all peer-group interactions regardless of home language.

While there are concerns that language policy does not reflect the linguistic ideologies on the ground (Selleck 2013: 38), Williams (2008: 279) makes it clear that 'language revitalisation measures and the devolution process have opened new spaces and created new resources with which to construct a bilingual society'. The Welsh-language movement has, during the course of the twentieth century, managed to normalise the idea of official bilingualism. The challenge for the twenty-first century is to normalise Welsh-language use and promote language choice.

It is within this background of language use, non-use and revitalisation that we now turn more specifically to the sociolinguistic situation in Wales.

Previous Work on Sociolinguistics in Wales

This section begins with a review of previous dialectological and variationist work on varieties of Welsh, Welsh English, and Welsh–English bilingual speech. It will then outline work which encompasses different aspects of the interplay between language and society such as language use, identity, and attitudes.

Dialectology and Variationist Studies of Welsh

There is a long tradition of Welsh dialectological research, beginning in the first half of the twentieth century (e.g. Anwyl 1901; Awbery 1986; Darlington 1902; Davies 1934; Fynes-Clinton 1913; G.E. Jones 2000; Sommerfelt 1925). Reflecting the wider field, this type of work has tended to focus on phonological, grammatical, or lexical descriptions of specific local areas (see B. and P.W. Thomas 1989 for an overview). A.R. Thomas's Linguistic Geography of Wales (1973) and The Welsh Dialect Survey (2000) are the most comprehensive and large-scale attempt to map dialectal variation in the language. Dialectological research in Welsh has found a three-way distinction between Northern, Midlands, and Southern dialect areas (with the Midlands dialect area being a transition zone between the North and South, Rees 2013: 13). Further differences in lexicon, grammar, and phonology mean that the three areas can each be divided into East and West, resulting in six traditional dialect areas (A.R. Thomas 1973: 14; B. Thomas and P.W. Thomas 1989).

From the 1970s, in line with the growth of variationist sociolinguistics internationally, there was a shift of focus towards more variationist research and an examination of external factors to better understand the patterns found. Roberts's (1973) work on the North Wales town of Pwllheli was among the earliest to employ these methods for Welsh. Not in Wales, but looking at Welsh nonetheless, R.O. Jones's work (e.g. 1984) examined phonological variation in the Welsh-speaking population of Chubut, Argentina. Both dialectological and early variationist work on Welsh tended to focus on close-knit areas where the language was a strong community language. In addition to the usual external factors (speaker sex, age, and education level) studied in variationist sociolinguistics, C.M. Jones (1987, 1989) differentiates between home language in her work in New Moat in Pembrokeshire. B. Thomas's (1988) work on the small mining village of Pont-rhyd-y-fen is frequently cited as a counterexample to evidence that men use more vernacular forms than women (e.g. Holmes 1992: 181), as she found that women were more likely to use local forms despite having access to 'prestige variants' (B. Thomas 1989: 60).

The chapters in Ball (1988) and, to a lesser extent, Ball and G. Jones (1984) are a good representation of language variation and change work in Welsh undertaken during this period. Many of these chapters are English summaries of the work described above (e.g. R.O. Jones 1984; Roberts 1988). Other chapters examine variation in consonant mutation (P.W. Thomas 1984), and generational differences in the devoicing of consonants in the Upper Swansea Valley (B. Thomas 1988). Ball and Müller's (1992) research on initial consonant mutation found that, like B. Thomas (1989), men produced more standard variants in some contexts. Second, they also found that engagement or 'acculturation' to Welsh was also significant though this also seemed to be correlated with age (Ball and Müller 1992: 255).

M.C. Jones's (1998) work not only examines variation in more bilingual areas but also focuses on the linguistic differences between communities. Her study suggests that, in areas where English is the dominant language, traditional dialects may be losing many features and undergoing levelling (Jones 1998: 236). The disparate findings of research on the close-knit communities compared to more bilingual areas suggests that the new generation of Welsh speakers in the East, of whom the vast majority come from English-speaking homes, are not acquiring the local dialect features. Instead, speakers acquire a variety of Welsh which is an intermediary form between Literary Welsh and local dialects. The Welsh acquired in schools is, perhaps more precisely, a 'closely linked set of standards [...] for education purposes' (Coupland and Ball 1989: 17), rather than a unified form. The description of such forms remains a question for further research.

More recently, we also find synchronic descriptions of Welsh and variationist work. In addition to the research presented in this volume, there is research on phonological variation in the oft-neglected Midlands (Rees 2013); stylistic variation (Prys 2016) and morphosyntactic variation and change (Willis forthcoming). It is clearly an opportune time to revisit variation and change in the Welsh context, especially in light of the societal changes which have affected Welsh-speaking communities since the earlier dialectal work.

This period has also seen increased interest in sociolinguistic aspects of bilingualism. Work from Bangor University's ESRC Centre for Research on Bilingualism has applied variationist methods to code-switching in Welsh–English bilinguals' speech (e.g. Carter et al. 2011). Morris (2013) examined the extent to which linguistic and extra-linguistic factors (such as sex, proportion of Welsh speakers in the community, and home language) influence phonetic and phonological variation in both English and Welsh. This, and further work in both North and South Wales (Morris 2014; Mennen et al. 2015; Mayr et al. 2015) indicates that certain features are phonetically identical in both languages due to long-term language contact. It also appears, however, that extra-linguistic factors influence the realisation of some phonological features.

Dialectology and Variationist Studies of Welsh English

There have also been large dialect surveys of Welsh English, most notably the two-volume Survey of Anglo-Welsh Dialects (Parry 1977, 1979) and

The Anglo-Welsh dialects of North Wales (Penhallurick 1991, 1993) in addition to various overviews (e.g. Thomas 1984, 1994; Awbery 1997; Penhallurick 2004, 2007; Paulasto 2013).

Welsh English can be viewed as an umbrella term for the varieties of English which are spoken in Wales. For example, Wells (1982: 377) states that 'the main influence on the pronunciation of English in Wales is the substratum presented by the phonological system of Welsh'. Regional variation within Welsh English is largely influenced by the extent to which Welsh is, or has been, spoken in a particular region. Awbery (1997) distinguishes between three distinct varieties of Welsh English. There are areas of Wales where English has been a community language for many centuries (such as parts of Pembrokeshire and some border areas) and as such show little influence from Welsh. In many other areas, Welsh has been (and in many cases remains) the main language of the community, and it is here where a more direct influence from Welsh can be seen. Awbery (1997: 88) calls the third area 'the Conurbations' which contains the more urban areas in both South-East and North-East Wales. In many areas, such as the historically English-speaking border areas and parts of the North-East, influence is noted from neighbouring dialects such as those of the West Midlands and Liverpool (A.R. Thomas 1994: 112–113).

Some work has focused on Cardiff, the largest urban area in Wales. Mees (1983) examined language variation and real-time change in the speech of 36 Cardiff school children. Speakers were stratified in terms of sex and social background, and stylistic variation was also investigated. Most interestingly, glottalisation of /t/ was found to be a prestige feature and was most frequent in the speech of middle-class young women (see also Mees 1990; Collins and Mees 1990; Mees and Collins 1999).

Much of Coupland's work has also examined the sociolinguistic aspects of variation. Coupland (1985), for instance, focused on variation in the pronunciation of place names in Cardiff (many of which contain phonemes specific to Welsh) to examine correlations between ethnic identity and pronunciation. Coupland (1980, 1988) concentrated on stylistic variation in an analysis of workers in a Cardiff travel agency. This work challenged the parameters which style was operationalised under and promoted a more detailed analysis of speakers' repertoires in order to understand the motivations of stylistic or contextual variation (see Coupland 2001a for an overview). The idea of how Welshness was 'performed' is another focus of Coupland's work: for example, dialect stylisation in English-language radio broadcasts in Wales (Coupland 2001b) and by a pantomime dame (Coupland 2009).

Coupland and A.R. Thomas's (1990) edited volume focused on varieties of English in Wales and provided an overview of the field as it was at the time. The volume presents both descriptive accounts of Welsh English varieties as well as studies on the influence of Welsh on children's English and the social meaning of Welsh English (Giles 1990). In the years after the appearance of the volume, various publications have focused on Welsh English, either providing further, necessary, descriptions (e.g. Podhovnik 2008, 2010; Walters 1999, 2003) or answering broader sociolinguistic questions using Welsh English data (Hejná 2015; Paulasto 2006; Roller 2016). Beyond that, much work in the 1990s and 2000s turns to the debate about the status of Welsh English (and indeed Welsh) as a marker of Welsh identity and attitudes towards these varieties. It is to these aspects of sociolinguistic research which we now turn.

Attitudes and Identity

While there are few studies of attitudes towards varieties of Welsh (see, however, Robert 2009), studies of attitudes towards Welsh English have been extensive (see Giles 1990 for an overview). Giles (1970) found that the Welsh English accent was perceived quite favourably by Welsh school children even if it was seen as less prestigious than received pronunciation. Subsequent work, for example, Bourhis et al. (1975), suggests that while Welsh English is perhaps not viewed as being as prestigious as more standard accents of English, it is seen as more trustworthy and a symbol of belonging to the community (see Paulasto, this volume).

Coupland, Garrett and Williams applied a perceptual dialectology approach to the study of Welsh English through an examination of teachers' attitudes in a number of papers (e.g. Coupland et al. 1994, 1999; Garrett et al. 1995, 1999; Williams et al. 1996). They found evidence for degrees of Welshness attached to varieties of Welsh English, with the more 'Welsh' accents of English being perceived in the West, but also a more complex pattern of distinctions. Williams et al. (1996) compared their results with the three-Wales model (Balsom 1985), an attempt to characterise the link between cultural identity in Wales and geography. Balsom (1985) distinguished between *Y Fro Gymraeg* to the West (where Welsh is widely spoken and people identify as Welsh), Welsh Wales (in the Valleys and Swansea areas which are not predominantly Welsh speaking but where Welsh identity is relatively strong), and British Wales (the East where the population is not largely Welsh speaking and identify as British). Williams et al. (1996) found some evidence for this distinction, yet note that differences exist within British Wales (Williams et al. 1996: 196). Interestingly, subsequent work has hinted that the three-Wales model may no longer be valid and that Welshness is perceived in accents across Wales (albeit to variable degrees, Garrett et al. 1999) and also seen as a marker of identity across the country regardless of Welsh-language ability. Coupland et al. (2005: 15), in a study of 16-year-olds, note that "first-language Welsh language competence may provide a 'topping up' symbolic resource for focusing ethnic pride and ingroup subjectivity, on top of the positive ethnic sensitivities that are shared by most young Welsh people".

The Current Volume

Having presented previous research from the twentieth and early twenty-first centuries, we now turn to the studies in this volume. In designing the volume, our aim was to present the wealth of sociolinguistic research currently taking place in Wales. We have included investigations into language variation and change in Welsh and Welsh English (Davies; Paulasto), perceptual dialectology and attitudinal studies (Durham; Montgomery), Welsh–English bilingual speech (Deuchar, Donnelly and Piercy; Morris, Mayr and Mennen), linguistic ethnography and multi-lingualism (Rock and Hallack), and language policy and language planning (Carlin and Mac Giolla Chríost; Evas and Cunliffe). The structure of the volume is designed to reflect linguistic diversity in Wales and is divided into three sections. The first section examines recent research on

Welsh, the second section focuses on English, and the third section deals with Welsh–English bilingualism and multilingualism. There is, however, synergy across sections as a number of contributions examine different aspects of sociolinguistics in Wales using similar methodological and theoretical frameworks.

In the first section, on Welsh, Davies (Chap. 2) investigates two variable and changing features and considers the extent to which speakers' age offers insight into the shift towards a new form. Evas and Cunliffe (Chap. 3) consider behavioural economics and how it could help increase take up of Welsh-language e-services. Carlin and Mac Giolla Chríost (Chap. 4) present an overview of the Welsh Language Measure and its legal ramifications.

The second section, on Welsh English, begins with Paulasto (Chap. 5). She presents a quantitative study of morphosyntactic variation and the extent to which dialect contact is influencing Welsh English. Montgomery (Chap. 6) compares dialect maps drawn by secondary school children on both sides of the Wales-England border and establishes the extent to which perceptions of Welsh English dialects differ between them. Durham (Chap. 7) presents data from Twitter in order to investigate attitudes towards the Welsh English accent.

The final section turns to language in Wales more broadly and presents work on bilingual and multilingual language use. Deuchar, Donnelly, and Piercy (Chap. 8) analyse code-switching in Welsh–English bilingual speech using a variationist framework and examine the influence of a range of external factors. Morris, Mayr, and Mennen (Chap. 9) aim to establish the extent to which the linguistic background of young Welsh–English bilinguals influences sound variation. Finally, Rock and Hallack (Chap. 10) study the ways in which multiple languages are incorporated into the linguistic landscape of Cardiff.

Future Sociolinguistics in Wales

The sociolinguistic situation in Wales is rapidly changing. As elsewhere, factors such as inward and outward migration and greater social mobility are leading to more diverse communities. In contrast to other countries of the UK, however, these factors are coupled with societal and official bilingualism (albeit to varying degrees) and an increased awareness of a Welsh national and cultural identity. Our aim with this volume is to show how current research on sociolinguistics in Wales considers this unique context in different ways and to highlight avenues for future research.

The changing demographics of the Welsh-speaking population has been widely discussed in this chapter, but there are unanswered questions regarding how the changes to Welsh-speaking communities and the increasing proportion of Welsh speakers who have acquired the language through formal education will affect language ideologies and use. As much of the work on language attitudes and use has focused on school children, it remains to be seen how these change over people's lifetimes. Although the use of Welsh has been shown to correlate with a number of factors, such as the proportion of Welsh speakers in the community, it is not known whether wider patterns of use can be found amongst all speakers and there is evidence to suggest that, for some people, there is a functional diglossic relationship between Welsh and English, whereby English is the main or only language used in official or formal situations, despite official bilingualism.

The relationship between Welsh identity and Welsh English amongst different groups of speakers also merits attention. How have the communities with more English contact managed to maintain their sense of Welsh identity and what are the linguistic features that they use to do this?

The increase of non-official languages in Wales is also inherently interesting from a sociolinguistic perspective. Not only can transmission and preservation of heritage languages be examined, but the processes of language contact more generally can be investigated. The immigration into Cardiff, for example, will potentially influence the English spoken there and possibly lead to a multicultural variety similar to those found in London and Manchester.

The breadth of studies in this volume highlight the extent to which the linguistic situation also differs between communities in Wales. The fact that communities differ in the extent to which there are first-language Welsh speakers, those who have acquired the language through education, adult Welsh learners, English monolinguals, and bilingual and multilingual speakers of other languages, provides an opportunity for sociolinguistic analysis. Research is needed on language variation in different communities, which consider community dynamics and sociolinguistic influences on Welsh, English, and on other languages, and which consider how changes in communities have affected language change. In particular, this volume shows that the diverse nature of Cardiff and the largely ignored Wales-England border area present exciting opportunities for further research.

Overall, we hope that this volume will confirm that Wales is a prime location for sociolinguistic research and that it will continue to be so for many years to come. The long-term contact of two languages, combined with the border which separates Welsh English from the English spoken in England, along with the increased multilingualism found in larger UK cities today offers many opportunities to further our understanding of how language can be transformed by contact and by diverse societies.

References

Abalain, Hervé. 1989. *Destin des Langues Celtiques*. Paris: Editions Ophrys.

Aitchison, John W., and Harold Carter. 1994. *A Geography of the Welsh Language 1961–1991*. Cardiff: University of Wales Press.

Anwyl, Edward. 1901. Report of the dialect section of the guild of graduates. In *Transactions of the University of Wales guild of graduates*, 33–52. Cardiff: University of Wales Press.

Awbery, Gwenllian. 1986. *Pembrokeshire Welsh: A phonological study*. Llandysul: Gomer.

———. 1997. The English language in Wales. In *The Celtic Englishes*, ed. Hildegard L.C. Tristram, 86–99. Heidelberg: Winter.

Ball, Martin J. (ed). 1988. *The use of Welsh: A contribution to sociolinguistics*. Clevedon: Multilingual Matters.

Ball, Martin J., and Glyn E. Jones (ed). 1984. *Welsh phonology: selected readings*. Cardiff: University of Wales Press.

Ball, Martin J., and Nicole Müller. 1992. *Mutation in Welsh*. London: Routledge.

Balsom, Denis. 1985. The three-Wales model. In *The national question again: Welsh political identity in the 1980s*, ed. John Osmond, 1–17. Llandysul: Gomer.

Beverley Smith, Llinos. 1997. Yr iaith Gymraeg cyn 1536. In *Y Gymraeg yn ei Disgleirdeb: yr Iaith Gymraeg cyn y Chwyldro Diwydiannol*, ed. Geraint H. Jenkins, 15–43. Cardiff: University of Wales Press.

Bourhis, Richard Y., Howard Giles, and Wallace E. Lambert. 1975. Social consequences of accommodating one's style of speech: A cross-national investigation. *International Journal of the Sociology of Language* 6: 55–72.

Carter, Diana, Margaret Deuchar, Peredur Davies, and María del Carmen Parafita Couto. 2011. A systematic comparison of factors affecting the choice of matrix language in three bilingual communities. *Journal of Language Contact* 4(2): 153–183.

Collins, Beverley, and Inger M. Mees. 1990. The phonetics of Cardiff English. In *English in Wales: Diversity, conflict, and change*, ed. Nikolas Coupland, 87–103. Clevedon: Multilingual Matters.

Coupland, Nikolas. 1980. Style-shifting in a Cardiff work-setting. *Language in Society* 9(1): 1–12.

———. 1985. Sociolinguistic aspects of place–names. Ethnic affiliation and the pronunciation of Welsh in the Welsh capital. In *Focus on: England and Wales (=Varieties of English around the World 4)*, ed. Beat Glauser, and Wolfgang Viereck, 29–44. John Benjamin's: Amsterdam/Philadelphia.

———. 1988. *Dialect in use: Sociolinguistic variation in Cardiff*. Cardiff: University of Wales Press.

———. 2001a. Dialect stylization in radio talk. *Language in Society* 30: 345–375.

———. 2001b. Language, situation, and the relational self: Theorizing dialect style in sociolinguistics. In *Style and sociolinguistic variation*, ed. Penelope Eckert, and John R. Rickford, 185–210. Cambridge: Cambridge University Press.

———. 2009. Dialect style, social class and metacultural performance: The pantomime dame. In *The new sociolinguistics reader*, ed. Nikolas Coupland, and Adam Jaworski, 311–325. Basingstoke/New York: Palgrave Macmillan.

Coupland, Nikolas, and Michelle Aldridge. 2009. Introduction: A critical approach to the revitalisation of Welsh. *International Journal of the Sociology of Language* 195: 5–13.

Coupland, Nikolas, and Martin J. Ball. 1989. Welsh and English in contemporary Wales: Sociolinguistic issues. *Contemporary Wales* 1: 7–40.

Coupland, Nikolas, and Alan R. Thomas (ed). 1990. *English in Wales: Diversity, conflict, change*. Clevedon: Multilingual Matters.

Coupland, Nikolas, Angie Williams, and Peter Garrett. 1994. The social meanings of Welsh English: Teachers' stereotyped judgements. *Journal of Multilingual and Multicultural Development* 15(6): 471–489. doi:10.1080/0 1434632.1994.9994585.

———. 1999. 'Welshness' and 'Englishness' as attitudinal dimensions of English language varieties in Wales. In *Handbook of perceptual dialectology, 1*, ed. Dennis R. Preston, 333–343. Amsterdam: John Benjamins.

Coupland, Nikolas, Hywel Bishop, Angie Williams, Betsy Evans, and Peter Garrett. 2005. Affiliation, engagement, language use, and vitality: Secondary school students' subjective orientations to Welsh and Welshness. *International Journal of Bilingual Education and Bilingualism* 8(1): 1–24.

Cunliffe, Daniel, Delyth Morris, and Cynog Prys. 2013. Young bilinguals' language behaviour in social networking sites: The use of Welsh on Facebook. *Journal of Computer-Mediated Communication* 18(3): 339–361.

Darlington, Thomas. 1902. Some dialectal boundaries in mid Wales: With notes on the history of the palatalization of long a. *The transactions of The Honourable Society of Cymmrodorion (1900–01)*: 13–39.

Davies, J. J. Glanmor. 1934. *Astudiaeth o Gymraeg Llafar Ardal y Ceinewydd: Ei Seineg gydag Ymchwiliadau Gwyddonol, ei Seinyddiaeth a'i Ffurfiant gyda Geirfa Lawn, a Chyfeiriad at ei Semanteg*. Unpublished PhD Thesis, University of Wales, Aberystwyth.

Davies, Cynog. 1973. Cymdeithas yr Iaith Gymraeg. In *The Welsh language today*, ed. Meic Stephens, 248–263. Llandysul: Gomer.

Davies, John. 1990. *Hanes Cymru*. London: Penguin.

Evans, Neil. 2015. Immigrants and minorities in Wales, 1840-1990: A comparative perspective. In *A tolerant nation? Revisiting ethnic diversity in a devolved Wales*, ed. Charlotte Williams, Neil Evans, and Paul O'Leary, 24–50. Cardiff: University of Wales Press.

Ferguson, Gibson. 2006. *Language planning in education*. Edinburgh: Edinburgh University Press.

Filppula, Markku, Juhani Klemola, and Heli Paulasto. 2008. *English and Celtic in contact*. New York/London: Routledge.

Fynes-Clinton, Osbert H. 1913. *The Welsh vocabulary of the Bangor district*. Oxford: Oxford University Press.

Garrett, Peter, Nikolas Coupland, and Angie Williams. 1995. 'City Harsh' and 'the Welsh version of RP': Some ways in which teachers view dialects of Welsh English. *Language Awareness* 4(2): 99–107.

———. 1999. Evaluating dialect in discourse: Teachers' and teenagers' responses to young English speakers in Wales. *Language in Society* 28: 321–354.

Gathercole, Virginia (ed). 2007. *Language transmission in bilingual families in Wales*. Cardiff: Welsh Language Board.

Giles, Howard. 1970. Evaluative reactions to accents. *Educational Review* 22: 211–227.

———. 1990. Social meanings of Welsh English. In *English in Wales: Diversity, conflict, and change*, ed. Nikolas Coupland, 258–282. Clevedon: Multilingual Matters.

Great Britain Historical GIS Project. 2004. Great Britain historical GIS. University of Portsmouth. Available at: http://www.visionofbritain.org. uk/footer/doc_text_for_title.jsp?topic=credits&seq=4. Accessed 24 May 2016.

Hejná, Míša. 2015. *Pre-aspiration in Welsh English: A case study of Aberystwyth*. PhD thesis, University of Manchester.

Hodges, Rhian. 2009. Welsh language use among young people in the Rhymney Valley. *Contemporary Wales* 22(1): 16–35.

Holmes, Janet. 1992. *An introduction to sociolinguistics*. London/New York: Longman.

Jones, Robert Owen. 1984. Change and variation in the Welsh of Gaiman, Chubut. In *Welsh phonology: Selected readings*, ed. Martin J. Ball, and Glyn E. Jones, 208–236. Cardiff: University of Wales Press.

Jones, Christine M. 1987. Astudiaeth o Iaith Lafar Y Mot (Sir Benfro), Unpublished PhD thesis, University of Wales, Lampeter.

———. 1989. Cydberthynas Nodweddion Cymdeithasol ag Amrywiadau'r Gymraeg yn Y Mot, Sir Benfro. *Bwletin y Bwrdd Gwybodau Celtaidd* 36: 64–83.

Jones, Robert Owen. 1993. The sociolinguistics of Welsh. In *The Celtic languages*, ed. Martin J. Ball, 536–605. London/New York: Routledge.

Jones, Barry. 1997a. Welsh politics and changing British and European contexts. In *British regionalism and devolution: The challenges of state reform and European integration*, Regional policy and development, vol 16, ed. Jonathan Bradbury, and John Mawson, 55–74. London: Routledge.

Jones, Robert Owen. 1997b. *Hir Oes i'r Iaith: Agweddau ar Hanes y Gymraeg a'r Gymdeithas*. Llandysul: Gomer.

Jones, Mari C. 1998. *Language obsolescence and revitalization: Linguistic change in two sociolinguistically contrasting Welsh communities*. Oxford: Clarendon Press.

Jones, Glyn E. 2000. *Iaith Lafar Brycheiniog: Astudiaeth o'i ffonoleg a'i Morffoleg*. Cardiff: University of Wales Press.

Jones, Hywel M. 2008. The changing social context of Welsh: A review of statistical trends. *International Journal of Bilingual Education and Bilingualism* 11(5): 541–557.

———. 2012. *A statistical overview of the Welsh language.* Cardiff: Welsh Language Board. Available at: http://www.comisiynyddygymraeg.cymru/Cymraeg/Rhestr%20Cyhoeddiadau/Darlun%20ystadegol%20Cymraeg.pdf. Accessed 23 May 2016.

———. 2013. *The intergenerational transmission of the Welsh Language.* Available at: http://www.comisiynyddygymraeg.cymru/English/Publications%20List/20130814%20DG%20S%20Poster%20BSPS%20trosglwyddo.pdf. Accessed 24 May 2016.

Jones, Kathryn, and Delyth Morris. 2009. Issues of gender and parents' language values in the minority language socialisation of young children in Wales. *International Journal of the Sociology of Language* 195: 117–139.

Lewis, Robyn. 1973. The Welsh language and the law. In *The Welsh language today*, ed. Meic Stephens, 195–210. Llandysul: Gomer.

Löffler, Marion. 1997. *Englisch und Kymrisch in Wales: Geschichte der Sprachsituation und Sprachpolitik.* Hamburg: Dr. Kovač.

Markaki, Yvonni. 2016. Migration trends report: Migration flows and population trends in Wales. Available at: http://www.welshrefugeecouncil.org/sites/default/files/msiw/pdf/Trends%20Report-Migration%20Flows%20&%20Population%20Trends.pdf. Accessed 23 May 2016.

Mathias, Roland. 1973. The Welsh language and the English language. In *The Welsh language today*, ed. Meic Stephens, 32–63. Llandysul: Gomer.

Mayr, Robert, Jonathan Morris, Ineke Mennen and Daniel Williams. 2015. Disentangling the effects of long-term language contact and individual bilingualism: The case of monophthongs in Welsh and English. *International Journal of Bilingualism.* Published first online at: http://dx.doi.org/10.1177/1367006915614921. Accessed 24 May 2016.

McAllister, Fiona, Adam Blunt, Cynog Prys, Carys Evans, Eilir Jones and Iwan Evans. 2013. Exploring Welsh speakers' language use in their daily lives. Beaufort Research.

Mees, Inger M. 1983. *The speech of Cardiff schoolchildren: A real time study.* Unpublished PhD thesis, University of Leiden.

———. 1990. The phonetics of Cardiff English. In *English in Wales: Diversity, conflict, and change*, ed. Nikolas Coupland, 167–194. Clevedon: Multilingual Matters.

Mees, Inger M., and Beverley Collins. 1999. Cardiff: A real-time study of glottalisation. In *Urban voices: Accent studies in the British Isles*, ed. Paul Foulkes, and Gerard Docherty, 185–202. London: Routledge.

Mennen, Ineke, Robert Mayr, and Jonathan Morris. 2015. Influences of language contact and linguistic experience on the production of lexical stress in Welsh and Welsh English. In *Proceedings of the 18th international congress of phonetic sciences*, ed. The Scottish Consortium for ICPhS 2015. Glasgow: The University of Glasgow.

Ministry of Education. 1949. *Bilingualism in the secondary school in Wales*. London: His Majesty's Stationery Office.

———. 1953. *The place of Welsh and English in the schools of Wales: Summary of the report of the central advisory council for education (Wales)*. London: Her Majesty's Stationery Office.

Morris, Delyth. 2010. Young people and their use of the Welsh language. In *Welsh in the twenty-first century*, ed. Delyth Morris, 80–98. Cardiff: University of Wales Press.

Morris, Jonathan. 2013. *Sociolinguistic variation and regional minority language bilingualism: An investigation of Welsh–English bilinguals in North Wales*. Unpublished PhD thesis, University of Manchester.

———. 2014. The influence of social factors on minority language engagement amongst young people: An investigation of Welsh–English bilinguals in North Wales. *International Journal of the Sociology of Language* 230: 65–89.

Musk, Nigel. 2006. *Performing bilingualism in Wales with the spotlight on Welsh. A study of the language practices of young people in bilingual education*, Studies in language and culture, vol 8. Linköping: Linköpings Universitet.

Office for National Statistics. 2012. *2011 census: Key statistics for Wales*, March 2011. Available at: http://www.ons.gov.uk/peoplepopulationandcommunity/populationandmigration/populationestimates/bulletins/2011censuskeystatisticsforwales/2012-12-11#household-language. Accessed 23 May 2016.

Parry, David. 1977. *The survey of Anglo-Welsh dialects. Volume 1: The South-East*. Swansea: University College Swansea.

———. 1979. *The survey of Anglo-Welsh dialects. Volume 2: The South-West*. Swansea: University College Swansea.

Paulasto, H. 2006. *Welsh English syntax: Contact and variation*, University of Joensuu Publications in the Humanities, vol 43. Joensuu: Joensuu University Press.

Paulasto, Heli. 2013. English in Wales. In *World Englishes, The British isles*, vol I, ed. T. Hopkins, and J. McKenny, 241–262. London/New Delhi/New York/Sydney: Bloomsbury Academic.

Penhallurick, Robert. 1991. *The Anglo-Welsh dialects of North Wales: A survey of conservative rural spoken English in the counties of Gwynedd and Clwyd.* Frankfurt am Main: Lang.

———. 1993. Welsh English: A national language? *Dialectologia et Geolinguistica* 1: 28–46.

Penhallurick, Rob. 2004. Welsh English: Morphology and syntax. In *A handbook of varieties of English*, Morphology and syntax, ed. Bernd Kortmann, Kate Burridge, Rajend Mesthrie, Edgar Schneider, and Clive Upton, Vol. 2, 102–113. Berlin/New York: Mouton de Gruyter.

———. 2007. English in Wales. In *Language in the British Isles*, ed. David Britain, 152–170. Cambridge: Cambridge University Press.

Podhovnik, Edith. 2008. The phonology of Neath English: A socio-dialectological survey. Unpublished PhD thesis, Swansea University.

———. 2010. Age and accent-changes in a Southern Welsh English accent. *Research in Language* 8: 1–18.

Prys, Myfyr. 2016. *Style in the vernacular and on the radio: Code-switching and mutation as stylistic and social markers in Welsh.* Unpublished PhD thesis, Bangor University.

Rees, I. 2013. *Astudiaeth o amrywiadau ffonolegol mewn dwy ardal yng nghanolbarth Cymru.* Unpublished PhD thesis, Aberystwyth University.

Robert, Elen. 2009. Accommodating "new" speakers? An attitudinal investigation of L2 speakers of Welsh in south-east Wales. *International Journal of the Sociology of Language* 195: 93–115.

Roberts, Anna E. 1973. *Geirfa a Ffurfiau Cymraeg Llafar Cylch Pwllheli.* Unpublished MA thesis, University of Wales.

———. 1988. Age-related variation in the Welsh dialect of Pwllheli. In *The use of Welsh*, ed. Martin J. Ball, 104–123. Clevedon: Multilingual Matters.

Roller, Katja. 2016. *On the relation between frequency and salience in morphosyntax: The case of Welsh English.* Unpublished PhD thesis, Freiburg University.

Selleck, Charlotte. 2013. Inclusive policy and exclusionary practice in secondary education in Wales. *International Journal of Bilingualism and Bilingual Education* 16: 1–20.

———. 2015. Re-negotiating ideologies of bilingualism on the margins of education. *Journal of Multilingual and Multicultural Development* 2015: 1–13.

Sommerfelt, Alf. 1925. *Studies in Cyfeiliog Welsh.* Oslo: Jacob Dybwad.

StatsWales. 2012. Welsh speakers by local authority, gender and detailed age groups, 2011 Census. Available at: https://statscymru.cymru.gov.uk/Catalogue/Welsh-Language/WelshSpeakers-by-LocalAuthority-Gender-DetailedAgeGroups-2011Census. Accessed 24 May 2016.

Thomas, Alan R. 1973. *The linguistic geography of Wales: A contribution to Welsh dialectology*. Cardiff: University of Wales Press.

Thomas, Peter Wynn. 1984. Variation in South Glamorgan consonant mutation. In *Welsh phonology: Selected readings*, ed. Martin J. Ball, and Glyn E. Jones, 208–236. Cardiff: University of Wales Press.

Thomas, Beth. 1988. A study of calediad in the Upper Swansea Valley. In *The use of Welsh*, ed. Martin J. Ball, 85–96. Clevedon: Multilingual Matters.

———. 1989. Differences of sex and sects: Linguistic variation and social networks in a Welsh mining village. In *Women in their speech communities*, ed. Jennifer Coates, and Deborah Cameron, 51–60. London/New York: Longman.

Thomas, Alan R. 1994. English in Wales. In *The Cambridge history of the English language. Volume V – English in Britain and overseas: Origins and development*, ed. R. Burchfield, 94–147. Cambridge: Cambridge University Press.

———. 2000. *The Welsh dialect survey*. Cardiff: University of Wales Press.

Thomas, Beth, and Peter Wynn Thomas. 1989. *Cymraeg, Cymrâg, Cymrêg: Cyflwyno'r Tafodieithoedd*. Cardiff: Gwasg Tâf.

Toorians, L. 2000. Flemish in Wales. In *Languages in Britain and Ireland*, ed. Glanville Price, 184–196. Oxford: Blackwell.

Walters, J. Roderick. 1999. *A study of the segmental and suprasegmental phonology of Rhondda Valley's English*. Unpublished Ph.D. thesis, University of Glamorgan.

———. 2003. On the intonation of a South Wales 'Valleys accent' of English. *Journal of the International Phonetic Association* 33(2): 211–238.

Welsh Government and Welsh Language Commissioner. 2015. *Welsh language use in Wales 2013–15*. Cardiff: Welsh Government. Available at: http://llyw.cymru/statistics-and-research/Welsh-language-use-survey/?skip=1&lang=en. Accessed 27 Nov 2015.

Welsh Government. 2012. A living language: A language for living. Available at: http://gov.wales/docs/dcells/publications/122902wls201217en.pdf. Accessed 24 May 2016.

Welsh Language (Wales) Measure. 2011. Available at: http://www.legislation.gov.uk/mwa/2011/1/pdfs/mwa_20110001_en.pdf. Accessed 24 May 2016.

Wells, John. 1982. *Accents of English 2: The British Isles*. Cambridge: Cambridge University Press.

Williams, Jac L. 1973. The Welsh language in education. In *The Welsh language today*, ed. Meic Stephens, 91–109. Llandysul: Gomer.

Williams, I.W. 2003. Y Gymraeg mewn addysg: Ddoe a heddiw. In *Addysg Gymraeg, addysg Gymreig*, ed. Gareth Roberts, and Cen Williams, 6–23. Bangor: University of Bangor Department of Education.

Williams, Colin H. 2008. *Linguistic minorities in democratic context.* Basingstoke: Palgrave MacMillan.

———. 2009. Commentary: The primacy of renewal. *International Journal of the Sociology of Language* 195: 201–217.

Williams, Angie, Peter Garrett, and Nikolas Coupland. 1996. Perceptual dialectology, folklinguistics, and regional stereotypes: Teachers' perceptions of variation in Welsh English. *Multilingua* 15(2): 171–200.

Willis, David. Forthcoming. Investigating geospatial models of the diffusion of morphosyntactic innovations: The Welsh strong second-person singular pronoun *chdi. Journal of Linguistic Geography.*

Part 2

Welsh

2

Age Variation and Language Change in Welsh: Auxiliary Deletion and Possessive Constructions

Peredur Davies

Yn y bennod hon trafodir oedran fel newidyn mewn amrywiaeth morffo-gystrawennol mewn Cymraeg cyfoes, gan gyflwyno dadansoddiad o ddata corpws. Yn gyntaf, trafodir dileu'r ferf gynorthwyol, lle mae amrywiaeth oedran cydamserol yn cael ei ddehongli fel arwydd o newid iaith, ac mae tystiolaeth fewnol yn awgrymu bod y strwythur yn dangos cydgyfeiriant tuag at drefn geiriol mwy tebyg i'r Saesneg. Yn ail, trafodir amrywiaeth yn nefnydd gwahanol fathau o strwythurau meddiannol Cymraeg: mae dadansoddiad o amrywiaeth oedran yn nefnydd strwythurau meddiannol person 1af lluosog a 3ydd person unigol yn dangos mwy o ddefnydd o strwythur newydd—un a oedd gynt yn cael ei chysylltu gydag iaith plant ar y cyfan—gan siaradwyr ifanc, sydd eto yn cael ei ddefnyddio fel dadl am newid iaith, er bod y newid yn edrych fel ei fod wedi datblygu'n wahanol ar draws y ffurfiau person 1af a 3ydd person.

P. Davies (✉)
Bangor University, Bangor, UK
e-mail: p.davies@bangor.ac.uk

© The Author(s) 2016
M. Durham, J. Morris (eds.), *Sociolinguistics in Wales*,
DOI 10.1057/978-1-137-52897-1_2

Introduction

Synchronic age variation in linguistic data can be a snapshot of long-term diachronic change in the language. An increase or decrease in the use of a variant across speakers of different ages, where young speakers use more of a variable than older speakers, for example, can be interpreted as change in progress via the apparent time construct (e.g. Bailey et al. 1991; Cukor-Avila and Bailey 2013), which posits that 'differences among generations of similar adults mirror actual diachronic development in a language' (Bailey et al. 1991: 241). It has been argued that Welsh is undergoing language change, often because of direct influence from English (e.g. Thomas 1982; Phillips 2007). With this in mind, my aim in this chapter is to examine two features of grammatical variation in contemporary spoken Welsh which are examples of language change. I will show from my analysis how different patterns of age variation can indicate different stages of language change by highlighting the difference between changes which are nearing completion (where the new variant has almost entirely displaced the old) or which are still underway (where there will be more substantial generational differences). Furthermore I will be considering how we can look at age variation data to find out more precisely when changes started to propagate and spread in relation to one another. This paper also hopefully contributes to the study of Welsh linguistics as it comprises a discussion of two hitherto little-discussed parts of Welsh grammar.

After describing the corpus from which the data will be taken, I shall report on the results of the two studies. First, I will consider auxiliary verb deletion in Welsh. Davies and Deuchar (2014) argued that the change under examination (deletion of the second person singular present tense auxiliary *wyt* in certain constructions) is nearing completion, since all speakers now delete the auxiliary very frequently, although there is a small but statistically significant change between older speakers and speakers from other age groups. In this chapter, I will elaborate on the nature of the change found in the different forms of the same auxiliary by focusing on the parts of Davies and Deuchar which considered age variation. I will compare the pattern found with that feature with that found with the second feature being considered, namely Welsh possessive constructions, where a non-traditional construction shows increased frequency of use by younger generations, but where the change seems to still be underway. I will then discuss the ramifications of the findings from both studies, and compare what they show about the nature of age variation and language change.

Methodology

Given the increased availability of Welsh linguistic corpora today, it is now possible to use corpus data to analyse the grammar used by a wide range of Welsh speakers from different backgrounds. In particular, the *Siarad* corpus of the speech of Welsh–English bilinguals, collected between 2005 and 2008 by a research group based at Bangor University, Wales, is a valuable resource for this purpose, and both analyses I report on in this chapter use data from this corpus (see Deuchar et al. in this volume for further research on/description of this). *Siarad* consists of about 40 hours of spontaneous, informal speech by 151 participants, recorded in conversation in pairs or small groups where those conversing know one another well and recorded in informal surroundings without a researcher participating in the conversations. The primary research aim of the corpus as designed was to analyse code-switching by Welsh speakers. The corpus has been fully transcribed, glossed and translated, and is available for researchers at http://www.bangortalk.org.uk. All the analyses presented in this chapter will use data extracted from *Siarad*.

The corpus was collected with the aim of representing the informal speech (primarily Welsh) of Welsh–English bilinguals from a range of backgrounds and from across Wales and beyond, the only prerequisite being that they be speakers of both Welsh and English. We aimed for a broadly balanced distribution of major sociolinguistic factors where possible. The participants, each, were given a questionnaire to collect information about their background. Below are some of the variables which we tried to account for when recruiting participants:

- *Gender:* 54% of speakers were female, 46% were male, which is representative of the overall gender distribution in Wales.[1]
- *Age:* The participants recruited were primarily adults (18 years old or above), although a small number of participants of school age were also

---

[1] In the 2011 UK Census, out of Wales' population of 3.06 m, it was recorded that 1.50 m were men (49%) and 1.56 m were women (51%). We considered the gender distribution in *Siarad* to be close enough to this distribution as to be representative of Wales in general.

recruited. The age range of participants is between 12 and 89. The aim was to recruit participants from across the age range. The corpus is slightly more biased towards younger participants than older participants—for example, as there are 27 participants who are under 20 years old, whereas there are only 15 participants who are 70 or older—which may be related to the university environment from which the data collection was organised, and/or the generally young social networks of the researchers.

- *Place where they grew up*: The town or area where a participant grew up was used as a guide to their dialectal variety. The majority (111 or 74%) of participants in *Siarad* grew up in north-west Wales—for example, Gwynedd, Anglesey—which probably represents the project team, who were based in this area, using their local networks to recruit participants. Thirty-four participants came from other parts of Wales and six participants were not born in Wales.

- *First language*: The majority of the participants had Welsh as their first language (94 or 63%), which may represent again the area where the project team were based, where native Welsh speakers are commonly found. Thirty-four (23%) reported they had acquired Welsh and English simultaneously, while 20 (13%) had English as their first language. Two speakers had neither Welsh nor English as their first language. The corpus therefore primarily represents the speech of people who have spoken Welsh from birth/an early age, as opposed to second-language learner speech.

- *Education level*: The majority of participants (113 or 75%) reported that they had qualifications of A-levels[2] or higher, and indeed 48% of participants had a University degree (Bachelor's or higher). Only 38 (25%) participants only had educational qualifications below A-level. Thus, the speakers in *Siarad* tend to have relatively high levels of formal education.

The ratios above represent the challenges of collecting a corpus with such a broad speech population. Nevertheless, I would argue that the large number of participants included in the corpus allows for any analysis of the whole corpus to be generally representative of Welsh speech.

For the study on auxiliary verb deletion reported in section "Results: Variation in Auxiliary Verb Deletion", 28 speakers' speech was analysed, while for the study on possessive constructions, the output of all speak-

---

[2] UK qualifications that school students attain if they stay in school until they are 18.

ers in the *Siarad* corpus were included in the analysis. Further details on specific analyses are provided in the relevant sections of this chapter.

Further details on the participants included in *Siarad* can be found in Deuchar et al. (2014) and in Deuchar et al. (forthcoming).

Results: Variation in Auxiliary Verb Deletion

Welsh sentence structure allows for periphrastic constructions where a finite auxiliary verb precedes the subject and a nonfinite main verb comes later in the clause. Periphrastic constructions are very frequent in the informal spoken language. An example of an auxiliary construction from the *Siarad* corpus is given in (1) below, where the auxiliary *wyt*, a second person singular present tense form of *bod* 'be', precedes the subject *ti* 'you'; and the nonfinite main verb *byw* 'live' comes later in the sentence; these words have been highlighted in bold.

1)	*oh*	*yeah*	*os*	**wyt**	*ti*	*'n*	***byw...***	*yn*	*Chirk*
	oh	yeah	if	be.2s.PRES	2s	PRT	live.NONFIN	in	Chirk
	ynde.								
	eh								
	'Oh yeah, if you live... in Chirk, eh'.			[davies11-Rachel][3]					

In spoken Welsh it is common (Borsley et al. 2007: 260–1) for the auxiliary verb to be omitted, at least in some contexts (e.g. for a particular person, number, tense, depending on the speaker or dialect), resulting in a sentence like that shown in (2). In this example, the second person singular auxiliary verb, *wyt* in the previous example, has not been produced, resulting in a clause-initial second person singular subject pronoun *ti* and a nonfinite main verb *jocian* 'joke'. The particle *'n* in both (1) and (2) denotes nonperfective aspect.

2)	*ti*	*'n*	*jocian.*
	2s	PRT	joke.NONFIN
	'You're joking.'		[davies6-Daniel]

---

[3] References in square brackets following examples are to specific files in the Siarad Welsh–English bilingual corpus which we collected and have made available on www.talkbank.org/BilingBank. Transcripts of recorded conversations are referred to by the filename, for example, davies1, fusser27, and the pseudonym of the participant is then supplied.

I call this AUXILIARY DELETION (AuxD), and it can be observed primarily with auxiliary forms of *bod* 'be' in periphrastic constructions in informal Welsh, although each of the different inflections of the auxiliary do not delete equally, as will be discussed below.

While in Davies and Deuchar (2014) we suggested that AuxD in Welsh may have first appeared during the twentieth century (see below), recent research by Willis (forthcoming) finds that AuxD is in fact first attested in Welsh, albeit in a restricted fashion, considerably earlier in history. Willis finds many examples of AuxD in some Welsh translations of Harriet Beecher Stowe's novel *Uncle Tom's Cabin* published between 1852 and 1854 by various translators. In several of these translations AuxD (or copula deletion) is used in the translated speech of the black slave characters to represent their speech variety: for example, 'I rides a leetle ahead' is translated by Hugh Williams in his 1854 translation as *fi dipyn bach o'u blaen nhw* 'I am a little bit ahead of them', rather than *(r)wyf fi dipyn bach o'u blaen nhw*, that is, with a deleted first person singular present tense verb *(r)wyf*. Willis argues that this linguistic choice shows the author seeking to represent a kind of pidgin Welsh intended to reflect the creolised English of black Americans of that time period. Willis finds an even earlier appearance of AuxD from an 1850 text by William Rees, *Llythyrau 'Rhen Ffarmwr [The letters of the Old Farmer]*, where the narrator is a landowner who professes to not being able to speak or write Welsh well, implying that AuxD is a feature of imperfectly learnt second-language Welsh. Indeed, Willis points to repeated use of AuxD in writings throughout the nineteenth and early twentieth century as a tool used by Welsh authors to characterise the speech of non-fluent second-language learners of Welsh, which Willis argues is a strong indicator that this change was perceived as coming from outside, that is, via English, with AuxD later spreading to the speech of native Welsh speakers through prolonged language contact. Linguistic influence of English on Welsh has deep historical roots, and is most clearly evident via the extensive lexical borrowing from English found in Welsh (e.g. Parry-Williams 1923). Contact between the two languages dates back ultimately to the period of Anglo-Saxon settlement but certainly became more intense in recent centuries (Davies 1994), given that bilingualism in Welsh and English is now universal for adult Welsh speakers and that English is spoken by almost everyone in Wales.

These facts point to AuxD being considered historically highly non-standard, and indeed the deleted form is absent from many grammar books as recently as the late twentieth century, such as Williams (1980) and Thorne (1996), which only provide the full, undeleted form. Nonetheless, there are linguistic discussions of AuxD of the second person singular present tense form of *bod* 'be', *wyt*—probably the most common type—which indicate that it was a feature of informal Welsh at least as early as the 1970s (Jones and Thomas 1977; Roberts 1988, describing data collected in the early 1970s). Authors describing twenty-first century Welsh note that AuxD of *wyt* is 'particularly common' (Borsley et al. 2007: 261), and that deletion of other forms of *bod* varies according to dialect. There is also evidence that AuxD is becoming more frequent, at least in some dialects: research by Jones (1998) on Welsh in two communities, Rhosllanerchrugog in north-east Wales and the Rhymney Valley in south-east Wales, which she identified as undergoing dialect obsolescence and language shift, finds that speakers are more likely to delete the auxiliary the younger they are, which one can explain as representing a change in progress, where deleting the auxiliary is increasingly becoming the norm. While Jones focused on communities where Welsh is arguably undergoing language shift, Davies and Deuchar (2014), presenting analysis first shown in Davies (2010), looked at the speech of a wide range of different speakers from diverse communities across Wales and also identified significant age variation, which the authors argued to show a change in progress. I summarise the results of that study here, focusing on the age variation we identified, and then elaborate by suggesting the ways in which the change might spread in the future.

In Davies and Deuchar, we presented a corpus analysis of the speech of 28 speakers, from 13 different recorded conversations in the *Siarad* corpus, who had been selected to be generally diverse and balanced in terms of age and gender: half the speakers were male and half female and the age range was 12–81 (mean = 43)—although all but one speaker analysed was 18 or older. The places where the selected speakers grew up were as follows: 18 from north Wales, 8 from south Wales, 1 from mid-Wales and 1 from England. All spoke Welsh and English fluently.

The analysis focused on auxiliaries with the second person singular present tense form of *bod* 'be', which is *wyt* and pronounced variously [ut], [uɪt], [it] etc. This form was chosen because it was common across all the *Siarad* data and was a type of AuxD that speakers of all dialects appear to use (see discussion above). One reason for its commonness in the data

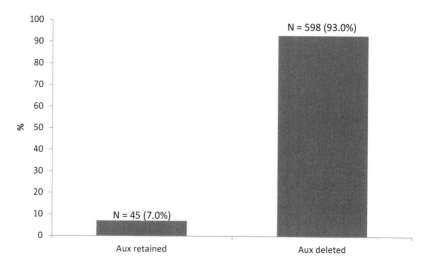

Fig. 2.1 Overall frequency of deleted versus retained second person singular present tense auxiliary *wyt* in the dataset

is probably that the conversations in *Siarad* are usually between pairs of friends or family and are thus overwhelmingly in an informal style, which results in the familiar second person address form being used frequently. A total of 643 tokens were extracted from the dataset and were labelled for whether they DELETED or RETAINED the auxiliary verb *wyt*.

The aggregate variation (retained vs. deleted auxiliary) is illustrated in Fig. 2.1. Overall, the pattern found was that the deletion of the auxiliary *wyt* is very common, with 93.0% of clauses, 598 out of 643 tokens, having a deleted auxiliary.

Furthermore, the authors found that at least 50% of the tokens for each speaker analysed had a deleted auxiliary, indicating that none of the speakers never delete the auxiliary, and some speakers even deleted the auxiliary in 100% of their tokens, although the authors assume that this does not mean they lack +A in their repertoire entirely (e.g. they might well prefer to retain the auxiliary for formal speech, but analysing stylistic variation is out of the scope of the *Siarad* corpus as it contains only informal speech).

One explanation for the AuxD change we gave in Davies and Deuchar (2014) linked to convergence, which we classify as the grammar of one

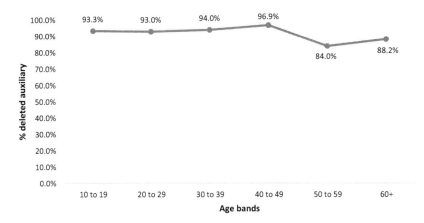

Fig. 2.2 Age variation (by age band) in frequency of deleting the auxiliary *wyt* in the dataset

language changing to be more similar to that of another language which it is in contact with. The auxiliary-deleted form of a Welsh sentence typically results in the subject being the first overt constituent (AuxSVO becomes SVO), which is superficially similar to the SVO word order normally found in English main clauses. In Davies and Deuchar, we argued that speakers may be being influenced by the prevalence of this word order in English and are increasing the frequency of SVO clauses in their Welsh by deleting the auxiliary.

We then analysed the data according to the variable of age, dividing speakers into age bands (10–19, 20–29, etc., up to 60+) to see if speakers of different ages were more or less likely to delete *wyt*.[4] The age variation is illustrated in Fig. 2.2 and the data is given in Table 2.1.

A Chi-square test for independence showed statistically significant variation at the 5% level across age bands (χ^2 = 4.389, p = 0.036, without continuity correction; Cramer's V = 0.083), with speakers below 50 deleting *wyt* more frequently than those 50 or older did. However, speakers

---

[4] As Table 2.1 shows, the number of tokens per age band is not balanced. There are more tokens for the groups for speakers aged between 20 and 49 than for the younger and the older speakers, and there are very few tokens for the oldest speakers. I acknowledge that analysing more balanced age bands in the future might affect the statistical analysis presented below.

Table 2.1 Age variation (by age band) in frequency of deleting the auxiliary *wyt* (-A) in the dataset

Age bands	Auxiliary retained (% within group)	Auxiliary deleted (% within group)	Total number of tokens
10–19	93.3	6.67	75
20–29	93.0	7.04	199
30–39	94.0	5.98	117
40–49	96.9	3.13	160
50–59	84.0	16.00	75
60+	88.2	11.8	17

aged 60 or older still produced high frequencies of auxiliary deletion, and the value of Cramer's V indicates that the difference identified is, while significant, not very strong.

Results: Variation in Possessive Construction Type Used by Speakers

Welsh possessive noun phrases traditionally follow one of two patterns: one option has a preposed possessive clitic (inflected for person and number of the possessor) which precedes the possessed noun, illustrated in (3), or with both this proclitic *and* with a dependent personal pronoun following the possessed noun, as illustrated in (4). Neither option appears to carry a different meaning or particular emphasis (Borsley et al. 2007; although cf. Morris-Jones 1931 who argues that the latter option can be used 'to add clearness or emphasis to a pronominal element already expressed' [1931: 81–2]). The possessive constructions are in bold in these examples.

3)	Gwelodd	Y	dyn	ei	arth.
	see.3s.PAST	DET	man	POSS.3s	bear
	'The man saw **his bear**'.				

4)	Gwelodd	y	dyn	ei	arth	o.
	see.3s.PAST	DET	man	POSS.3s	bear	3SM
	'The man saw **his bear**'.					

While there is no clear semantic difference between the two types, one distinction between them is dependent on the medium or formality of the discourse. Typically, the type illustrated in (3) is considered more appropriate for a literary and/or formal style than the one shown in type (4). Watkins (1977) discusses the relationship between the two types, noting that the former is associated with the written language and the latter with the spoken language, even to the point that novelists will use the former type in narration but the latter type when representing spoken dialogue. The 'sandwich'construction (I call it so because the possessum is sandwiched between two elements) seen in (4) is probably the prototypical option in present-day spoken Welsh (Watkins 1977; John Morris-Jones stated that '[i]n the spoken language the affixed pronoun [i.e. found in the 'sandwich' type] is almost always heard even when unemphatic, whenever it is admissible' [1931: 84]) but that both can be found in the spoken language (as acknowledged by, e.g., Morris-Jones and identified in data by, e.g., Awbery 1994). In this paper, I will use the following shorthand to distinguish between types: I will refer to the possessive construction in (3) as the LITERARY CONSTRUCTION (LC) and the construction in (4) as the SANDWICH CONSTRUCTION (SC). These are only labels, however, and are not intended to imply that, for example, the LC is *only* found in written or high-register Welsh (as will be seen, both types are found in the *Siarad* data I analysed).

It has been shown (Awbery 1994) that, at least for some speakers, coreferential features dictate which of the two types is selected. Awbery found that old Welsh speakers (b. 1890–1900) from Pembrokeshire in south-west Wales would categorically only use the literary type when the referent of the possessive NP matched the referent of the clause's subject, and conversely only used the sandwich type where the referent of the possessive NP did not match the subject's referent. However, Borsley et al. (2007) suggest that not all speakers adhere to this rule categorically. Thus, it is reasonable to assume that for some speakers the selection of SC over LC is driven by factors other than referentiality (although I will not be considering referentiality in the analysis I present here). Note also that the use of either LC or SC is not permissible in certain idiosyncratic constructions,[5] as detailed by, for example, Watkins (1977), but I will also not consider such exceptions here as they are not numerous.

A third option for constructing a Welsh possessive noun phrase, which I will call the COLLOQUIAL CONSTRUCTION (CC), has apparently become increasingly frequent in recent years, at least among certain speakers and/or in certain dialects (e.g. M.C. Jones 1998; Borsley et al. 2007), and used to be associated primarily with children's speech (e.g. Jones and Thomas 1977; Awbery 1994; Jones 1990). This option lacks a possessive proclitic and instead just uses a postnominal pronoun, as illustrated in (5).

5)	Gwelodd	y	dyn	arth (f)o.
	see.3S.PAST	DET	man	bear 3s
	'The man saw **his bear**'.			

Authors like Borsley et al. (2007) have proposed that the CC pattern is an extension or analogical levelling of the normal construction used in Welsh for nonpronominal noun phrases, where the possessor follows the possessum, as shown in (6), where the proper noun *Dafydd* follows *arth* 'bear'.

6)	Gwelodd	y	dyn	**arth Dafydd.**
	see.3S.PAST	DET	man	bear Dafydd
	'The man saw **Dafydd's bear**'.			

One could link this extension to language shift (M.C. Jones 1998), in the form of grammatical simplification resulting from lack of input of the historical possessive forms.

The CC possessive is another linguistic feature which Willis (forthcoming) identifies as a feature used by some nineteenth century Welsh authors to represent the speech of second-language and/or non-fluent

---

[5] One such example is *ei gilydd* (etc.) 'each other', which is a grammaticalisation of (now archaic) *cilydd* 'companion', i.e. formerly *ei gilydd* 'his companion', and where using a pronoun, e.g., **ei gilydd o*, is ungrammatical.

learners of Welsh—discussed in the previous section—which, as (perhaps coincidentally) with AuxD, points to this construction being viewed as nonstandard—although the analysis I present below is not able to show whether it is more frequent in the speech of second-language speakers than first-language speakers. It has seemingly been used in Welsh for over a century and a half, but even as recently as the late 1970s the CC option was considered by some linguists as being highly 'sub-standard' (Jones and Thomas 1977: 172), with a 'disturbingly high frequency in the speech of young children' (ibid.); Borsley et al. (2007: 159) note that CC is 'considered non-standard'. Nevertheless, Roberts (1988) found that it was common in the speech of many speakers in Pwllheli, north-west Wales, in the 1970s, B.M. Jones (1990) identified it as being widespread in adult speech in the late 1980s, and M.C. Jones (1998), analysing speech in the 1990s in communities which she argued to be undergoing language shift, found that CC was present in most of her participants' speech and showed statistically significant age variation, with speakers more likely to produce the CC type the younger they were.

R.J. Davies (2012) examined the possessive constructions used in online Welsh writing on the social networking site Twitter, and found that 47.2% of 58 tokens used only the prenominal pronoun (LC), 19.2% used both a prenominal and postnominal pronoun (SC) and 32.9% used only a postnominal pronoun (CC); thus LC was the most frequent type used. She also found that participants from south Wales used more of the colloquial construction type than participants from north Wales, which—accepting that she looked at only a very small sample of data—points to a dialectal difference in usage (albeit that the data is typed and not spoken).

Several of these studies point to Welsh speakers from varying backgrounds using CC more frequently the younger they are, with differing reports on the frequency of CC in the speech of older speakers/adults. I present here an analysis which focuses on first person plural constructions (e.g. *ein hafal/ein hafal ni/afal ni* 'our apple') and both masculine and feminine third person singular constructions (e.g. *ei afal/ei afal o/afal fo* 'his apple'). The CLAN programme (MacWhinney 2000) was used to extract all clauses containing an appropriate construction from the corpus, and any inappropriate or incomplete constructions were excluded from analysis. The final sets of analyses consists of 134 tokens of first person plural constructions and 1055 tokens of third person singular constructions. I will discuss the findings of both analyses in turn before comparing the two sets.

Examples of first person plural possessive constructions in *Siarad*, of all three possessive types, are given below in (7), (8), and (9). The possessives are in bold in each example and a superscript label identifies which of construction types (SC, LC or CC) it is.

7)	*oedden*	*ni*	*wedi*	*cael*	***ein***	***bwyd*** LC...
	be.1PL.IMP	1PL	PRT.PAST	have.NONFIN	poss.1PL	food
	'We had had our food...'			[Fusser13-Beinon]		

8)	...*yn*	***ein***	***pwyllgor***	***ni*** SC	*nos*	*Lun*	*nesa*	*fydd*
	in	POSS.1PL	committee	1PL	night	Monday	next	be.3S.FUT
	raid	*ni*	*sôn*	*am*	*hynna.*			
	need	1PL	mention.NONFIN	about	that			
	'In our committee next Monday night we'll have to mention						[Fusser32-	
	that.'							Matthew]

9)	*oh,*	***pres***	***ni*** CC	*ydy*	*o*	*yn*	*diwedd,*	*te,*	*yeah.*
	oh	money	1PL	be.3S.PRES	3SM	in	end	TAG	yeah
	'Oh, it's our money in the end, eh, yeah.'				[Fusser23-Heledd]				

The frequency in *Siarad* of each type is illustrated in Fig. 2.3.[6]

As Fig. 2.3 shows, the colloquial construction is the most frequent construction used overall (98 or 73.1% of 134 tokens), while the other two types are used about as frequently as each other (sandwich construction 19 tokens or 14.2%; literary construction 17 tokens or 12.7%).

To analyse age variation, speakers were divided into age bands (10–19 years old, 20–29, etc.). The frequency of each first person plural possessive construction type is illustrated in Fig. 2.4 below and the data is shown in Table 2.2.

---

[6] An issue that arose in the analysis was categoricality, in particular with the frequent CC token *tŷ ni* 'our house', which was found in 19 tokens in the corpus but which only ever appeared as a CC construction, never SC (*ein tŷ ni*) or LC (*ein tŷ*). It could be that *tŷ ni* has become conventionalised as a set phrase which may mean something like '(our) home'.

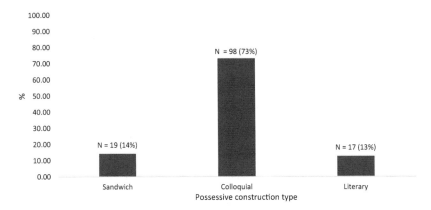

Fig. 2.3 Overall frequency of use of the different types of first person plural possessive construction in the *Siarad* corpus

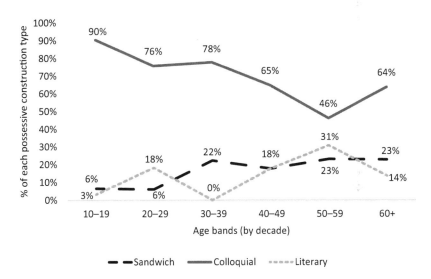

Fig. 2.4 Age variation in the frequency of the different types of first person plural possessive construction used by speakers in the *Siarad* corpus (by decade age bands; *p* = 0.066)

The pattern in Fig. 2.4 is not very clear, but broadly it can be seen that younger speakers (under 39) produce more CC than older speakers, although speakers 60 and over produce more CC than speakers in the 50–59 age group. A broad pattern of younger speakers producing

Table 2.2 Age variation in frequency of use of different first person plural possessive construction types

	10–19		20–29		30–39		40–49		50–59		60+	
	n	%	n	%	n	%	n	%	n	%	n	%
Sandwich type	2	6.5	2	6.1	4	22.2	3	17.6	3	23.1	5	27.8
Colloquial type	28	90.3	25	75.8	14	77.8	11	64.7	6	46.2	11	61.1
Literary type	1	3.2	6	18.2	0	0.0	3	17.6	4	30.8	2	11.1
Total	31	100.0	33	100.0	18	100.0	17	100.0	13	100.0	18	100.0

very little SC or LC compared to older speakers can also be identified, although note that CC is clearly the most frequently selected construction for all age groups.

A Chi-square test for independence was made to see if there is a relationship between age band and first person plural possessive constructions, but the relationship was not found to be statistically significant ($p = 0.066$, df = 12, Cramer's V = 0.274). Since there are not many tokens in each cell, however, this might affect the reliability of the statistical tests. The relationship between age and first person plural possessive use may be on the borderline of significance, and if more tokens were available then perhaps the pattern would be clearer.

I now turn to the third person singular (masculine and feminine) constructions. Examples from *Siarad* of all three types of possessive are shown in (10) through (15) below.

10)	*yeah*	*dw*	*i*	*meddwl*	*Jemimah*[7]	*oedd*	*ei*	*enw hi.*sc
	yeah	be.1s.PRES	1s	think. NONFIN	Jemimah	be.3s.IMP	POSS.3SF	name 3SF

'Yeah, I think her name was Jemimah.'   [davies2-Greta]

---

[7] *Siarad* uses pseudonyms for people named within the conversations as well as for the participants themselves.

11) | *oedd* | *ei* | *frawd* | *e^{sc}* | *yn* | *vet* | *neu* | *rywbeth?* |
|---|---|---|---|---|---|---|---|
| be.3s.IMP | POSS.3SM | brother | 3SM | PRT | vet | or | something |

'Was his brother a vet or something?'   [davies11-Rachel]

12) | *gynni* | *hi* | *'m* | *tyllau* | *yn* | *ei* | *chlustiau^{Lc}* | *chwaith...* |
|---|---|---|---|---|---|---|---|
| with.3SF | 3SF | NEG | holes | in | POSS.3SF | ears | either |

'She doesn't have holes in her   [robert9-Penri...]
ears, either.'

13) | *mi* | *losgodd* | *o* | *ei* | *geg.^{Lc}* |
|---|---|---|---|---|
| PRT | burn.3s.PAST | 3SM | POSS.3SM | mouth |

'He burnt his mouth.'   [davies10-Cledwyn]

14) | ...*a dyn* | *nhw* | *ddim* | *yn...* | *ailhysbysebu* | *swydd* | *hi.^{cc}* |
|---|---|---|---|---|---|---|
| and be.3PL.PRES.NEG | 3PL | NEG | PRT | readvertise.NONFIN | job | 3SF |

'...and they're not... readvertising her   [stammers6-Ifan]
job.'

15) | *wel* | *wnaeth* | *o* | | *a* | *'i* | *gariad* | *o* |
|---|---|---|---|---|---|---|---|
| well | do.3S.PAST | 3SM | | and | POSS.3SM | girlfriend | 3SM |
| *gorffen* | *fath* | *â* | *tra* | | *oedd* | *o* | *wneud* |
| finish.NONFIN | kind | with | while | | be.3S.IMP | 3SM | do.NONFIN |
| ***dissertation*** | *o.^{cc}* | | | | | | |
| dissertation | 3SM | | | | | | |

'Well, he and his girlfriend broke up while he was doing his dissertation.'
[davies12-Ceri]

For the purpose of this analysis, I combined the masculine and feminine pronouns. The frequency of each type is illustrated in Fig. 2.6 below.

Figure 2.5 shows that the most frequent type used for third person singular possessive constructions overall is, perhaps surprisingly, LC (427 or 40.5% of 1055 tokens), but the other types are also frequent (SC = 291 tokens or 27.6%; CC = 337 tokens or 31.9%).

To analyse age variation, speakers were again divided into age bands by decade. The frequency patterns across age bands are illustrated in Fig. 2.6 and the data is shown in Table 2.3.

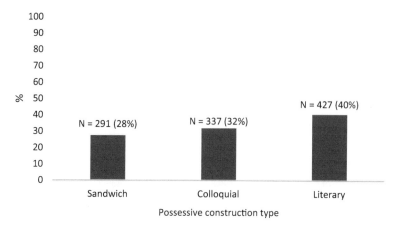

Fig. 2.5 Overall frequency of use of the different types of third person singular (masculine and feminine combined) possessive construction in the *Siarad* corpus

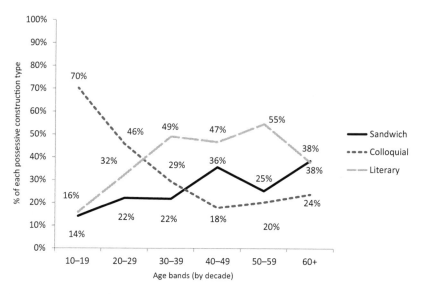

Fig. 2.6 Age variation in the frequency of the different types of third person singular possessive construction used by speakers in the *Siarad* corpus (by decade age bands; $p = 0.0005$)

Table 2.3 Age variation in frequency of use of different third person plural possessive construction types

	10–19		20–29		30–39		40–49		50–59		60+	
	n	%	n	%	n	%	n	%	n	%	n	%
Sandwich type	16	14.0	43	22.1	23	21.7	42	35.6	55	25.2	117	38.5
Colloquial type	80	70.2	89	45.6	31	29.2	21	17.8	44	20.2	72	23.7
Literary type	18	15.8	63	32.3	52	49.1	55	46.6	119	54.6	115	37.8
Total	114	100.0	195	100.0	106	100.0	118	100.0	218	100.0	304	100.0

The overall pattern of age variation in third person singular constructions is clearer than for the first person plural possessives. All generations produce all three possessive types, but with clear differences. LC, while most common overall (see Fig. 2.5) and used with fairly high frequency by most generations over 19 (see Fig. 2.6), is notably less frequent in the speech of the youngest speakers. An inverse pattern can be seen for SC, which is more common in the speech of the older generations than the younger generations. Most striking is the difference in use of third singular CC across generations. The youngest group (10–19 years old) heavily favour CC and disfavour the other two types, and there is an obvious spike in the data in frequency of CC for speakers aged under 40. The older the speaker, the more SC and LC they use and the less CC they use. A crossover point can be seen in the 30–39 age group, who use SC and CC as frequently as each other. A Chi-square test shows that the relationship between third person singular possessive type and age is statistically significant at the 5% level ($p = 0.0005$, df = 10, Cramer's V = 0.266). I discuss these findings in the next section.

Discussion

Generational differences were found in both studies, but with contrastive patterns. I will first discuss the ramifications of the auxiliary deletion analysis, before proceeding to compare the findings of the possessive construction analysis.

In Davies and Deuchar (2014), we argued that the age variation found in the data points to language change in progress, with apparent time representing a diachronic increase in deleting the auxiliary since when the eldest speakers were born (in the first half of the twentieth century). Even though the pattern on the graph is not a clear S-curve, the speakers under 50 all produce about the same frequency of auxiliary deletion, which suggests that the change has plateaued and perhaps reached completion. Since the frequency of deleting the auxiliary is high for most speakers, even elderly speakers (note that even the 60+ group produces 88.2% deletion), the authors suggest that this is a change which has been underway for a long time. Adding to this the recent findings by Willis (forthcoming) that AuxD may have been present in—or stereotypically indicative of—the Welsh speech of second-language learners of Welsh from the mid-nineteenth century, it is plausible here to propose that AuxD remained a novel but uncommon form until the middle of the twentieth century—the earliest explicit mention of Welsh AuxD in a grammar book that I have found is in Jones and Thomas (1977)—after which it spread and became more frequent. In Davies and Deuchar, we point to historical events which occurred in that period, like the increase in Welsh-medium education and an increase in awareness of Welsh identity and of language campaigning, and we suggest that this could have led to an increase in younger people taking up Welsh, which may have led to an acceleration of grammatical change.

In Davies and Deuchar, we argue that the small (albeit significant) gap between the younger and the older speakers may reflect late-life uptake of the novel form by older speakers once it has become the norm among younger speakers, a process called 'late adoption' by Boberg (2004) and 'lifespan change' by Sankoff and Blondeau (2007); the latter classify it as a change in the speech of individuals later in life in the direction of a change in progress by other speakers in the community.

Despite the statistically significant difference between the older and the younger groups in the frequency of deleting the auxiliary, then, the findings point to the change nearing completion. All age groups delete the auxiliary *wyt* with high frequency, and it can be predicted that real-time data collected in the future would show that the newest generation of speakers would delete *wyt* even more frequently than the current youngest age group. Given that even the oldest speakers are apparently now abandoning the auxiliary-retained form of the construction, I predict that the form that retains the auxiliary will become more and more restricted in use in the future, possibly only continuing to be found in formal or literary language. The indicator of a change having reached completion would be a lack of age variation, since all speakers will be presumed to delete the auxiliary *wyt* in this context.

While deletion of second person singular *wyt* is very frequent and seemingly in all informal varieties, deletion of other persons are limited to certain dialects, particularly in south Wales (cf. Borsley et al. 2007: 261). Consider the clause shown in (16), taken from the *Siarad* corpus (English code-switched words are underlined in examples).

16)	fi	just	yn	dibynnu	ar	y	style,	though,	yn	y	diwedd.
	1s	just	PRT	depend.NONFIN	on	DET	style	though	in	DET	end

'I just depend on the style,   [fusser27-Lisa]
though, in the end.'
[hypothetical form with a retained aux.: **wyf** *fi just yn dibynnu ar y* style
though *yn y diwedd*]

The auxiliary deleted in (16) is presumably a first person singular present tense of *bod* 'be'. The speaker here is from south Wales, where the form of this auxiliary is usually something like *wyf* [uiv] or *yf* [iv]. The form of the auxiliary for speakers of north Welsh varieties, however, is usually something like *ydw* [ədu] or *dw* [du]—and I have found no firm examples in *Siarad* of this auxiliary being deleted by speakers from north Wales. Based on this, and following Jones (2004), in Davies and Deuchar (2014) we argue that this difference between AuxD 'scope' in northern and southern varieties of Welsh is phonologically conditioned, whereby auxiliaries with an initial consonant[8] are resistant to deletion, whereas auxiliaries which do not *can* be deleted. This seems to be the pattern

---

[8] Perhaps this could be more strictly defined as verb which has a stressed syllable with an initial consonant, which explains non-deletion of bisyllabic verbs like *ydw*.

Table 2.4 Primary differences between the pronunciation of present tense auxiliary forms of *bod* 'be' in northern and southern varieties of Welsh

	Northern Welsh	Southern Welsh
First singular	dw [du]	w [u]
Second singular	wyt [ut]	wyt [uɪt]
Third singular	ma' [ma]	ma' [ma]
First plural	dyn [dən]	ŷn [in]
Second plural	dych [daχ]	ŷch [iχ]
Third plural	ma'n [man]	ma'n [man]

Adapted from Jones (2004: 88–9)

identifiable in *Siarad* and in Welsh speech in general. The paradigm in Table 2.4 below illustrates differences between the phonological form of the auxiliary in both dialects; I have given approximate pronunciations but there remain intra-regional differences which I have ignored for simplicity.

An eyeball of the *Siarad* data indicates that the following rules tend to apply with regards to deletion or non-deletion of auxiliary forms of *bod* 'be': forms which begin with [d] or [m]—like *dw* or *ma'* are seldom if ever deleted by most speakers, whereas forms which begin with a vowel—like *w*, *wyt* or *ŷn* can be deleted (and, going by the analysis presented here, are more likely to be deleted than retained). Phonologically, I propose that what may be going on is that the forms with initial consonants are considered 'heavy' enough that speakers choose not to phonologically reduce them, whereas conversely vowel-initial forms can be elided and reduced to the final consonant, which is in turn assimilated to the initial consonant of the following pronoun if applicable: for example, *ŷn ni'n mynd* [in nin mind] 'we are' > *ni'n mynd* [nin mind].

In northern speech only the second singular *wyt* has an initial vowel—the rest of the forms typically have an initial consonant—whereas in southern speech only the third person forms tend to have initial consonants.[9] The pattern, then, is that AuxD in southern varieties can take

---

[9] Again one must allow for dialectal differences, since the northern/southern distinction is a crude and perhaps overly generalistic one, and indeed there will also be individual speaker differences, such as southern L2 speakers who might have a more standard pronunciation due to the influence of 'school Welsh' (e.g. first plural *dyn* rather than *ŷn*).

place with more verb forms than it does in northern varieties, due to a phonological factor which restricts the scope of the change. The change occurs in both northern and southern varieties for second singular *wyt*, because its form happens to begin with a vowel in all varieties of Welsh. Furthermore, if I hypothesise that the same change in frequency of AuxD is not only happening in constructions involving second singular *wyt*— as argued in this section—but also, in southern Welsh speech, to other forms as well, then I would expect to see the same age variation patterns in the distribution of AuxD across age bands with southern forms like the first person singular or second person plural.

Note that, despite this, there *is* some limited evidence in *Siarad* of speakers of northern dialects deleting an auxiliary which does start with a consonant. An example from the corpus[10] is given in (17) below, where the presumed deleted auxiliary is the third person singular present *mae* [ma].

---

17) *honno*   *casáu*   *fi,*   *ydy.*
     that-one.F   hate.NONFIN   1s   be.3s.PRES

     'She hates me, doesn't she.'   [davies6-Daniel]

     [hypothetical form with a retained aux.: **mae** honno ('n) casáu fi, ydy]

This speaker, Daniel, is a young (25) male from north-west Wales. If examples such as this become more common in Welsh speech, then it might be a sign that the phonological constraints described above are no longer active, and that *any* auxiliary may in principle be deleted. Thus, I would propose that AuxD represents a change which initially involved deleting the phonologically 'open' forms of *bod*, like the second person singular present tense *wyt*, but is by now apparently starting to spread to verb forms which are phonologically 'closed', like the third singular present tense *mae* noted above. While the change with deletion of *wyt* seems to be nearing completion, changes with other forms of the verb may not yet have reached completion, and are still underway. A future analysis of

---

[10] This is one example I found in *Siarad* of this kind of deletion. Another example involves a proper noun subject; this is given as example (6) in Davies and Deuchar (2014). There are likely to be other similar instances in the corpus.

those forms would allow us to compare the age variation patterns across verb forms, so as to try to identify the ongoing scope of the change.

I now proceed to comparing these findings to the possessive construction analyses. Two analyses were made, one of first person plural constructions and another of third person singular constructions. The patterns found for both analyses differed somewhat, but overall we can see that the colloquial possessive type (CC) is more frequent in young people's speech than older people's speech for both first and third person constructions. The pattern for first person plural age data shows that CC is generally more common for younger speakers than older speakers (Fig. 2.4), although the difference is not significant, and the increase in CC for younger age groups looks like an S-curve and indicative of diachronic change. We could also perhaps interpret the fact that the older and younger groups produce more CC than the middle age groups do as a U curve, that is, a kind of age grading (e.g. Chambers 2003; Sankoff and Laberge 1978; Labov 2001). whereby middle-aged speakers restrict their use of CC and increase their use of SC and LC. The small number of tokens in each group here may affect the results, however.

In Fig. 2.6 we can see that the line for CC frequency in third singular constructions is not strictly speaking a true S-curve: although the youngest speakers clearly use much more CC than the oldest speakers, the speakers aged 40–49 actually use slightly less CC than the speakers older than them, and so the middle-aged speakers are those least likely to use CC. Nevertheless, the older speakers (above 40) use CC markedly less than the younger speakers, and instead prefer SC or LC. I argue that the difference seen between the oldest and the youngest speakers' use of CC in both analyses indicates that CC has become more frequent over time, and that this is a change in progress, where CC is becoming more and more common in speech. Indeed, the higher use of CC by the oldest speakers in both the first and third person analyses may indicate late adoption/lifespan change, as proposed above for the AuxD analysis, although one might expect that to occur when a change is nearing completion, whereas neither of the increases in CC appears to be near a completed change.

The major difference between the two datasets is that the change (increase in frequency of CC) seems to have started its increase earlier in time for the first person plural type than for the third person singular type. CC in the first person plural has high frequency even for the 60+ year old speakers, whereas CC in the third person singular has low frequency in age groups older than 39, after which there is a clear jump in frequency of use, which I take to indicate that the change propagated later in time for the third person singular than for the first person singular. Perhaps the presence of CC in the first person allowed its spread to the third person.

The trend for both constructions is that CC is becoming more common, while SC and LC are becoming less common. If we posit SC or LC as the historical prototype, it is reasonable to interpret these data as showing that CC taking over from SC and LC as the norm (this crossover is more apparent in the third singular data than in the first plural data). The logical end point of such a change would be the disappearance of SC/LC from the spoken language. Note that LC is nevertheless present in the speech of speakers of all ages in these data, to a varying extent, and it could be that this possessive type lingers in the spoken language as a result of its use in more formal, literary Welsh, which in turn may lend it a higher prestige.[11]

The contrasting patterns found between the two possessive construction analyses are reflective of the spread of the change in AuxD I proposed above, in which the change began with second person singular *wyt*, and is nearing completion, but is now perhaps spreading beyond its initial phonological constraints to other forms, like the third person singular. With the possessive constructions, I argue that the change in frequency occurred in the first person plural before it spread to the third person singular, although future analyses of the other pronominal forms of the possessive constructions would be required to shed more light on the exact nature of that change.

---

[11] Jones (1998) found that school-aged children in Rhosllanerchrugog tended to use standard or literary grammatical forms of certain constructions, rather than the dialectal forms used by older Welsh speakers in the community (such as preferring the more formal/neutral nominal plural suffix <-au> [aɨ] to the dialectal <-e> [e]), presumably because of the influence of 'school Welsh' as perhaps their primary input source for Welsh. The reasons for the persistence of the LC possessive in even the younger generations' speech may be similarly-motivated, whereby speakers retain forms which are common in written or formal Welsh even though they are not the most common constructions found in speech (and, therefore, in the input).

One thing that should be borne in mind when considering an analysis of the whole *Siarad* corpus—as the possessive constructions analysis is—is that the speakers are from very diverse linguistic backgrounds. While the majority are first-language Welsh and the majority from north Wales, not all are, and so the analysis is not of one homogeneous group. It may be, for example, that the changes identified via the age variation are also conditioned by dialect. This would be a fruitful future avenue for study of this feature.

What do these results suggest about our theories of age variation and language change in general? The data all support the notion that variation according to age reflects language change, and I have argued that the differences in age variation patterns across the three datasets analysed give us an indicator that similar types of changes, even within the same paradigm, can start in one form before spreading to others. I have also suggested that, in the AuxD analysis at least, there is evidence of older speakers adapting their speech to mirror a community change, and this may be a more common feature of language change than was previously assumed. Phonological constraints, as seen in the AuxD analysis, can limit the extent and nature of a change, but it seems that such constraints are not invulnerable (as seen in example 17). Speakers will, it seems, embrace a change and extend it where the circumstances allow.

Conclusion

In this chapter, I have presented two studies of grammatical variation in contemporary spoken Welsh. My aim was to show how an analysis of age variation can indicate whether or not change is in progress, and, furthermore, what stage that change might be at. The analysis of auxiliary deletion shows a long-standing change, where the deletion of *wyt* increases in frequency, which I argue is nearing completion, as seen by its high frequency of use among speakers of all ages, albeit that older speakers still currently delete the auxiliary slightly less than younger speakers. The possessive construction analysis reveals interesting patterns of usage which differ between the first person plural data and the third person singular data analysed. In fact, there is evidence that the increase in use of the first plural colloquial construction started at an earlier point in history than the same increase in the third singular, as evidenced by the different shapes of the lines on Figs. 2.5 and 2.6. It seems reasonable to suggest that the change (increase in CC) began in limited contexts, for example, in the first person plural, and then spread to other inflections. Both of the studies I have presented here give early indicators of the nature of the variation and change featuring these two constructions in Welsh, but future analysis may add weight to the arguments I propose here. Analysing AuxD of other verb forms[12] would also allow us to see to what extent the deletion of *wyt* is typical.

References

Awbery, Gwen. 1994. Echo pronouns in a Welsh dialect: A system in crisis? *Bangor Research Papers in Linguistics* 5: 1–29.

Bailey, Guy, Tom Wikle, Jan Tillery, and Lori Sand. 1991. The apparent time construct. *Language Variation and Change* 3: 241–264.

Boberg, Charles. 2004. Real and apparent time in language change: Late adoption of changes in Montreal English. *American Speech* 79: 250–269.

Borsley, Robert D., Maggie Tallerman, and David Willis. 2007. *The syntax of Welsh*. Cambridge: Cambridge University Press.

Chambers, Jack K. 2003. *Sociolinguistic theory: Linguistic variation and its social significance*, 2nd edn. Cambridge, MA: Blackwell.

Cukor-Avila, Patricia, and Guy Bailey. 2013. Real time and apparent time. In *The handbook of language variation and change*, 2nd edn, ed. Jack.K. Chambers, Peter Trudgill, and Natalie Schilling-Estes, 239–262. Maiden: Wiley-Blackwell.

Davies, John. 1994. *A history of Wales*. London: Penguin.

Davies, Peredur. 2010. *Identifying word-order convergence in the speech of Welsh–English bilinguals*. Unpublished PhD dissertation. Bangor University.

---

[12] And indeed verbs other than *bod* 'be', since AuxD appears to be largely confined to forms of *bod*, and it would be of interest to identify why. Perhaps it is due largely to the high frequency of *bod* as an auxiliary.

Davies, Rhian J. 2012. *The development of the Welsh possessive and its current use in the online informal written domain.* Unpublished BA dissertation. Bangor University.

Davies, Peredur, and Margaret Deuchar. 2014. Auxiliary deletion in the informal speech of Welsh–English bilinguals: A change in progress. *Lingua* 143: 224–241.

Deuchar, Margaret, Peredur Davies and Kevin Donnelly. Forthcoming. *Building and using the Siarad Corpus of spoken Welsh: Bilingual conversations in Welsh and English.* Monograph.

Deuchar, Margaret, Peredur Davies, Jon Russell Herring, M. Carmen Parafita Couto, and Diana Carter. 2014. Building bilingual corpora. In *Advances in the study of bilingualism*, ed. Enlli Môn Thomas, and Ineke Mennen, 93–111. Clevedon: Multilingual Matters.

Jones, Bob Morris. 1990. Linguistic causes of change in pronominalization in children's Welsh. *Bulletin of the Board of Celtic Studies* 37: 43–70.

Jones, Mari C. 1998. *Language obsolescence and revitalization: Linguistic change in two sociolinguistically contrasting Welsh communities.* Oxford: Clarendon Press.

Jones, Bob Morris. 2004. The licensing powers of mood and negation in spoken Welsh: Full and contracted forms of the present tense of *bod* 'be'. *Journal of Celtic Linguistics* 8: 87–107.

Jones, Morris, and Alan R. Thomas. 1977. *The Welsh language: Studies in its syntax and semantics.* Cardiff: University of Wales Press for the Schools Council.

Labov, William. 2001. *Principles of linguistic change: Social factors.* Malden: Wiley-Blackwell.

MacWhinney, Brian. 2000. *The CHILDES project: Tools for analyzing talk*, 3rd edn. Mahwah: Lawrence Erlbaum Associates.

Morris-Jones, John. 1931. *Welsh syntax: An unfinished draft.* Cardiff: University of Wales Press.

Parry-Williams, T.H. 1923. *The English element in Welsh: A study of English loanwords in Welsh.* London: Honourable Society of Cymmrodorion.

Phillips, John D. 2007. Mae nodweddion hynotaf y Gymraeg ar ddiflannu. *Journal of the Literary Society of Yamaguchi University* 57: 261–282.

Roberts, Anna E. 1988. Age-related variation in the Welsh dialect of Pwllheli. In *The use of Welsh: A contribution to sociolinguistics*, ed. Martin J. Ball, 104–124. Clevedon: Multilingual Matters.

Sankoff, David, and Suzanne Laberge. 1978. The linguistic market and the statistical explanation of variability. In *Linguistic variation: Models and methods*, ed. David Sankoff, 339–350. New York: Academic Press.

Sankoff, Gillian, and Hélène Blondeau. 2007. Language change across the lifespan: /r/ in Montreal French. *Language* 83(3): 560–588.

Thomas, Alan R. 1982. Change and decay in language. In *Linguistic controversies: Essays in linguistic theory and practice in honour of F. R. Palmer*, ed. David Crystal, 209–219. London: Edward Arnold.

Thorne, David. 1996. *Gramadeg Cymraeg*. Llandysul: Gomer Press.

Watkins, T. Arwyn. 1977. The Welsh personal pronoun. *Word* 28(1-2): 146–165.

Williams, Stephen J. 1980. *A Welsh grammar*. Cardiff: University of Wales Press.

Willis, David. Forthcoming. Cyfieithu iaith y caethweision yn *Uncle Tom's Cabin* a darluniadau o siaradwyr ail iaith mewn llenyddiaeth Gymraeg.

3

Behavioural Economics and Minority Language e-Services—The Case of Welsh

Jeremy Evas and Daniel Cunliffe

Mae'r bennod hon yn trafod y defnydd isel o e-wasanaethau yn y Gymraeg, gan gynnig sawl rheswm am hyn a sawl ffordd o fynd i'r afael â'r sefyllfa. Mae'n cynnig modelau Economeg Ymddygiadol fel dull amgen, ar ffurf lens i weld y 'broblem' hon drwyddi a hefyd fel fframwaith y gellid ei ddefnyddio i ymchwilio i ymraethau. Yn benodol, mae'n canolbwyntio ar e-wasanaethau Cymraeg (e.e. ar wefannau, peiriannau arian parod a meddalwedd) ac yn ystyried y potensial i godi'r defnydd drwy ddefnyddio Economeg Ymddygiadol. Rydym yn cyflwyno canlyniadau astudiaeth empeiraidd sydd â'r nod o ddarparu cyfeiriad i ymchwil ac arfer yn y dyfodol.

J. Evas (✉)
School of Welsh, Cardiff University, Cardiff, UK

D. Cunliffe
School of Computing and Mathematics, University of South Wales, Pontypridd, UK

© The Author(s) 2016
M. Durham, J. Morris (eds.), *Sociolinguistics in Wales*,
DOI 10.1057/978-1-137-52897-1_3

Introduction

The legislative framework surrounding the Welsh language in Wales aimed to increase the provision of Welsh language services and to normalise their use. However, despite increased provision and a continuing desire expressed by speakers for that provision, we shall see that actual use of these services appears to be low.

This chapter discusses the low use of Welsh language services and offers possible reasons and remedies for this. It proposes Behavioural Economic models as an alternative approach, as both a lens through which to view this 'problem' and a framework under which interventions could be researched. In particular, it focusses on Welsh language e-services (e.g. on websites, ATMs, and software) and considers the potential for increasing usage through the application of Behavioural Economics. We present the results of an empirical study which aims to provide a direction for further research and practice.

Welsh Language Service Provision and Use

The Welsh Language Act 1993 (HM Government 1993) came into being after a long period of pro-Welsh language, non-violent, civil disobedience in Wales (Phillips 1998a, b). One of the main provisions of the Act was that a statutory Welsh Language Board be established to promote and facilitate the use of the Welsh language in Wales. As part of this mission, 'Welsh Language Schemes' (Welsh Language Board 1996) were to be established, which would detail how a given public sector organisation would provide a bilingual service to the public. Such schemes included how each organisation would:

- answer correspondence
- provide signage
- answer telephone calls
- make information available on websites

By late 2015, 566 Welsh Language Schemes were in force (Welsh Language Commissioner 2015a). It would be fair to say that the public sector linguistic landscape in Wales has been transformed, in large part, by the 1993 Act, with the Welsh language at least a passive part of most people's daily experience. There have, however, been frequent criticisms of the Act (Williams 2010; O'Flatharta et al. 2013), from user groups and from opponents of the language (Owen 2013). These objections range from the semi-philosophical (criticisms of the legislation's overarching 'hands off' neoliberal discourse), to the practical (poor quality of Welsh service provision which some view as inaccessible and begrudgingly offered (Evas 2001)). A narrative has also developed suggesting that there is no groundswell call for, or sufficient use of such services (Cairns 2015; Evas 2015). At worst this narrative also notes that, 'they all speak English anyway' (Davies 2001b) and that as such Welsh language services are a waste of tax pounds which could more gainfully be expended elsewhere.

The narrative against Welsh language services is often predicated on the low use of such services. A naïve analysis based solely on the statistical evidence would appear to support this. According to the 2011 Census, 18.56% of the population of Wales (some 562,000 people aged three and above) could speak Welsh (Welsh Language Commissioner 2013). However:

- The legislative framework mentioned above enables driving examinations to be taken in English or Welsh in Wales. The number of theory driving tests taken in Welsh in 2013–14 was 78 (0.17% of the total). 46,309 such tests were taken in English. 276 practical tests were taken in Welsh (0.76% of the total). 28,418 such tests were taken in English in Wales (Welsh Government 2015: 39).
- Of all the visits to the NHS Direct Wales website in 2014–15, 0.1% were to the Welsh language version, and 0.7% of the telephone calls answered by NHS Direct Wales were made in Welsh (Welsh Government 2015: 40).[1]
- In 2012, the Chief Executive of National Savings and Investments wrote to the Welsh Language Commissioner, noting '[...] after 14

---

[1] This document sounds a note of caution regarding the reliability of such figures, however, stating that 'there are a number of difficulties in terms of the standard of some of these administrative systems, such as documenting recording the information or the ability of the systems to report the necessary information. There is also a problem with data continuity [for NHS Direct] owing to system changes.' (p. 85)

years of offering a Welsh Language Scheme, NS&I had 107 customers who corresponded with us in Welsh, representing 0.007% of the 1,549,577 customers who live in Wales, and only 0.06% of Welsh deposits. At an annual cost of £899 per Welsh speaking NS&I customer, or an additional cost of 3.78% for every pound of their deposits, our Welsh Language Scheme is not an effective use of public funds.' (See the tribunal Judgement handed down in R (Welsh Language Commissioner) v NS&I, CO/9841/2013).

• The Wales Office Minister, and future Secretary of State for Wales, Alun Cairns (2015) noted in a strident public lecture, 'You would never believe just how depressingly low are the number of visitors to Welsh language content that is available on GOV.UK. To date, there have been only TWO, yes TWO, Welsh language applications completed for a Carer's Allowance and there are several other examples I could share.'

As the figures quoted above for the NHS Direct and GOV.UK websites illustrate, the low levels of use of Welsh language e-services appears to broadly mirror the situation of Welsh language services generally (Jones 2007; Deudraeth Cyf. 2008; Evans 2008; Jones and Hughes 2008; Evas 2011).

Arguments based on evidence of low usage, however, run counter to continuing evidence of Welsh speakers' stated desire to be able to access services through the medium of Welsh. For example, several empirical surveys (Welsh Office 1995; Beaufort Research et al. 2013; Citizens' Advice Bureau 2015) state that Welsh speakers would welcome more opportunities to use Welsh.

Whilst the evidence may initially appear paradoxical (high-stated desire, but low actual use), we posit that many Welsh language services are based on a 'build it and they will come' tradition, ill-informed with respect to recent thinking in human behaviour. Such a neoclassical economical approach would aver that the mere fact that a service is available, and that possible service users are aware of its existence, would lead to its use. Why would this not be the case, given the large-scale historical civil disobedience in Wales that led to the creation of the services? This coincides with current thinking around *homo economicus* (the theoretical rational actor who weighs and measures all options studiously before coming to a decision and the theory of rational action (Monroe 1991)). The latest thinking is that behaviour is far more complex than this, and that humans tend to 'go with the flow' of the options presented to them first, rather than expending energy in seeking out alternatives.

Towards a Behavioural Economic Perspective on Low Service Use

One of the main things we should note is that believing that information alone or that merely *instructing* someone to change behaviour will result in behaviour change is one of the main misunderstandings when applying behavioural change techniques (Fogg et al. 2010; Institute for Government 2010; Halpern 2015). Telling prospective users of Welsh language services that 'they have a choice' (as did the Welsh Language Board's campaign, 'Mae gen ti ddewis...') when a given service is not actively available, needs to be sought out, or is of poor quality is likely to reap poor results. This then feeds into the established negative narrative—and the cycle of low use is perpetuated.

The prevailing discourse in language planning in Wales has centred on the *provision* of Welsh language services and, more recently, a rights-based approach to language normalisation and official status. Little has been written regarding how *exactly* the service provision that has thus been achieved should be offered to the end user. Thomas (2010: 21) offers a salutary opinion which chimes with those of the doyens of Nudge theory, Thaler and Sunstein (2008), who argue in a provocatively titled journal article that 'libertarian paternalism is not an oxymoron.' Thomas emphasises that:

> [...] no one [should] think that the right to use Welsh and increasing Welsh language use always go hand in hand. Nor that a new Welsh language act will contribute substantially to language revival unless detailed attention is given to how the majority of Welsh speakers can be 'nudged' into taking advantage of the resultant opportunities [to use the language]. As well as rights, a nudge is needed.

Thomas' opinion dovetails well with that of Halpern et al. (2004: 9) who observed that:

> The exercise of personal responsibility or choice is not without cost for the individual—it involves time and energy in assessing information. [...] In

our busy lives, we sometimes look to the state to ensure that the default choice is a safe and appropriate one. Indeed, often, the setting of a default option […] cannot be avoided. This had led some to argue that the role of the state is to engage in 'libertarian paternalism'—setting default options in the interests of the public but enabling them to opt for alternatives.

In order to provide Welsh language services on an equitable basis with English, an Active Offer of that service is needed, as research (Sunstein and Thaler 2003; Institute for Government 2010) shows that people tend to follow the default settings provided in a given situation.[2] A clear, equitable language choice is the advice to the public sector in Wales in terms of technological provision by the Welsh Language Commissioner and others (Welsh Language Board et al. 2006; Welsh Language Commissioner 2015c). However, this advice is often begrudgingly implemented, misinterpreted, or lost in corporate governance structures (O'Flatharta et al. 2013), and a default language is chosen *for* the end user—usually the English language. The findings of Citizens' Advice Bureau (2015: 46) confirm that there was 'low awareness or visibility of the Welsh language, particularly online' and that this might comprise the 'core principle of effective service.' Our research investigates whether increasing visibility of a language choice would increase take-up of that choice.

Cairns (2015) announced that his office would commission independent research into the reasons Welsh speakers did not use the Welsh language versions of websites. The resultant report by the Government Digital Service and Wales Office (2015) found that 'The language participants use/d in their higher education and professional environment (Welsh or English) impacts on how confident they are using Welsh government services online.' It also found that:

- When Welsh users want to stay in the Welsh version, but need assistance with particular words, they often switch backwards and forwards between Welsh and English versions. They will also do this to check that the Welsh version is as up to date and complete as the English version (often not the case).

---

[2] The essence of the Active Offer Concept is that a given Service is offered *proactively* in either language, rather than begrudgingly, without the user having to request it.

- An end-to-end Welsh experience is rarely offered. People are frustrated that services in Welsh are not as good as the English services, and that they are presented as Welsh services but are not entirely in Welsh.
- Social media and blogs are perceived as non-threatening digital spaces because Welsh is usually conversational. These channels also offer Welsh speakers an opportunity to serendipitously discover new Welsh content.

In addition to these factors, it should be noted that there is not a strong tradition of expecting Welsh language services (Eaves 2007, 2015). Indeed, it could be argued that a strong social norm in Welsh-speaking Wales *is* that one must not make oneself different by requesting a Welsh language service. Nelde et al. (1996), Evas (1999) and Davies (2001a) note that the collective conscience which developed over the centuries of being steeped in the 'national' mentality and the subsequent 'othering' of minority languages has deeply pierced the psyche of minority language groups (see, e.g. Davies 2001a for a vigorous psychiatric analysis of 'colonised' peoples, with a specific emphasis on the case of the Welsh speakers in Wales). Such ingrained expectations of what one's language is good for becomes an integral part of social normativity. Played out in the field, this could mean that an individual actively seeking out a Welsh language service, when use of such services is not a widespread behaviour, could mark themselves out as different from the group. Being aware of this, the individual may not adopt the behaviour.

Towards the Application of Behavioural Economics in Welsh Language e-Services

The idea that the way technology is presented to an end user can be used to achieve behaviour change has moved into mainstream thinking, manifesting itself in a variety of guises, for example, 'persuasive technology' (Fogg et al. 2003); 'design with intent' (Lockton et al. 2010); 'seductive interaction' (Anderson 2011); and 'Evil' design (Nodder 2013). There have also been a number of successful commercial applications based on these ideas, such as Fitbit (www.fitbit.com) and Nest Thermostat (www. nest.com). There has, however, been little direct application of these ideas to language behaviour change through technology.

The scant research conducted into minority language behaviour in the context of human computer interaction and behavioural science has hitherto concentrated on changing language settings and manipulating language choice mechanisms (Keegan and Cunningham 2008). Initial research by Evas and Keegan (2012) has asked to what degree theories of 'libertarian paternalism' espoused by so-called 'Nudge' proponents could be used to increase take-up of Welsh language computer interfaces.

One of the most popular models of behaviour change is the MINDSPACE model. We describe this mnemonic briefly here, with its relevance for the research instruments we used. From MINDSPACE, the simplified EAST model (Behavioural Insights Team 2015) (i.e. that behaviour change should be Easy, Attractive, Social and Timely) has also developed.

- *Messenger*—who exactly conveys a behaviour change message to a target, for example a government organisation, or a member of a peer group?
- *Incentives*—is a change worth the perceived effort?
- *Norms* entail the perceived opinion of others regarding a target behaviour. To what degree does such a behaviour break a group norm?
- Research shows that humans tend to follow *default* options. Would defaulting an interface to Welsh increase the number of Welsh speakers that used it?
- Use of a language also depends on how *salient* the language choice mechanism is. For example, does a 'splash page' engender more use of Welsh than an English default page with a Welsh language choice?
- *Priming* regards the sub-conscious stimulations that could affect behaviour. If a target behaviour has been adopted in one sphere, will that behaviour 'spill over' to another?
- *Affect* (emotion) can trump rational processes. Indeed, we are 'predictably irrational' (Ariely 2008). Could an appeal to emotion be employed to achieve the target behaviour?

- Public *commitments* have been shown to increase the likelihood of successful behaviour change.
- Lastly, the *ego* is a factor that has been used by language planners in Wales over the years. In many opinion polls, positive attitudes towards the Welsh language have been found (e.g. NOP Social and Political 1996).

Our study examines whether use of Welsh language e-services could potentially be improved by implementing small reconfigurations in how exactly those services are offered. We explore this new thinking, in particular 'choice architecture,' as expounded in the domain of Behavioural Economics (Halpern et al. 2004; New Economics Foundation 2005; Thaler and Sunstein 2008), by researching the effect of graphical mock-ups of language choice scenarios for Welsh language e-services.

The Study

In order to explore *how* Behavioural Economics could be applied to the design of e-services, and to investigate its potential effect on user behaviour we conducted a questionnaire-based study. The questionnaire consisted of two main sections—an attitudinal survey and a series of graphical mock-ups of language choice scenarios for Welsh language e-services based on the MINDSPACE elements.

Between October 2014 and June 2015, we collected data from a total of 147 respondents using the bilingual Bristol Online Survey platform. The survey was presented in English and Welsh. Participants were recruited by email invitation, university distribution lists, and via contact databases of the Coleg Cymraeg Cenedlaethol (the national Welsh language College, an all-Wales federal institution placing Welsh language teaching posts in Higher Education establishments in Wales). Word of mouth also played a part in the recruitment process, and social networks ensured that the survey details were further shared.

The sample comprises fluent and frequent users of Welsh (96% of the respondents noted that they spoke Welsh fluently, 94.6% that they speak it daily, and that 78.2% of them mainly learnt Welsh at home). The respondents of the survey were overwhelmingly young (82% were 29 or under) and 71% were students. 39.5% were male and 60.5% female. Recent national Welsh Language Use Surveys (Welsh Language Board 2008; Welsh Government and Welsh Language Commissioner 2015) have shown that fluent Welsh speakers are much more likely to use their Welsh language skills frequently (according to the 2015 figures, they are three times more likely than non-fluent speakers to do so on a daily basis). Fluent Welsh speakers are also 'most comfortable using Welsh or equally as comfortable using both languages' (Welsh Government and Welsh Language Commissioner 2015: 47).

The majority of the respondents have a high level of Welsh language capability and are likely to be technologically adept due to their age. Therefore, there are no overt *a priori* reasons why they could not make use of a Welsh language e-service if it were offered.

Attitudinal Survey

As mentioned above, previous studies had indicated low service use despite positive attitudes towards the language and a desire for Welsh language service provision. In order to understand the respondents' attitudes, they were asked their level of agreement or disagreement with a series of attitudinal statements.

A reliability test was conducted using SPSS, to gauge the level of accuracy in the scale used in 'Note how strongly you agree or disagree with the following statements on a scale where 1 means you strongly disagree and 7 means you strongly agree.'

The derived Cronbach's Alpha (α) value measured the accuracy of the responses gathered from applying a seven-point Likert Scale, determining the level of agreement of the participants possessed towards the 18 statements tested. The internal consistency of this scale was 'acceptable' ($\alpha = 0.762$), indicating that the scale had served its purpose.

The statements are shown below; the mean scores show a high level of support for promotional policy for the Welsh language, and in information technology. They also showed that the respondents had a positive image of the language. Text in square brackets in the table refers to responses for which data is 'reverse coded.' This means, for example, that an original question was negative, for example, 'Welsh is an unsophisticated language.' Reverse coding such responses enabled us to calculate an overall positivity score towards the Welsh language (Table 3.1).[3]

Table 3.1   Results of attitudinal statements regarding the Welsh language

Questions about Welsh in technology	Mean score
It is important that large corporations such as Microsoft, Google, and Apple, provide products in Welsh	6.67
It is important that Facebook provide a Welsh language interface	6.53
It is important that Twitter provide a Welsh language interface	6.52
It is important that Amazon.co.uk provide a Welsh language interface	6.19
Bank cards should remember language preferences so receipts in shops are automatically available in my chosen language	6.09
Questions about Welsh as a modern language	
Welsh is a modern language	5.73
Welsh is [not] an unsophisticated language	6.41
Welsh is a language fit for the twenty-first century	6.33
Questions about the language	
Welsh is a beautiful language	6.54
Welsh is a literary language	5.56
Welsh is a good language for literary purposes	5.67
Questions about attitudes towards using the language	
It is [not] impolite to speak Welsh in front of people who do not understand it	5.5
The ability to speak Welsh is something to be proud of	6.63
The ability to speak Welsh is [not] something to be ashamed of-	6.77
Questions about the enduring value of the language	
It is important that Welsh is taught in every school in Wales	6.75
[No] benefit will come from speaking Welsh	6.54
In 20 years Welsh will [not] be a dead language	6.22

---

[3] The Likert reversed-scale items are reproduced below in their original form:

- It is impolite to speak Welsh in front of people who do not understand it
- Welsh is an unsophisticated language
- The ability to speak Welsh is something to be ashamed of
- No benefit will come from speaking Welsh
- In 20 years Welsh will be a dead language

The results indicate that the respondents have a positive attitude towards the language and its relevance in the modern world. They also indicate support for Welsh provision across a number of e-services. There is nothing in this data to suggest they would not make use of a Welsh language e-service if it were offered.

Language Choice Scenarios

A language choice 'splash' page is a commonly used choice architecture in technology in Wales, especially on websites. The sole purpose of a 'splash' page is to provide a language choice, with no other functionality. This approach is also taken on certain ATMs and other e-service interfaces. Indeed, the Welsh Language Commissioner (2015c: 111) recommends a splash page as an ideal proactive language entry point to a system where no other 'reliable implicit determination of the preferred language for the user' can be ascertained. Amongst such implicit determinations is the use of an URL in a particular language, or browser locale choice. In the absence of prior language choice knowledge, a splash screen is a simple and obvious point at which a language choice must be made. We investigate such splash screens below. The language choice scenarios investigated the respondents' beliefs about their behaviour and the behaviour of others when presented with a number of language choice 'splash' page style interfaces. The design of the interfaces was informed by consideration of the MINDSPACE elements, therefore the designs themselves can be seen as an exploration of how the elements might be realised in a language choice interface design.

Scenarios were created for three commonly used e-service settings:

- Websites
- ATMs
- Office software setup

The results are analysed below.

Website Choice Architecture

We created a series of three mocked-up website home pages for a ficti-
tious establishment, 'The University of Abertaff.' A single home page
version per question was presented to respondents (all screens are
reproduced below). The first screen (q17) defaulted to Welsh on the
initial page with an option to switch to English supplied in 'the Sweet
Spot' (Welsh Language Commissioner 2015c: 113) at the top right-
hand side of the page. The second mock-up (q18) defaulted to English,
with an option to switch to Welsh at the Sweet Spot. The third option
presented (q19) was a 'splash' page, as described above. In the case of
the first two mock-ups, the site could be used, read, and navigated
without necessarily having to view the other language. The third mock-
up—the splash version—used what the literature in behaviour change
would call a 'coerced choice model' (Sunstein and Thaler 2003), that
is, in every case, an end user would have to make a conscious choice
of which language to continue in. All three mock-ups shared the same
brand, and look and feel. For each, respondents were asked to 'Imagine
the page below is the 'very first' page of an organisation you wish to
know more about. In which language would you continue browsing
this site?'

In the case of the website defaulting to Welsh (q17), 88.4% (n = 130)
of the respondents indicated that they would continue browsing that
website in Welsh. In the next mock-up, (q18) where the default page was
in English, the percentage of the respondents who indicated that they
would continue in *English* was 46.9% (n = 69). This again suggests that
the default language of a website has a large bearing on people's language
use on websites; this, of course, ties in with behavioural change literature
regarding defaults.

In the case of the last mock-up (the 'splash screen'), the percentage of
the respondents who noted they would continue in Welsh is the highest
score for all three of the mock-ups: 90.5% (n = 133). The message that
these results conveys is a common sense one—if the language choice is
hidden, fewer Welsh speakers will use Welsh. If the default language is

Welsh, or if a coerced choice (splash screen) model is offered, the acceptance and take-up is likely to be much higher. To use the parlance of
the EAST model (Behavioural Insights Team 2015), 'friction' has been
removed. Indeed, Halpern (2015: 65) notes that removal of such friction
is 'so simple, so obvious, it should hardly need saying at all. And yet,
across the world, governments and scholars have been slow to learn the
importance of this most basic behavioural principle.'

In terms of the website language choices we tested, the results are
clear—the respondents indicate that they will use the Welsh language
versions if the language choice architecture is clear and easily accessible,
the average acceptance score for the Welsh language on these mocked-
up websites being 77% ($n = 113$). However, it is important to note that
there may well be a difference between what people state (or believe)
they would do and what they might actually do in practice. Their actual
behaviour is likely to be influenced by factors such as the type of information they were looking for, who that information was to be used by,
and so on. Language choice behaviours are not abstract choices; they are
rooted in a rich and complex context (Fig. 3.1).

ATM Choice Architecture

Since the early 1990s, many banks and building societies in Wales have
provided a language choice on their ATMs. Although we do not spend
large amounts of time on ATMs at single sessions, we do use them
often. The exact choice architecture on these ATMs differs from bank to
bank, some offering the coerced choice model as described above, where
users *must* choose a language to continue with their transactions, others
defaulting to a transaction screen in English, whilst offering an optional
Welsh language choice on that screen. We have found no cases where
ATMs defaulted to a Welsh language screen. Many use flags to denote
languages, contrary to much advice (World Wide Web Consortium
2013; Welsh Language Commissioner 2015c). Information regarding

Fig. 3.1 The three models of website language choice architecture surveyed

actual use of ATMs by Welsh speakers is extremely hard to come by, as banks tend to be reticent about giving out such data.[4]

ATMs provide an interesting research focus for a number of reasons, not least because they meet many of the suggested user needs for a Welsh language service:

- A large number of ATMs in Wales provide a Welsh language service in addition to an English language service, so the opportunity to use a Welsh language service is often available. Users would therefore be familiar with being offered a language choice, via whichever means.
- The number of different paths through the service are limited, so an end-to-end service in Welsh is typically provided when Welsh is chosen.
- The language used on a cash machine, be it English or Welsh, is relatively limited, simple, and predictable.
- An ATM typically makes an offer of English or Welsh language at the start of the interaction with the service. So the availability of Welsh service is advertised and language selection is reasonably straightforward.
- Research (Beaufort Research et al. 2013: 52) suggests that using Welsh at an ATM is an activity associated with no perceived risk of having one's Welsh language capabilities judged.
- As no human is involved in an ATM transaction (apart from the person using the ATM), no marker effect/fear of offending others will be a factor in language choice.
- The one point on which the ATM may fail to meet the user needs is that language choice is fixed for the duration of the transaction and offers no subsequent page-level language switching mechanism.
- Research shows that in the shift to online and mobile banking there are fewer opportunities for customers to use Welsh when dealing with their banks (Welsh Language Commissioner 2015b), with ATMs being one of the few opportunities.

---

[4] The only figures we have been able to ascertain are for one company (offering cockney language choice on their ATMs) as reported by BBC News. 2012. *Cockney cash: Lady Godivas and speckled hens* [Online]. London: BBC. (Available at: http://www.bbc.co.uk/news/business-17535156 [Accessed: 26/11/15]). This news story states that 'less than 1% of people opt for the Welsh language.' However, this does not break data down by geographical area (i.e. the territory of Wales) or, more saliently, by language ability.

We wanted to explore the potential effect that different choice architecture designs, based on Behavioural Economic approaches, might have in encouraging the use of the Welsh language on ATMs. As in the case of websites, we created mock-ups of different language choice architectures for ATMs, each using a different combination of Behavioural Economic approaches. Several elements of the MINDSPACE model were used, together with typical designs used by UK banks for offering a language choice at ATMs. Respondents were asked 'Which one of these cashpoint screens would be most likely to encourage a Welsh speaker to use Welsh?'

The questionnaire presented 11 different language choice scenarios (in sets of three or four). The English version of the language choice for all but one option read as follows 'Which language do you require?' and was placed above the Welsh on each mock-up (in terms of buttons and explanatory text). The screen design mostly varied only the Welsh language offer in order to persuade the Welsh speaker to choose Welsh. The Welsh version of the language choice varied according to each behavioural approach chosen. The 'look and feel' of all 11 designs was identical.

The first question (q. 11) contrasted a set of three ATM designs. The first of these designs (A) had a 'Working Welsh' (Welsh Language Commissioner 2015d) badge superimposed on the 'Cymraeg' choice. Working Welsh has existed in its present brand since 2004, was established by the former Welsh Language Board, and is now run by the Welsh Language Commissioner. It is a reasonably common sight in organisations around Wales, on badges worn by staff, embroidered into their uniforms, or on lanyards containing identity/security cards. Research by Ivey et al. (2007) has shown that this approach engendered brand loyalty when attached to a human, rather than to a point of sale (which could have multiple humans working on it). Given that the scheme had been running for nine years, it was our assumption that awareness of the logo would be considerable, and that it would be widely identified with a Welsh language service.

The second ATM design (B) used a social-norming approach, picturing a stock photo of an imaginary 'Siân' from Bangor, noting that she 'chooses Welsh at all times—will you?' This direct approach—passive aggressive, almost—attempts to pique the user's in-group sentiment, noting that the typical Welsh speaker in an area chooses the Welsh language.

The final design in this question superimposed a set of lipstick lips on the 'Cymraeg' language choice, instructing the user to 'Love your language—use your Welsh.' This appeal to the 'affect' was intended to ascertain whether emotion could be used to increase language use (Fig. 3.2).

Over half the respondents (53.7%, $n = 79$) chose design 'A,' with 23.1% ($n = 34$) each choosing B and C. This would *suggest* that the majority of the respondents preferred a simple language choice with no attendant messaging, and that such a clear choice, when identified with a long-standing language brand trumps social norming and affect (Fig. 3.3).

Whilst the designs in question 11 all position the Welsh service in a positive way, in question 12 we examine choice through fear of adverse consequences. This question contained two designs, the first (A) with a sentence under the Welsh sentence, and not reproduced in English, not-

Fig. 3.2 ATM language choice architecture (1)—'Working Welsh' logo v. social norming v. affect

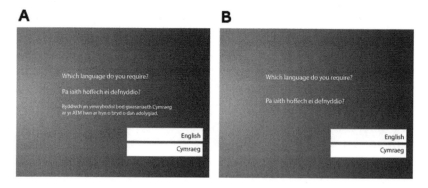

Fig. 3.3 ATM language choice architecture (2)—Loss aversion v. simple coerced choice

ing that the user should 'Be aware that the Welsh language service on this ATM is currently under review.' The intended implication is that if the Welsh service is not used, then it may be withdrawn, piquing a sense of responsibility towards the language.

The second design (B) contained a standard language choice with no intervention at all, and inasmuch, is fairly typical of the language choice architecture of many ATMs in use in Wales today.

The effect tested for in this question was 'loss aversion.' Literature in behaviour change (Institute for Government 2010) notes that in certain cases, people are more motivated by the possible loss of something, than the gain of an equivalent something, for example, effective cash for weight loss programmes were ones that had penalties as well as bonuses—noting the powerful effect of loss aversion meaning that losing £10 was more powerful than gaining £10. The large majority of the respondents (71.4%, $n = 105$) believed that design 'B,' that is, plain coerced language choice with no behavioural/loss aversion gloss would be most likely to encourage Welsh speakers to use the Welsh language on a given ATM. This would again appear to suggest that the majority of the respondents do not agree that a threat of withdrawal of a Welsh language service, however passive that threat may be, is a motivating factor for use of a Welsh language service.

Question 13 contained three designs, the first (A) contained a line from *Hen Wlad fy Nhadau* (the National Anthem of Wales), that is, 'O bydded i'r heniaith barhau' [may the old language live on]. This was chosen as an appropriate line from the anthem, itself chosen to pique the affect of respondents, our assumption being that the majority of them would recognise the line and possibly equate a Welsh language choice with patriotism for Wales.

Design B attempts to motivate choice through concern for societal values and desire for self-approval noting 'Your language, your choice.' Design C, attempts to motivate the choosing of the Welsh language through social norms and peer approval—'Rhys in Bangor just chose Welsh—will you?' This locates a Welsh language choice in the relationship the user of the ATM has with a Welsh-speaking community, family or friends—now with added immediacy and an implied sharing of behaviours (Fig. 3.4).

Fig. 3.4 ATM language choice architecture (3)—Patriotic 'affect' (Welsh National anthem) v. Emphasis of personal choice v. Immediacy of other person's Welsh language use

Whilst 30.6% (*n* = 45) of the respondents chose design A, the line from the Welsh national anthem, over half (55.1%, *n* = 81) believed that design B, 'your language, your choice,' would encourage the most use of Welsh. A small proportion, 14.3% (*n* = 21) believed that the social-norming design (C) would be the most conducive to the use of Welsh. This would suggest that excessively overt messaging of the user, when compared to a coerced language choice with weak intervention, would be less likely to encourage use of the Welsh language.

The final question on ATMs again used three different Behavioural Economic approaches. Design A attempts to motivate choice through social norms and peer approval noting in both English and Welsh that 'Our ATMs have been used in Welsh 2,703 times.' This arbitrary figure was meant to normalise the use of such technology in Welsh in the minds of the respondent, anecdotal feedback having been received during the research design phase that certain users could be worried that they would be viewed as 'odd' or engaging in non-normative behaviour were they to choose the Welsh language option. The figure was meant to suggest that choice of the Welsh language is a commonplace behaviour. It also hints, however, that the use of the Welsh language interface is monitored, thereby giving the user an opportunity to have their Welsh use recorded, consequently demonstrating the need for the Welsh service.

Design B attempts to motivate choice through concern for societal values and desire for self-approval, celebrity endorsement, role models, and humour. The figure chosen for this was Saunders Lewis, one-time university lecturer, language activist, playwright, and novelist—still famed

Fig. 3.5 ATM language choice architecture (4)—Normative (and monitored) use of Welsh v. Saunders Lewis snow clone v. Passive aggressive loss aversion

today for his 1962 Radio Lecture *the Fate of the Language*, widely credited with inspiring a generation of civil disobedience and non-violent protests, which led to many of the developments of the status of the Welsh language (Lewis 1962). The question, 'What would Saunders Lewis do?', a snowclone of the 'What would Jesus do?' a phrase, was intended to pique users' possible nationalist sentiment juxtaposed with the perceived behaviour of a doyen of Welsh language activism, as well as injecting a humorous note.

Design C attempts to motivate choice through a passive threat of adverse consequences 'Isn't it time you used your Welsh?' the implication being that they may lose their Welsh (or the Welsh language provision) if they do not use it. This direct, aggressive question was intended to raise the hackles of the respondents to see how they responded to quasi-authoritarian prompts. It also suggests that the ATM knows that the user was about to use English (Fig. 3.5).

Again, the more emotive or authoritarian/passive aggressive designs were deemed less likely to encourage Welsh language use (designs B and C respectively gaining 14.3% ($n = 21$), and 27.2% ($n = 40$) of the respondents' responses). The largest percentage (58.5%, $n = 86$) was apportioned to the social-norming design (A).

It is interesting to note that the responses across all four sets of designs appear to favour those that are closest to the conventional and familiar language choice architecture available on many ATMs in Wales. It may be that the unfamiliarity of the other designs was in itself a factor influencing their perceived lack of effect. It would appear that the respondents believe that a plain and simple language choice, which does not use affect, guilt or aggression—passive or otherwise—is more likely to encourage Welsh language use. Social norming appeared to be useful only in the case where no individual was named, and no prompt (e.g. 'will you?') was included. Where the arbitrary figure of 2703 was included, this gained traction, possibly because it gave the impression to respondents that they would not be alone in choosing the Welsh language version, that it would be normative, normal, thereby subverting the discourse that 'nobody uses the Welsh language version.'

Office Setup Results

Free language interfaces for many Microsoft products have been available since 2004, but the low usage of Welsh language software as evidenced in several surveys (Beaufort Research 2007; RMG Clarity 2013). We therefore wanted to ascertain whether applying a choice architecture intervention to the setup of Office software would potentially increase the number of people using that software in Welsh. With many workers using office suites such as Microsoft Office for a large proportion of their working day, we posit that passive exposure to the language for such periods would further normalise Welsh in the domain of computer and technology use. We referred earlier to the concept of 'friction' removal in the terms of behaviour change. The current process for ensuring a complete user experience in Welsh on a computer running Microsoft software at present entails changing many settings, and having a high degree of self-efficacy in order to implement these. The following conditions need to be satisfied for such an installation:

- Awareness that a Welsh language interface is available
- A desire to use the Welsh language interface
- The requisite administration rights on a given machine
- Download of two Language Interface Packs (LIPs), one for Microsoft Office and another for Microsoft Windows
- Certainty as to which version of Windows and Office one is using, and which 'bit' version of the software one has

- Browser locale and date and time settings need to be changed independently (manually, depending on which version of the software is being used)
- The appropriate keyboard for Welsh must be activated, and the user must have knowledge of how to use accent marks (no tuition is available on the way to obtain accents)
- Both LIPs need to be switched to Welsh independently via separate switching mechanisms, and a log-off must be ensured.

With such a high degree of friction involved in the setup, it is hardly surprising that the usage of Microsoft Office and Windows in Welsh would appear to be low. In terms of the results of our study, 89.1% (n = 131) of the respondents used Microsoft products at home and 79.6% (n = 117) were aware that there is 'a Welsh language version available for Microsoft Office/Windows.' However, awareness of a provision/behaviour, as so often noted in literature on behaviour change, does not necessarily lead to widespread adoption of that provision or behaviour, as respondents noted that their use of the Welsh language packs at home was 36.1% (n = 53) (training had been provided to some students on how to use the LIPs at home).

In response to the open-ended question, 'If you do not use the Welsh versions of this software, what one thing would make you use them' the vast majority of the respondents noted that they would use it if the choice was made available to them and it was easy to use (with several noting the fear that they would not understand the terminology).

We tested the coerced choice methodology on setup of Microsoft Office, using the mocked-up dialogue box below (Fig. 3.6).

The prompt asked respondents to imagine that they had just received a new computer, and they were in the process of setting it up.

The text in the mocked-up dialogue noted that a geo-sensing function had observed that the user was in Wales, and that the computer could be shared with people in same household who did not speak same language.

A large majority (79.6%, n = 117) indicated that they would choose Welsh, and 20.4% (n = 30) English in such a 'de-frictionised' choice architecture scenario. If this predicted behaviour were realised, it would

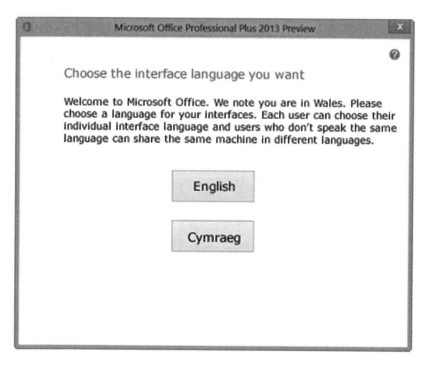

Fig. 3.6 Geosensing and language choice architecture: mock version of Microsoft Office setup process

more than double the percentage of the respondents using Welsh language interface packs at home.

Of course, for such an easy-to-access language choice scenario to exist, certain software architecture solutions would have to be implemented by the software manufacturer.

Conclusion

We conducted research in order to explore how Behavioural Economics could be applied to the design of e-services, using the Welsh language in Wales as our field of study. We wanted to ascertain what the potential effects of this approach could be on end-user behaviour. The results of our research show that that Behavioural Economic models provide a valuable framework for substantially increasing the uptake of Welsh language e-service provision.

The fact that our study confirms that there is a demand for Welsh language e-services that could potentially be harnessed and converted into increased use of those services contravenes a persistent narrative in Wales that few people want a Welsh language service, as they are fluent in English. We explored the application of MINDSPACE elements to the design of three commonly used e-service settings: websites, ATMs, and software setup. Whilst our results mirror those of other research carried out in Behavioural Economics (behaviour changed in the light of manipulation of defaults and use of a coerced choice model), some of the more elaborate approaches appear less appealing to respondents, perhaps due to their unfamiliarity. These merit further research. That further research could include monitoring and even observation of actual, rather than predicted behaviour at the point of use of a given e-service—it may be that other designs could be even more effective than manipulation of the default language. What is clear is that the Behavioural Economic approach has much to offer to the field of bilingual service provision in Wales and beyond.

References

Anderson, Stephen. 2011. *Seductive interaction design: Creating playful, fun, and effective user experiences.* Berkeley: Pearson Education.

Ariely, Dan. 2008. *Predictably irrational: The hidden forces that shape our decisions.* New York: Harper Collins.

BBC News. 2012. *Cockney cash: Lady Godivas and speckled hens* [Online]. London: BBC. Available at: http://www.bbc.co.uk/news/business-17535156. Accessed 26 Nov 2015.

Beaufort Research. 2007. *Omnibus survey of Welsh businesses (Cwmnibus) of Beaufort research: The use of Welsh by small and medium sized enterprises March 2007.* Cardiff: Welsh Language Board. Available at: http://www.webarchive. org.uk/wayback/archive/20120330040108/http://www.byig-wlb.org.uk/ english/publications/pages/publicationitem.aspx?puburl=/English/publications/Publications/B2730-1+WLB+Tabulations+report+and+questions+as ked.pdf. Accessed 28 Aug 2015.

Beaufort Research, et al. 2013. *Exploring Welsh speakers' language use in their daily lives*. Cardiff: Welsh Government. Available at: http://gov.wales/docs/dcells/research/130808-wels-lang-research-en.pdf. Accessed 26 Nov 2015.

Behavioural Insights Team. 2015. *EAST: Four simple ways to apply behavioural insights*. London: Behavioural Insights Team with HM Cabinet Office. Available at: http://www.behaviouralinsights.co.uk/publications/east-four-simple-ways-to-apply-behavioural-insights/. Accessed 11 Jan 2016.

Cairns, Alun. 2015. *The Welsh language: A duty and a challenge* [Online]. Cardiff: Cardiff University. Available at: https://www.gov.uk/government/speeches/the-welsh-language-a-duty-and-a-challenge. Accessed 27 Nov 2015.

Citizens' Advice Bureau. 2015. *English by default—Understanding the use and non-use of Welsh language services*. Cardiff: Citizens Advice. Available at: http://www.citizensadvice.org.uk/index/policy/policy_publications/english_by_default.htm. Accessed: 29 Mar 2016.

Davies, Dilys. 2001a. Within and without (the story of the Welsh) the impact of cultural factors on mental health in the present day in Wales. In *Colonialism and psychiatry*, ed. Dinesh Bhugra, and Roland Littlewood, 185–231. Oxford: Oxford University Press.

Davies, Elaine. 2001b. *'They all speak English anyway': The Welsh language and anti-oppressive practice*. Cardiff: Central Council for Education Training in Social Work.

Deudraeth Cyf. 2008. Promoting the use of Welsh information technology: Gwynedd and Conwy (Deudraeth Cyf.). Cardiff: Deudraeth Cyf. Available at: http://www.webarchive.org.uk/wayback/archive/20120330041228/http://www.byig-wlb.org.uk/english/publications/pages/publicationitem.aspx?puburl=/English/publications/Publications/reportBYIGe2.doc. Accessed 23Dec 2015.

Eaves, Steve. 2007. Cyfraniad hyfforddiant ymwybyddiaeth am yr iaith Gymraeg at gynllunio ieithyddol a'r broses o greu Cymru newydd. *Contemporary Wales* 20: 82–105.

———. 2015. *Hyfforddiant Ymwybyddiaeth Feirniadol am yr Iaith Gymraeg, a'i Gyfraniad at Gynllunio Ieithyddol Cynhwysol yng Nghymru*. Unpublished PhD thesis, Cardiff University. Available at: http://orca.cf.ac.uk/73554/. Accessed 28 Aug 2015.

Evans, Tudur. 2008. *Promoting the use of Welsh information technology: Gwynedd and Conwy*. Cardiff: Coleg Harlech. Available at: http://www.webarchive.org.uk/wayback/archive/20120330041225/http://www.byig-wlb.org.uk/

english/publications/pages/publicationitem.aspx?puburl=/English/publications/Publications/20080820+AD+S+Coleg+Harlech+Final.doc.   Accessed 28 Aug 2015.

Evas, Jeremy. 1999. *Rhwystrau ar lwybr dwyieithrwydd.* Unpublished PhD thesis, Cardiff University. Available at: http://orca.cf.ac.uk/42030/. Accessed 20 July 2015.

————. 2001. *Snapshot survey: Websites of organisations complying with statutory Welsh language schemes.* Cardiff. Available at: http://orca.cf.ac.uk/43868/. Accessed 20 July 2015.

————. (ed.). 2011. *Language technology for multilingual societies.* Meta-Forum: Solutions for a Multilingual Europe. Budapest. Berlin: META-NET. Available at: http://orca.cf.ac.uk/45373/. Accessed 20 July 2015.

————. 2015. *Polyanna Maes yr Iaith* [Online]. BBC. Available at: http://www.bbc.co.uk/cymrufyw/31639995. Accessed: 27 Nov 2015.

Evas, Jeremy, and Te Taka Keegan. 2012. 'Nudge!' Normalising the use of minority language ICT interfaces. *Alternative: An International Journal of Indigenous Peoples* 8(1): 42–52.

Fogg, B. J., Cathy Soohoo, David Danielson, Leslie Marable, Julianne Stanford, Ellen Tauber. (eds). 2003. *How do users evaluate the credibility of Web sites?* Proceedings of the 2003 conference on Designing for user experiences. ACM. Available at: http://dl.acm.org/citation.cfm?id=997097. Accessed 11 Jan 2016.

Fogg, B. J., Kara Chanasyk, Margarita Quihuis, Neema Moraveji, Jason Hreja and Mark Nelson. 2010. *Top 10 mistakes in behavior change* [Online]. Stanford: Stanford University. Available at: http://www.slideshare.net/captology/stanford-6401325. Accessed 16 Jan 2016.

Government Digital Service and Wales Office. 2015. *Why do fluent Welsh speakers use government services in English?* London: Government Digital Service. Available at: https://userresearch.blog.gov.uk/2015/09/15/the-welsh-experience-on-gov-uk-a-qualitative-research-study/. Accessed 25 Sept 2015.

Halpern, David. 2015. *Inside the nudge unit: How small changes can make a big difference.* London: W.H. Allen.

Halpern, David, Clive Bates, Geoff Mulgan, Stephen Aldridge, Greg, Beales, and Adam Heathfield. 2004. *Personal responsibility and changing behaviour: The state of knowledge and its implications for public policy.* London. Available at: http://webarchive.nationalarchives.gov.uk/20100125070726/http:/cabinetoffice.gov.uk/strategy/work_areas/personal_responsibility.aspx. Accessed 11 Jan 2016.

HM Government. 1993. *Welsh language act 1993*. London: HM Stationery Office. Available at: http://www.legislation.gov.uk/ukpga/1993/38/contents. Accessed 15 May 13.

Institute for Government. 2010. Mindspace: Influencing behaviour through public policy. London: Institute for Government. Available at: http://www. instituteforgovernment.org.uk/sites/default/files/publications/ MINDSPACE.pdf. Accessed 17 April 2015.

Ivey, Darren, Carla Chatfield and Rhian Richard. 2007. *Impact assessment of the working Welsh scheme: Report of findings*. Cardiff: Welsh Language Board. Available at: http://www.webarchive.org.uk/wayback/archive/201203300 40105/http://www.byig-wlb.org.uk/english/publications/pages/publication-item.aspx?puburl=/English/publications/Publications/Working+ Welsh+final+report_english+19oct.doc. Accessed 11 Jan 2016.

Jones, Eleri Wyn 2007. *Survey of promoting technology in Welsh: Experimental project—Anglesey*. Cardiff: Monitor Cymru. Available at: http://www.webarchive.org.uk/wayback/archive/20120330014023/http://www.byig-wlb.org. uk/English/publications/Pages/PublicationItem.aspx?puburl=/English%2fp ublications%2fPublications%2f4970.doc. Accessed 11 Jan 2016.

Jones, Eleri Wyn and Eirian Hughes. 2008. *Promoting Welsh medium information technology: Revisiting the 2007 project in Anglesey*. Cardiff: Monitor Cymru. Available at: http://www.webarchive.org.uk/wayback/archive/2012 0330041234/http://www.byig-wlb.org.uk/english/publications/pages/publicationitem.aspx?puburl=/English/publications/Publications/20080320+AD +S+Promoting+Technology+Report+2008+-+Monitor+Cymru.doc. Accessed 11 Jan 2016.

Keegan, Te Take, and Sally Jo Cunningham. 2008. What a difference a default setting makes. In *Research and advanced technology for digital libraries*, 264–267. New York: Springer.

Lewis, Saunders. 1962. *The fate of the language* [English translation]. BBC Wales. Available at: http://quixoticquisling.com/testun/saunders-lewis-fate-of-the-language.html. Accessed 17 April 2015.

Lockton, Dan, David Harrison, and Neville Stanton. 2010. The design with intent method: A design tool for influencing user behaviour. *Applied Ergonomics* 41(3): 382–392.

Monroe, Kirsten Renwick. 1991. The theory of rational action: What is it? How useful is it for political science? In *Political science: Looking to the future*, 77–98. Evanston: Northwestern University Press.

Nelde, Peter, Miquel Strubel, and Glyn Williams. 1996. *Euromosaic: The production and reproduction of the minority language groups of the EU*. Luxembourg: Office for Official Publications of the European Communities.

New Economics Foundatiorn. 2005. *Behavioural economics: Seven principles for policy makers*. London: NEF (New Economics Foundation). Available at: http://b.3cdn.net/nefoundation/cd98c5923342487571_v8m6b3g15.pdf. Accessed 11 Jan 2016.

Nodder, Chris. 2013. *Evil by design: Interaction design to lead us into temptation*. Indianapolis: Wiley.

NOP Social and Political. 1996. *Public attitudes to the Welsh language*. Cardiff: Welsh Language Board. Available at: http://www.webarchive.org.uk/wayback/archive/20120330040047/http://www.byig-wlb.org.uk/english/publications/pages/publicationitem.aspx?puburl=/English/publications/Publications/1136.pdf. Accessed 28 Aug 2015.

O'Flatharta, Peadar, Siv Sandberg and Collin H. Williams. 2013. *From act to action: Implementing language legislation in Finland, Ireland and Wales*. Dublin: Dublin City University. Available at: http://orca.cf.ac.uk/55360/. Accessed 11 Jan 2016.

Owen, Morgan. 2013. Attitudes towards the Welsh language in the letters page of the Western mail. Unpublished Research Poster: *Cardiff undergraduate research opportunities scheme*. Cardiff: Cardiff University.

Phillips, Dylan. 1998a. *Pa Ddiben Protestio Bellach?* Talybont: Y Lolfa.

———. 1998b. *Trwy ddulliau chwyldro…?: hanes Cymdeithas yr Iaith Gymraeg, 1962–1992*. Llandysul: Gwasg Gomer.

RMG Clarity. 2013. *Results of a survey of small and medium-sized enterprises March/April 2013*. Cardiff: Welsh Language Commissioner. Available at: http://www.comisiynyddygymraeg.cymru/English/Publications List/J11264 SMEs Welsh Language Survey – Technical Report (English) – v2.pdf. Accessed 11 Jan 2016.

Sunstein, Cass, and Richard Thaler. 2003. Libertarian paternalism is not an oxymoron. *The University of Chicago Law Review* 70(4): 1159–1202.

Thaler, Richard, and Cass Sunstein. 2008. *Nudge: Improving decisions about health, wealth, and happiness*. New Haven: Yale University Press.

Thomas, Roy. 2010. Damcaniaeth yr Hergwd. Barn. Mawrth 2010, pp. 20–21.

Welsh Government. 2015. *A living language: A language for living—Annual report 2014–15*. Cardiff: Welsh Government. Available at: http://gov.wales/docs/dcells/welsh-language/publications/150716-wls-annual-en.pdf. Accessed 11 Jan 2016.

Welsh Government and Welsh Language Commissioner. 2015. *Welsh language use in Wales 2013–15*. Cardiff: Welsh Government. Available at: http://llyw. cymru/statistics-and-research/Welsh-language-use-survey/?skip=1&lang=en. Accessed 27 Nov 2015.

Welsh Language Board. 1996. *Welsh language schemes; their Preparation and approval in accordance with the Welsh Language Act 1993*. Cardiff: Welsh Language Board Available at: http://www.webarchive.org.uk/wayback/ archive/20120330015019/http://www.byig-wlb.org.uk/english/publica-tions/pages/publicationitem.aspx?puburl=/English/publications/Publications/120.pdf. Accessed 10 April 2015.

———. 2008. *The Welsh language use surveys of 2004–2006: The report*. Cardiff: Welsh Language Board. Available at: http://www.webarchive.org.uk/way-back/archive/20120330031325/http://www.byig-wlb.org.uk/english/publi-cations/Pages/PublicationItem.aspx?puburl=/English/publications/Publications/Welsh%20Language%20Use%20Surveys%202004-06.pdf. Accessed 10 April 2015.

Welsh Language Board, et al. 2006. *Guidelines and standards for bilingual soft-ware*. Cardiff: Welsh Language Board. Available at: http://orca.cf.ac. uk/44056/. Accessed 20 July 2015.

Welsh Language Commissioner. 2013. *2011 Census: results by age*. Cardiff: Welsh Language Commissioner. Available at: http://www.comisiynyddygy-mraeg.org/English/Assistance/Dataandstatisitcs/Pages/2011Censusresults byage.aspx. Accessed 10 April 2015.

———. 2015a. *Annual report 2014–15*. Cardiff: Welsh Language Commissioner. Available at: http://www.comisiynyddygymraeg.cymru/English/Publications%20List/Adroddiad%20Blynyddol%202014-15%20(Gwefan). pdf. Accessed 27 Nov 2015.

———. 2015b. *Statutory review of the Welsh language services of high street banks in Wales*. Cardiff: Welsh Language Commissioner. Available at: http://www. comisiynyddygymraeg.cymru/English/Publications%20List/Statutory%20 review%20of%20banks.pdf. Accessed 26 Nov 2015.

———. 2015c. *Technology, websites and software: Welsh language considerations*. Cardiff: Welsh Language Commissioner. Available at: http://www.comisi-ynyddygymraeg.org/English/Publications%20List/Technoleg,%20 Gwefannau%20a%20Meddalwedd%20-%20Technology,%20Websites%20 and%20Software.pdf. Accessed 11 jan 2016.

———. 2015d. *Working Welsh Resources* [Online]. Cardiff: Welsh Language Commissioner. Available at: http://www.comisiynyddygymraeg.cymru/English/Commissioner/Pages/ordercymrbadges.aspx. Accessed 26 Nov 2015.

Welsh Office. 1995. *Welsh social survey 1992, report on the Welsh language.* Cardiff: Welsh Office.

Williams, Colin H. 2010. From act to action in Wales. In *Welsh in the twenty-first century*, ed. Delyth Morris, 36–60. Cardiff: University of Wales Press.

World Wide Web Consortium. 2013. *Indicating the language of a link destination* [Online]. Available at: http://www.w3.org/International/questions/qa-link-lang. Accessed 19 Nov 2015.

4

A Standard for Language? Policy, Territory, and Constitutionality in a Devolving Wales

Patrick Carlin and Diarmait Mac Giolla Chríost

Mae'r bennod hon yn trafod arwyddocâd Mesur y Gymraeg 2011 i'r gymuned wleidyddol Gymreig ac i'r DG ehangach. Ar ôl trafodaeth gychwynnol am y sefydliadau a'r mecanweithiau a grëwyd gan y Mesur, dadansoddir y berthynas rhwng statws swyddogol y Gymraeg a'r hyn y gall dinasyddion ei ddisgwyl o safbwynt darparu gwasanaethau yn y Gymraeg. Yna, ystyrir natur ddemocrataidd mecanwaith rheoleiddio'r safonau iaith yn y Mesur yn ogystal â pha mor briodol yw'r ddisgwrs ynghylch hawliau iaith a gysylltir â'r safonau. Mae'r bennod yn cloi gyda nifer o fyfyrdodau ynghylch y graddau y bydd yr agweddau cydgysylltiedig hyn yn rhan o drafodaethau cyfansoddiadol yn y Gymru sy'n datganoli a'r tu hwnt yn y DU.

Introduction

The passing of the Welsh Language Measure (WLM) by the Welsh legislature in 2011 represented a new framework for engagement with language policy

---

P. Carlin (✉) • D.M.G. Chríost
Cardiff University, Cardiff, UK

© The Author(s) 2016
M. Durham, J. Morris (eds.), *Sociolinguistics in Wales*,
DOI 10.1057/978-1-137-52897-1_4

in both Wales and the devolving UK. It is novel in at least three aspects. Firstly, it is the culmination of policy deliberations, for the first time, by the devolved Welsh Government and legislature on the matter of national language policy, gradually replacing the contents of the Welsh Language Act (WLA) passed at Westminster in 1993. Secondly, mechanisms and institutions through which previous language legislation was implemented have been remodelled, with the Welsh Language Commissioner (WLC) and Welsh Government taking on regulatory and promotional roles previously undertaken by the now defunct Welsh Language Board (WLB), whilst the WLA language scheme model has been for the most part replaced by language standards (which stipulate how organisations are expected to provide services to citizens in Welsh). Thirdly, the official status of the Welsh language now explicitly forms part of the legislation. The significance of these three overarching and interlinked aspects of the WLM is discussed through the chapter, consisting of seven sections. Firstly, the development of language-related legislation during the twentieth century is briefly discussed. After an introductory discussion of the linguistic demography of the Welsh language in section "The Welsh Language and the Demolinguistic Context", the growth of 'Welsh-facing' institutions are then examined in section "The Incremental Growth of Welsh-Facing Institutions. In section "Language Policy in a Devolving Polity", the institutions and mechanisms of the WLA and WLM are then introduced as they relate to language policy in the devolution period after 1999. Section "Official Status of the Welsh Language, the Citizen and the Political System" deals with the relationship between the official status of the Welsh language in the WLM and how this could impact upon citizen expectation of Welsh language service provision. The democratic quality of the language standards regulatory mechanism is considered in section "Language Policy and Regulation" and linked in section "A Right to Language? Sub-state Language Policy in a Transforming UK" to the appropriateness of the language rights discourse as they relate to the official status of Welsh and standards. The chapter concludes with reflections on how these interlinking aspects of the WLM may in the future interact with evolving Welsh and broader UK constitutional debates.

Analysing language policy within and across political systems offers empirical insight into how language knowledge and use is situated, interpreted, and assigned values within society, bringing together sociolinguistics, the sociology of language, political studies, history, and political philosophy. In the case of the Welsh language, for the vast majority of the twentieth century, language policy developed away from a 'Wales-facing' democratic mandate, being administered for politically, legislatively, and institutionally at the UK level of government (Williams 2007). It is with the onset and deepening of asymmetrical devolution—differing powers resting within and across the UK constituent nations—in the past 15 years (Jeffery and Wincott 2006) that language policy in Wales is now more fully appropriated and linked to an emerging sub-state political, legislative, and administrative system. This has resulted in the role of the Welsh language within a bilingual civil society being more deeply legitimated, albeit institutionally, by the National Assembly for Wales (NAfW) as a public good worthy of policy and legislative scrutiny by the Welsh executive and legislature (Morgan 2007). Assessing the degree to which the grafting of political and constitutional values onto language policy in Wales through the incremental growth of 'Welsh-facing' institutions lies at the heart of this chapter. In order to contextualise current language policy, the following paragraphs briefly discuss Welsh language legislation over the past 80 years.

Legislation dealing specifically with the Welsh language was passed three times during the twentieth century. These were the Welsh Courts Act of 1942 and the WLAs of 1967 and 1993, all of which were enacted at Westminster. The determining factors leading to the passing of each of these pieces of legislation should be understood in the context of a belief throughout the twentieth century by Welsh-speaking civil society that there was a lack of adequate provision for the language in the judicial and public administration system. Those who held this belief employed various tactics including protesting, lobbying, and petitioning against public bodies to increase the visibility and use of Welsh (Löffler 2000: 205–6), eventually leading to legislation. The Welsh Courts Act 1942 provided for the use of Welsh 'in any court in Wales by any party or witness who considers that he would otherwise be at any disadvantage by reason of his natural language of communication being Welsh' (Welsh Courts Act 1942). This piece of legislation was soon deemed not fit for purpose, and the Member of Parliament for Denbighshire, Sir Henry Morris-Jones, who was heavily involved in the drawing up of the legislation, stated in his diaries that the Welsh language 'will probably never be adequately settled outside a Welsh Parliament' (Prys Davies 2000: 233).

Scarcely 20 years had passed when in 1963, following the remit of a House of Commons inquiry which was set up to deliberate whether the status of the Welsh language could be based upon the principles of necessity, bilingualism, and equal validity in respect of English, the WLA 1967 ensued and acknowledged the use of the Welsh language in public life, with formal provision for the Welsh language in certain legal proceedings and in statutory forms and signage in Wales (Roddick 2007: 273). The legislation paved the way for an increase of government forms in Welsh: over 250 were available in 1969 compared with only 11 in 1964 (Johnes 2012: 227). However, the mechanism for the 'further provision' for the use of Welsh 'with the like effect as English, in the conduct of other official or public business' was not stipulated in the legislation, with the ensuing result that its implementation was subject to both maximalist and minimalist interpretations (Prys Davies 2000: 243).

The implementation of the concept of equal validity developed in the 1967 Act was thus seen to be unsatisfactory, with civil disobedience resulting in dozens of cases of imprisonment during the 1980s and 1990s (Williams and Morris 2000: 169) and added to more formal civil society methods of protest and engagement with the political and legislative process. By the early 1990s, the status of 'an official language' had been linked to the desire to flesh out how practical meaning could be given to equal validity (Prys Davies 2000: 246). Following on from the passing of the WLA, the WLB was established as the principal agency for the promotion of Welsh in public life. As the policy process which developed from the WLA matured, there remained significant structural weaknesses in terms of the implementation of public body language schemes, partly due to an inability to successfully resolve public and lobbyist expectation regarding uniform access to Welsh language services at the point of delivery but also to the perception that the language scheme mechanism was open to claims of fragmentation and misunderstanding due to the heterogeneous nature of schemes operating throughout the territory, thus making it difficult for citizens to be fully aware of which services in Welsh could be attained within a given geographical area or public sector function (Williams 2015: 191). The pattern of recurrent language legislation throughout the twentieth century continued into the twenty-first century with the passing in 2011 of the WLM and this piece of legislation will be used as a core reference point in the chapter in order to discuss the societal relevance of the Welsh language to the ever-devolving political system in Wales.

The Welsh Language and the Demolinguistic Context

A sketching of the demographics of the Welsh language paints a partial yet telling picture of a twentieth century of immense changes in society impacted upon by a number of factors: population movement with subsequent labour and individual mobility later on in the century, technological developments, and perceptions around the usefulness of Welsh and English in everyday life. These trends are the backdrop to two overarching and related themes, firstly, the decrease in knowledge and use of Welsh throughout the century and, secondly, the societal, institutional and political response to these demographic changes, culminating around the growth in Welsh-medium education and the struggle for increased official recognition of the language (Jenkins and Williams 2000: 2–6).

In 1901, census figures detail that Welsh was the first language of virtually half the population (929,824) with 30% of those being monolingual speakers and living in areas of the country where 90% of the population were Welsh speakers, linking thus the use of the language to specific territories. The relation, however, between learning and using English to modernity, progress, and economic and social betterment (Johnes 2012: 206) can be discerned in the reduction by more than two-thirds of monolingual Welsh speakers between 1891 and 1911 (Census of England and Wales 1911). Towards the twentieth century's end, census figures for 1991, showing 508,098 (18.6%) being able to speak Welsh, with 56% of those living in the north-west and western 'heartlands' of Gwynedd and Dyfed (Jenkins and Williams 2000), demonstrate the numerical and percentage decline of Welsh spoken and the changing geographic distribution of where the language is spoken. Figure 4.1 (below) illustrates the decline in numbers of Welsh speakers across all age groups throughout most of the twentieth century until 1981, by which time developments in favour of the language in the fields of television broadcasting, Welsh-medium education, and a more 'Wales-facing' curriculum began to embed the relevance of the language within the non-devolved Welsh political system (Edwards et al. 2011: 537–8).

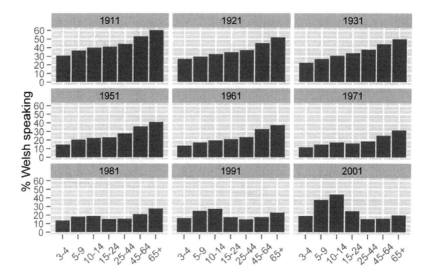

Fig. 4.1 Percentage of the population able to speak Welsh (Jones 2012: 12)

The geographical distribution of Welsh has changed in the past decades, clearly discerned when comparing national percentages of people able to speak Welsh within the population as a whole (Fig. 4.2) with those at the community level (Fig. 4.3), the latter showing clearly that the capacity for Welsh to be spoken exists territory-wide. This geographical distribution has significant repercussions for language policy as the objectives for the transmission and promotion of Welsh gain legitimacy on a national basis, impacting thus upon education curricula and the development of bilingual public services. In policy terms, the challenge thus exists how capacity building in the decades ahead can help foster a bilingual civil society.

The Incremental Growth of Welsh-Facing Institutions

Political communities may or may not coincide with the boundaries of a state, but self-ascribing nations may exert influence on *some* level of government, and the increasingly plurinational UK is no different

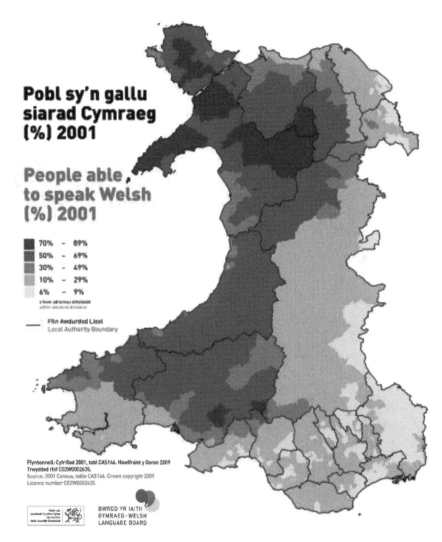

Fig. 4.2   Percentage able to speak Welsh in 2001 (Jones 2012: 21)

in this aspect. Interpreted as a union state, the UK has over the centuries sanctioned, and to some degree subsequently given free rein to, the growth of cultural and administrative flexibility within its constituent nations (Wyn Jones 2005). In the case of Wales, in the absence of

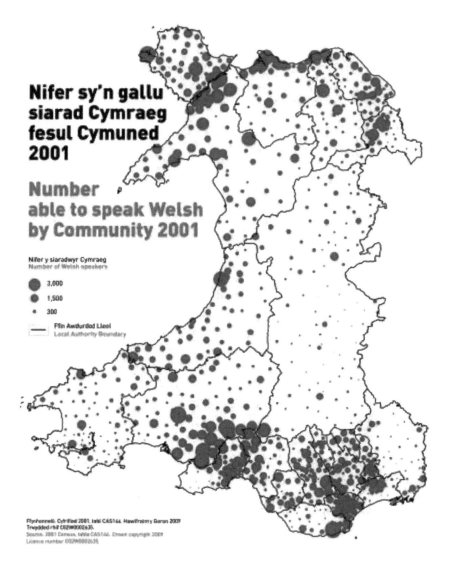

Fig. 4.3 Number able to speak Welsh by community 2001 (Jones 2012: 22)

political institutions at the sub-state national level until 1999, local government represented to a large degree elected government in Wales, taking on significant sub-state symbolism (Carlin 2013). In the case of the

Welsh language, the 'flawed consociationalism' of policy-making which is attributed to the pre-devolution system became terrain to be negotiated by a multifaceted movement comprising of policy communities seeking to extract concessions from the UK government (Thomas 1997), with bilingual statutory education at the vanguard of broad civil society lobbying during the second half of the twentieth century (Thomas and Williams 2013). It is argued here that the development of language policy in Wales reflects the incremental growth of Wales as a converging political, legal, and institutional system over and above a nation predicated on solely cultural and linguistic traits. Such a development opens an alternative path for a '*complex* normative language policy' which is premised upon 'the acknowledgement that the interface between power and language does not operate in a linear or predictable fashion' (Peled 2014: 313).

Despite the fact that the UK qua legal and political system intermittently sanctioned cultural and linguistic heterogeneity within its territory (Colley 1992), until the turn of the millennium the UK (or at least, England and Wales) remained essentially a centralised political system with power residing formally within a strong sovereign parliament. The 450 years between the Acts of Union (1536 and 1543) and the present period can be seen as two macro-historical 'tendencies' explaining broad-stroke historical change (Carter 1970). The first tendency was the creation of formal English administration in Wales and the suppressing of various jurisdictions which at that time existed in Wales. It was during this period that legal structures and administrative areas which would treat England and Wales as one unit began to develop. A corollary of the integration of Wales into the developing union state resulted in increasing linguistic homogenisation, although there would be 'certainly no consistent, sustained effort in this direction' (Wyn Jones 2005: 29).

A counter-tendency developed from the end of the nineteenth century with the individuality of Wales within the UK being increasingly recognised following social, religious, and political pressures. This led to the gradual growth of 'Welsh-facing' institutions and Wales-related legislation at Westminster. Additionally, in an age of increasing suffrage, the Representation of the People Act 1884 increased suffrage in Wales to approximately 60% of the male adult population. This piece of legislation is regarded, unwittingly perhaps, as a constituent element in the birth of Welsh political democracy (Morgan 1981). The Sunday Closing (Wales) Act of 1881, the Welsh Intermediate Act of 1889, the creation of the Central Welsh Board in 1897 in the field of education, the establishment of a Welsh department in the central government Board of Education in 1906, and the Welsh Church Act 1914 are all crucial building blocks in an appreciation of the degree to which the central UK state began to publicly accept the distinctiveness of Wales as a separate nation within the UK and that this would need to be consistently managed in an increasing number of areas of public life (Griffiths 1996). By 1945, 15 Whitehall departments had offices in Wales (Gowan 1970) and existing bodies such as the Welsh Board of Health had been given greater responsibilities (Rawlings 2003). By the time of the creation in 1964 of the UK ministerial cabinet post of Secretary of State for Wales and the Welsh Office, the governmental all-Wales administrative and policy coordination body subsequently subsumed by the devolved NAfW, a somewhat patchwork yet significant Wales-serving institutional framework was by now in existence.

Following a successful referendum vote of 1997 and the Government of Wales Act of 1998, the NAfW came into existence in 1999 with roughly the same powers as those assigned to the preceding Welsh Office, including subordinate legislation within a framework of UK primary legislation-making powers (Royles 2007). Although the opinion existed that significant constitutional change was unlikely to occur for a considerable amount of time (e.g. Pachett 2000), the 15 years following political devolution in Wales have witnessed sustained institutional incrementalism, creativity, and invention. In 2006, a formal split between the legislature and the executive (Wyn Jones and Scully 2008) occurred and, following an all-Wales referendum in 2011, primary legislative powers in 20 policy areas became the responsibility of the Welsh Assembly. These recent developments in the institutional and constitutional governance of Wales continue the incrementalism occurring in the Welsh polity over a period of more than a century. Due to the developments in administrative, political, and legislative devolution and the growth of policy areas now under the aegis of the Welsh Government and Assembly, an extensive regional institutional, legal, and political system and polity may now be said to exist in Wales. This is the sociopolitical hinterland writ large within which language policy operates. How, therefore, have we got to where we are?

Language Policy in a Devolving Polity

Although the WLA 1993 straddles the periods before and after devolution, it is a rather peculiar piece of pre-devolution legislation in that it was driven forward by Conservative party elites in Wales, pressured due to its inability to gauge the strength of lobbying groups calling for new language legislation, and subsequently accepted by a weakened central UK Conservative Party susceptible to compromise and enacted by the central UK Parliament at Westminster (Edwards et al. 2011: 551). Its statutory requirements based on the language schemes mechanism providing for Welsh-medium public services remain for the time being on the statute book. From a symbolic and cultural perspective, section 35 of the WLA is also significant that it repealed the Acts of Union, legislation which had determined, inter alia, English as the only language of official public administration and office in Wales.

As stated earlier in the chapter, a core element of the WLA was the establishment of the WLB, an arm's length governmental agency tasked with 'promoting and facilitating' the use of Welsh in public life. Public bodies both inside and outside Wales negotiated language schemes with the WLB, with each scheme stating how it would provide agreed services to citizens in Welsh. As the WLA policy process matured, significant structural weaknesses became evident in terms of the implementation of schemes, partly due to an inability to successfully resolve public and lobbyist expectation regarding uniform access to Welsh language services (Williams 2013). Additionally, the WLB did not have any independent powers of enforcement—indirectly confirmed in section 20 of the WLA—but rather it was the Secretary of State for Wales *before* the establishment of the NAfW, and the Welsh Government ministers *after* devolution, who were authorised to take enforcement actions, but were not obliged to do so.

The institutional architecture and light regulatory mechanism of this language policy model has been significantly remodelled following the WLM of 2011, one of the largest pieces of legislation to be enacted by the Welsh legislature and preceded by a committee-informed government policy statement entitled 'A Bilingual Future/Dyfodol Dwyieithog' (Welsh Assembly Government 2002)[1] followed by a national action plan entitled 'Iaith Pawb' (Welsh Assembly Government 2003). In this respect, irrespective of the future practicability and perceived outworking of the Measure, its passing by a Welsh legislature rather than at Westminster is significant. As a result therefore of the WLM, fruit of a Welsh Labour/Plaid Cymru coalition government between 2007 and 2011 (Welsh Assembly Government 2007), government language policy in Wales has morphed from straddling both a promotional and quasi-regulatory model, mediated through the language schemes mechanism of the WLA 1993 whereby schemes would be negotiated with public bodies to—on appearances at least—a more uniform and imposed regulatory model with perceived enhanced democratic accountability residing in both the Welsh executive and legislature. The Measure also provided for language standards to gradually replace the language schemes model over time.[2] The regulation of standards will be carried out by the WLC, with a Welsh Language Tribunal hearing any subsequent appeals on decisions made by the WLC. Crucially, the role of ministerial engagement, in its explicit delineation of both government and regulator responsibilities soon after the passing of the WLM (Welsh Government 2013a) marks the acceptance by the Welsh political system of, and responsibility for, language policy and its linkages to the wider regulated policy arena (section "Language Policy and Regulation"). In the light of these events, a deeper and more transdisciplinary engagement by sociolinguistic research to language policy qua politics in Welsh and wider UK society would appear to be both appropriate and necessary. With this in mind, the following section discusses the official status of Welsh as contained in the WLM

---

[1] The Welsh Assembly Government was subsequently renamed the Welsh Government.

[2] Language duties resulting from standards were applied to a first tranche of public organisations in March 2016, having previously been approved as regulations by the Welsh legislature.

and how this might impact upon how citizens understand their ability to access services in Welsh.

Official Status of the Welsh Language, the Citizen and the Political System

It is not yet clear how the institutional, conceptual, and implementation elements contained within the WLM of 2011 will interact, not least due to the lag in implementing a number of the statutory components of the legislation. Such a systemic delay in itself would suggest, at the very least, uncertainty on the part of political and institutional actors regarding the interpretation of, inter alia, the new language standards regime and the degree to which this new mechanism will be able to bridge the perceived gulf between government policy implementation, public and lobbyist expectation, and the demolinguistics of a minority language, albeit one which represents a significant cleavage in the Welsh polity (Johnes 2012: 430).

It is not perhaps unexpected that language legislation emanating from the newly established Welsh legislature contains a degree of conceptual novelty regarding the official status of the Welsh language. The first part of the legislation section states that 'the Welsh language has official status in Wales',[3] eight words which are then given legal and practical meaning in the following subsection of the legislation. This was to generate significant debate, particularly at the committee, expert evidence giving and plenary stage before the Measure's passing in the legislature (Mac Giolla Chríost et al. 2016). As previous language legislation has up to present encapsulated a legal customary 'culture' which has continually interpreted rather than stated that the status of the Welsh language was 'de facto' official, and therefore not requiring a declaration to that end in legislation (HC Deb 1993), a declaration of this kind regarding the status of Welsh in the WLM is significant both for language policy per se but quite possibly also for the relationship between the official use of two languages in the political, administrative, and jurisdictional system

---

[3] The Welsh legislature does not have legislative competence for the English language. On the significance of this, see Mac Giolla Chríost, 2016.

in Wales. The implications of official status in the legislation would seem to be multiple for both civil society in Wales and academic disciplines attempting to describe and account for the knowledge and use of the Welsh language as well as perceptions around it, as we shall see below.

A traditional view is that the customary and partly written UK constitution, of which the WLM now forms a part, is based upon pragmatism and adaptation, with practices being created through precedent rather than sweeping value-laden statements. It is often described as being a 'political' constitution in that it is *through political processes and institutions* that those who wield power are made accountable to citizens. UK sovereignty, thus, resides in Parliament (Gee and Webber 2010) as opposed to resting in the 'people', as in France and Spain, for example. The UK constitution develops as a result of a reasonable degree of conflict in politics whereby 'the democratic process *is* the constitution.' (Bellamy 2007: 5). Recently, however, it has been argued that the UK is gradually moving away from a 'political' to a more 'legal', increasingly fixed and Europeanised constitution (Claes 2007). Examples of this include the Human Rights Act (HRA) 1988, the creation of institutions such as the Supreme Court and the impact of devolution in the UK in general. The de jure declaration giving Welsh official status[4] may be seen as an example of such 'fixedness', albeit indirectly, in the possible wider move away to a more prescribed understanding of the UK customary constitution.

With this in mind, the former language schemes mechanism of the WLA can be understood as deriving from a 'political' constitution in that this piece of legislation represents a somewhat creative application in the early 1990s of the mechanism of commutation schemes which form part of the Welsh Church Act of 1914 (Williams 2013). The WLA thus constitutes an exceedingly ad hoc example of Welsh language planning using accrued learning from UK policy fixes of yesteryear. Since the arrival of full law-making powers in devolved areas and with a Welsh legal jurisdiction being mooted (Welsh Government 2012), it is necessary from a sociolinguistic, institutional, and political perspective to reflect on what might be the position of the Welsh language in such a jurisdic-

---

[4] The official status is itself circumscribed in section 1(2) of the WLM. For further details, see Mac Giolla Chríost et al. (2016).

tion whereby further attempts to embed the official status of the Welsh language may impact upon both competence and perceptions of identity.

Reference once more to the customary British constitution might shed some light on this point if one considers that the UK constitution is not as flexibly customary as portrayed. We are reminded that an embodiedness or 'firming up' in legislation and institution building has tended to follow on from periods of 'constructive political activity after phases of acute conflict and division' (Johnson 2004: 14–5). On such a view, recent constitutional changes in the UK such as the creation of a Supreme Court could be seen to be constitutive of such 'constructive political activity'. Similarly, it might be asked to what degree the *declaration* of the official status of the Welsh language in WLM, and in a subsequent declaration within future 'consolidated' legislation in Wales, such as a third Government of Wales Act or in legislation regarding the establishment of a Welsh legal jurisdiction, might resemble such constructive political activity? If this is the case, how might the official status of Welsh be operationalised in institutions serving Welsh citizens and in civil society generally?

On an initial view, however, the legislative drafting tradition in the UK does not seem to support the possibility of creative interplay between the conceptual development inherent in the official status of Welsh and the mechanics of language standards, understood as the result of 'constructive political activity'. According to lawyers at the Office of the Parliamentary Counsel, declarations do not form part of UK primary legislation (Williams 2013). In other words, primary legislation must be substantive, noting what is permissible in legislation and what is not, rather than having recourse to expansive, declaratory statements replete with norms and nebulous future possibilities. However, to what degree might the interpretation of UK law through declarations be comprehensive? Although declaratory statements do not often appear in legislation, it is not completely unknown either. An example of this, with undoubted constitutional ramifications, can be seen in the first section of the Northern Ireland Act 1998, whereby:

> It is hereby declared that Northern Ireland in its entirety remains part of the United Kingdom and shall not cease to be so without the consent of a major-

ity of the people of Northern Ireland voting in a poll held for the purposes of this section in accordance with Sch. 1. (Northern Ireland Act 1998)

This piece of legislation makes a *declaration* regarding the continuance of a specific territory within the UK until such time as citizens living there choose otherwise. It seems appropriate therefore, where a situation of substantial political and societal significance warrants it, to design legislation with declaratory effect in the British context. One possible reason for a declaration might be for reasons of absolute clarity, even when the matter under consideration, such as language policy, might be *normatively* linked to demolinguistic change. The repercussions for civil society in Wales loom large:

> The argument that it is not legitimate [declaratory statements] rests on the assertion that the sole purpose of legislation is to change the law. But if there is a real doubt as to the state of the law in respect of a particular matter, *removing the doubt by express provision does effect a change in the law.* (Greenberg 2008: 68)

One might consider, however, whether certain criteria under which a 'real doubt' is removed might be linked to a value-laden cultural sphere whereby declaratory claims in legislation offer signposts for clarity whilst couching subtle normative—and political—values? In the realm of language, might not the statement regarding the official status of Welsh begin to link political values with statutory language mechanisms and specific territories within Wales, perhaps leading to different language requirements and expectations by the public? It is thus conceivable that precedents exist within the British legal tradition which might facilitate the development of a language regime in Wales open to ever-increasing democratic scrutiny and diverging significantly from earlier versions. Seen thus, the still flexible British constitution, understood in the broad *political* sense referred to earlier, could provide the precedent for the statutory recognition—and operational delivery through follow-up secondary legislation—of the current WLM declaratory statement in future Welsh constitutional texts were political consensus in the NAfW obtained. The acceptance of such a mechanism could also form the legitimising basis for Welsh Government strategic plans and strategies in the form of non-binding 'soft' law for general promotional and sector-specific policy areas (such as promoting Welsh with prospective parents) as well as providing the required statutory framework for those local governments in Wales already engaged in working towards offering Welsh as a default service delivery language within a wider bilingual framework.

The former First Minister of Wales, Rhodri Morgan, stated in 2007 that the depoliticising of language during the 1980s and 1990s was the most appropriate strategy in the search for consensus (Morgan 2007). Such a path was tactically purposeful and, indeed, in line with government language policy throughout the twentieth century, with the baseline founded upon the growth of 'Welsh-facing' institutions in pre-devolution Wales. However, with the arrival of the Welsh executive and legislature and the further development of the Welsh political- and legal-administrative system, the possibility of a normatively informed and citizen-centred language policy is within reach. Such a policy need not necessarily be predicated on the moral grammar of language rights but rather on a contingent, context-driven process (Carlin 2015). Bringing territory into sharper relief posits the tendency towards blanket coverage of moral grammarians against a much more supple, political, and local approach. The argument forwarded here is that it is specifically, and perhaps unexpectedly, within the context of a flexible British constitutional setting that such a development might occur, representing an applied interpretation of language policy rather than being in thrall to a static and cumbersome prism which uses third-generational rights discourse. The appeal to politics within a broad institutional and civil society setting is clear:

> One cannot simply expect polities, languages and their interplay to remain unchanged through time, at least not outside a highly ideological perception ... [d]enying future generations the opportunity and responsibility for a meaningful participation in the shaping of their own political and linguistic circumstances effectively neutralises the dynamic prioritisation process of politics as a human activity. (Peled 2014: 313)

It goes without saying that a practical and adaptable policy of this description could only be viable were it to achieve party political consensus within the Welsh political system as well as the necessary support for its legitimation, design, implementation, and maintenance. An extended and inclusive 'national discussion' would invariably be needed for this purpose. At a time when the British constitution is rapidly adapting to the continuing relocation of power relations both within and outside the UK, might a more creative and flexible approach to language policy in Wales represent a partial recognition of, and response to, the language practices of citizens living in Wales? That question cannot be answered fully here. However, as policy tools of the local non-devolved system before 1999 and the current devolving Welsh polity, both language schemes and standards are linked to the family of regulated policy areas and to the wider implications as to how, as citizens, we protect and mediate social and public goods through central, devolved, and local state agencies. How, thus, can the regulatory state be understood as the hinterland for language policy mechanisms in Wales and how can we explain *in regulatory terms* the conceptual genesis for an agency such as the WLC, core to the innovation of the 2011 Measure? As the WLM now brings together regulation, democratically mandated ministerial direction and language policy together for the first time in Wales, the linkages between language policy and the institutions implicated in the regulatory turn contained in the WLM are now discussed.

Language Policy and Regulation

In the 1990s, scholars began to notice that although the state was less and less engaged in the day-to-day running of public services, it was in fact regulating more of them. The development of a *regulatory state* as shorthand to understand these phenomena in society began to gain currency at this time (Braithwaite 2008). In this age of governance, the proliferation of regulation includes many different actors, including government itself, regulatory agencies, and networks. A regulatory agency is commonly a non-departmental public organisation charged with the creation of compliance mechanisms as well as with the monitoring and enforcement of the regulated subject area (Levi-Faur 2011: 11), for example, food processing or data management. A relatively recent development in the regulatory turn has been in the area of social cohesion (Leisering 2011: 307) with the pertinent agencies entitled 'integrity' regulatory agencies (Levi-Faur 2011: 13).

This raises significant questions linking the democratic qualities of language policy in the context of regulation qua method of governance. There is consensus that the UK has experienced hyper-regulation during the past 30 years (Leisering 2011: 281) whereby the regulatory state is not 'marked by diminished ambitions' (Moran 2007: 20). If regulatory 'social cohesion' agencies, such as the WLC, are deemed to 'effectively smuggle social goals via the backdoor into the regulatory regime' (Dubash and Morgan 2012: 268–9), then a democratic challenge arises in that regulators are not directly elected, being accountable to the people indirectly through the executive and legislature, leading to debates about the degree of democratic deficit within regulatory systems (Levi-Faur 2011: 15). If the Welsh language is a social good which is being 'smuggled' via the back door, then the relationship between the WLC and the Welsh executive and legislature would seem to warrant ongoing and sustained scrutiny. Further questions going to the heart of a wider democratic debate arising from the WLM include

(i) have the roles and functions of the regulatory mechanisms within the WLM been hitherto sufficiently deliberated within the Welsh political system and civil society?

(ii) being a non-statewide language of the UK, how is this new language-based regulatory regime indexed to ongoing UK constitutional change, notwithstanding the perception that no 'settled procedures for dealing with constitutional reform in the UK' exist (Oliver 2011: 340)?

The final section of the chapter brings together the democratic imperative raised above and the 'engine room' of the WLM, that is, its regulatory standards mechanism and the linkage made by the WLC between standards and rights (Welsh Language Commissioner 2012: 3). What might this mean for how rights claims in respect of the Welsh language are constructed and interpreted in a devolving and constitutionally evolving UK?

A Right to Language? Sub-state Language Policy in a Transforming UK

To get a clearer picture as regards the nature of what language rights regarding the Welsh language might be constitutive of, we need to step back once again from Wales and look briefly at how rights are interpreted in UK legislation. Despite the UK's historical antipathy to a consolidated bill of rights (Hiebert 2006), a move was made when the Labour government came to power in 1997 to lessen the gaps between the UK's commitments to international rights-based agreements and the accommodating of these commitments in domestic law. This was realised when, in 1998, a significant constitutional building-block in the form of the HRA was put in place at Westminster (Kavanagh 2004). At one fell swoop, ministers, Parliament, public authorities, and judges were required to interpret primary and subordinate legislation in the light of the rights stipulated in the European Convention on Human Rights, ratified by the UK in 1951 but not incorporated into its domestic law until the passing of the HRA. Seen thus, how are rights-based guarantees in the HRA applied and evaluated in a constitutional arrangement like that of the UK where Parliament, in principle, takes sovereign primacy over the demos?

Partially, through the application of general standards. In other words, the *claim* to a right is given meaning through rules-based standards, as opposed to the mere *declaration* of a right or otherwise, for example, the declaration of the official nature of a given language as discussed above. An example of the use of standards at the UK level in a pre- and post-HRA scenario is the mechanisms contained within the Disability Discrimination Act (DDA) of 2005 compared with the DDA of 1995. From a regulatory point of view, the 2005 Act included standards which would be applicable to, and actionable by, public bodies. On this view, standards might be interpreted as a novel British mechanism for 'reading' rights off against a customary constitution which is itself adapting to an increasingly regulatory state. In one sense, this mirrors a Hohfeldian legal realist interpretation of right as *claim* (Hohfeld 1917) in that it limits, defines and, more to the point here, quantifies and parses what a claim means *practically* for the citizen, public bodies providing services, and any regulatory agencies involved in the regulation of such standards. Seen thus, language claims through standards are neither universal nor absolute but rather specific to given circumstances. On this alone, Welsh language standards align themselves with difficulty to the discourse of language rights. Nevertheless, a wider debate around how the concept of social progress has been interpreted and put into practice in the global north and south during the twentieth century through either rights-based legislation or social provisioning (Moyn 2014) could be argued to have been partially—for the time being—resolved in the UK through an innovative British application of standards to a wide range of social policy areas, including recently, language policy in Wales.

Standards have been an increasing part of governance (notably in the USA) and international social provisioning for the best part of 100 years (Majone 2011: 40). However, in their—much later—application in the evolving Welsh political system, standards qua regulatory mechanism were refocused, subsequently remoulded by the Welsh government and passed by the devolved legislature. Seen thus, it is not inconceivable that incorporation of the HRA a decade previously at Westminster presented itself as a means by which the 2007–11 coalition government and civil service in Wales, under pressure to provide a new model for language policy in Wales, was able to circumvent the traditional aversion to the language of rights in the UK. The policy process leading up to the WLM in 2011 shows constant endeavours to negotiate the path between the provision of services in Welsh as an absolute right or as negotiated and contingent social policy (Mac Giolla Chríost et al. 2016). It seems unlikely that language standards would have developed as service guarantee levels in the manner in which they have without the eruption of the HRA as a constitutional game-changer for the whole of the UK polity, devolved, and non-devolved.

Language standards, however, also trace their provenance back to the previous language scheme regime under the WLA of 1993 which can itself be considered an embryonic regulatory mechanism after a fashion. It could indeed be argued that the WLB, as the statutory body charged with implementing language schemes, was in many respects an early precursor and pre-devolution exemplar of the UK regulatory turn. This is demonstrated by the fact that by the time the WLB had been abolished under the WLM and its functions transferred to the WLC and the Welsh Government, there were approximately 550 language schemes in operation wherein tens of thousands of individual regulatory standards resided. Although the number of language standards pale in comparison with the previous language scheme regime, it is not completely clear that the public will more readily grasp the degree to which services will be accessed in Welsh at any given geographical location or otherwise platform (Mac Giolla Chríost et al. 2016).

Conclusion

This chapter has dealt with three encompassing and interlinked themes. That a Welsh executive and legislature is linked to language policy via legislation for the first time undoubtedly raises the question of how in the future citizens in Wales will engage with this policy through devolved and civil society institutions. Regulation by the WLC of the Welsh language under policy direction by the executive in Wales underscores a new democratic component of language policy, whilst the actual outworking of the WLM is somewhat clouded by the possible uncertainty of on the one hand a standards mechanism whereby uniform access by citizens to Welsh language services seems difficult to achieve and on the other hand a rights discourse which at least offers the appearance of such a scenario.

The innovative institutional learning and application by both civil servants and politicians in Wales of the regulatory standards mechanism as an example of increasingly rule-based governance in the UK is worthy of attention, not least because it would seem, paradoxically, to continue to mark its distance from an absolutist meta-narrative of rights 'talk' which underscores liberal visions of the good society (Waldron 2000). Reading off current language policy in Wales, legislation within the process-driven political constitution in the UK remains alive and well, with language standards formulated from an amalgam of policy mechanism spillover (such as the DDA), contingency, and political compromise. Moreover, standards would seem to speak to the combination of 'thinking linguistically and politically', *pace* Peled (above) as well as to the reaffirmation of a non-absolute, relational understanding of rights as claims firmly legitimated through the political process (Douzinas and Gearty 2014). By indexing language policy in such a clear manner to political contingency and the demography of language knowledge and use, the meta-narrative of rights talk might well take less prominence as an organising concept in the future whilst civil society language claims represented through the Welsh executive and legislature assume enhanced centrality.

References

Bellamy, Richard. 2007. *Political constitutionalism*. Cambridge: Cambridge University Press.

Braithwaite, John. 2008. *Regulatory capitalism*. Cheltenham: Edward Elgar.

Carlin, Patrick. 2013. Doing as they are told? Subregional language policies in the Basque Country, Catalonia and Wales. *Regional and Federal Studies* 23(1): 67–85.

———. 2015. Where were you, our friends on the inside? Language and contestation in Northern Ireland. *International Journal of the Sociology of Language* 235: 119–135.

Carter, Harold. 1970. Local government and administration in Wales, 1536–1939. In *Welsh studies in public law*, ed. John Andrews, 30–49. Cardiff: University of Wales Press.

Census of England and Wales. 1911. *General report with appendices, table 127: Wales and monmouthshire – Proportional numbers speaking English only, Welsh only, and both English and Welsh, 1901 and 1911*. Available at http://www.visionofbritain.org.uk/census/table_page.jsp?tab_id=EW1911GEN_M127&show=DB. Accessed 20 Jan 2016.

Claes, Monica. 2007. The Europeanisation of national constitutions in the constitutionalisation of Europe. *Croatian Yearbook of European Law and Policy* 3: 1–38.

Colley, L. 2005. *Britons: Forging the Nation 1707–1837*. New Haven: Yale University Press.

Douzinas, Costas, and Conor Gearty. 2014. *The meanings of rights*. Cambridge: Cambridge University Press.

Dubash, Navroz K., and Bronwen Morgan. 2012. Understanding the rise of the regulatory state of the south. *Regulation and Governance* 6: 261–281.

Edwards, Andrew, Duncan Tanner, and Patrick Carlin. 2011. The conservative governments and the development of Welsh language policy in the 1980s and 1990s. *The Historical Journal* 54(2): 529–551.

Gee, Graham, and Grégoire C.N. Webber. 2010. What is a political constitution? *Oxford Journal of Legal Studies* 30(2): 273–299.

Greenberg, Daniel. 2008. *Craies on legislation: A practitioner's guide to the nature, process, effect and interpretation of legislation.* London: Sweet and Maxwell.

Griffiths, Dylan. 1996. *Thatcherism and territorial politics: A Welsh case study.* Aldershot: Avebury.

Gowan, I. 1970. Government in Wales in the twentieth century. In *Welsh studies in public law*, ed. J.A. Andrews. Cardiff: University of Wales Press.

HC Deb. 1993. House of Lords Official Report, 6th Series, vol 228, cc.1138–58. Available at: http://hansard.millbanksystems.com/commons/1993/jul/15/official-status-of-the-welsh-language-no. Accessed 20 Jan 2016.

Hiebert, Janet L. 2006. Parliament and the Human Rights Act: Can the JCHR help facilitate a culture of rights? *International Journal of Constitutional Law* 4(1): 1–38.

Hohfeld, Wesley. 1917. Fundamental legal conceptions as applied in judicial reasoning. *Faculty Scholarship Series. Paper 4378.* Available at: http://digitalcommons.law.yale.edu/fss_papers/4378. Accessed 20 Jan 2016.

Jeffrey, Charlie, and Daniel Wincott. 2006. Devolution in the United Kingdom: Statehood and citizenship in transition. *Publius: The Journal of Federalism* 36(1): 3–18.

Jenkins, Geraint H., and Mari A. Williams. 2000. The fortunes of the Welsh language 1900–2000. In *Let's do our best for the ancient tongue*, ed. Geraint H. Jenkins, and Mari A. Williams, 1–27. Cardiff: University of Wales Press.

Johnes, Martin. 2012. *Wales since 1939.* Manchester: Manchester University Press.

Johnson, Nevil. 2004. *Reshaping the British constitution: Essays in political interpretation.* Basingstoke: Palgrave.

Jones, Hywel M. 2012. *A statistical overview of the Welsh language.* Cardiff: Welsh Language Board. Available at: http://www.comisiynyddygymraeg.cymru/English/Publications List/A statistical overview of the Welsh language.pdf. Accessed 20 Jan 2016.

Kavanagh, Aileen. 2004. The elusive divide between interpretation and legislation under the Human Rights Act 1998. *Oxford Journal of Legal Studies* 24(2): 259–285.

Leisering, Lutz. 2011. Varieties of the new regulatory state: Comparing the UK and Germany. In *The new regulatory state: Regulating pensions in Germany and the UK*, ed. Lutz Leisering, 275–288. Houndmills: Palgrave Macmillan.

Levi-Faur, David. 2011. Regulation and regulatory governance. In *Handbook on the politics of regulation*, ed. D. Levi-Faur, 1–25. Cheltenham: Edward Elgar.

Löffler, Marion. 2000. An exercise in quiet revolutions. In *Let's do our best for the ancient tongue*, ed. Geraint H. Jenkins, and Mari A. Williams, 181–215. Cardiff: University of Wales Press.

Mac Giolla Chríost, Diarmait, Patrick Carlin, and Colin H. Williams. 2016. *The Welsh language commissioner in context: Roles, methods and relationships*. Cardiff: University of Wales Press.

Majone, Giandomenico. 2011. The transformations of the regulatory state. In *The new regulatory state: Regulating pensions in Germany and the UK*, ed. Lutz Leisering, 31–56. Houndmills: Palgrave Macmillan.

Moran, Michael. 2007. *The British regulatory state: High modernism and hyper-innovation*. Oxford: Oxford University Press.

Morgan, Kenneth O. 1981. *Rebirth of a nation: Wales 1880–1980*. Oxford: Oxford University Press.

Morgan, Rhodri. 2007. The challenge of language equality. In *Language and governance*, ed. Colin H. Williams, 43–49. Cardiff: University of Wales Press.

Moyn, Samuel. 2014. *Human rights and the uses of history*. Edinburgh: Verso.

Northern Ireland Act. 1998. c. 47. Available at: http://www.legislation.gov.uk/ukpga/1998/47/section/1

Oliver, Dawn. 2011. The United Kingdom. In *How constitutions change: A comparative study*, ed. Dawn Oliver, and Carlo Fusaro, 329–356. Oxford: Hart Publishing.

Patchett, Keith. 2000. The Government of Wales Act 1998. In *The road to the National Assembly for Wales*, ed. J. Barry Jones, and Denis Balsom, 229–265. Cardiff: University of Wales Press.

Peled, Yael. 2014. Normative language policy: Interface and interfences. *Language Policy* 13: 301–315.

Prys Davies, Gwilym. 2000. The legal status of the Welsh language in the twentieth century. In *Let's do our best for the ancient tongue*, ed. Geraint H. Jenkins, and Mari A. Williams, 207–238. Cardiff: University of Wales Press.

Rawlings, Richard. 2003. *Delineating Wales: Constitutional, legal and administrative aspects of national devolution*. Cardiff: University of Wales Press.

Roddick, Winston. 2007. One nation – Two voices: The Welsh language in the governance of Wales. In *Language and governance*, ed. Colin H. Williams, 263–292. Cardiff: University of Wales Press.

Royles, Elin. 2007. *Revitalizing democracy?: Devolution and civil society in Wales*. Cardiff: University of Wales Press.

Thomas, Alys. 1997. Language policy and language in Wales: A comparative analysis. *Nations and Nationalism* 3(3): 323–344.

Thomas, Huw, and Colin H. Williams. 2013. *Parents, personalities and power.* Cardiff: University of Wales Press.

Waldron, Jeremy. 2000. The role of rights in practical reasoning: "Rights" versus "needs". *The Journal of Ethics* 4(1): 115–135.

Welsh Assembly Government. 2002. *A bilingual future: A policy statement by the Welsh Assembly Government.* Available at: http://www.wales.nhs.uk/sites3/documents/415/bilingualfuture-pdf.pdf. Accessed 5 Apr 2016.

———. 2003. *Iaith Pawb: A national action plan for a bilingual Wales.* Available at: http://gov.wales/depc/publications/welshlanguage/iaithpawb/iaithpawbe.pdf?lang=en. Accessed 5 Apr 2016.

———. 2007. *One Wales – A progressive agenda for the Government of Wales.* Available at: http://gov.wales/strategy/strategies/onewales/onewalese.pdf?lang=en. Accessed 20 Jan 2016.

Welsh Courts Act 1942, Chapter 40. London: The Stationery Office.

Welsh Government. 2012. *Consultation on a separate legal jurisdiction for Wales.* Available at: http://wales.gov.uk/consultations/finance/seplegaljurisdiction/?lang=en. Accessed 20 Jan 2016.

———. 2013a. *Letter to Welsh language commissioner Meri Huws re Welsh language standards: 23 January 2013.* Available at: http://gov.wales/newsroom/welshlanguage/2013/130225languagestandards/?lang=en. Accessed 20 Jan 2016.

Welsh Language Commissioner. 2012. *An introduction to the role of the Welsh language commissioner.* Available at: http://www.comisiynyddygymraeg.cymru/English/Publications List/20120319 GC Cyflwyniad i waith Comisiynydd y Gymraeg - fersiwn terfynol.pdf. Accessed 20 Jan 2016.

Williams, Colin H. 2007. Articulating the horizons of Welsh. In *Language and governance,* ed. Colin H. Williams, 387–433. Cardiff: University of Wales Press.

Williams, Colin.H. 2013. *Language law and policy.* Cardiff: University of Wales Press.

Williams, Colin H. 2015. Legislative devolution and the enactment of the official status of Welsh in Wales. In *Droits Culturels et Democratisation: Cultural rights and democratisation,* ed. Inigo Urrutia, Jean-Pierre Massia, and Xabier Irujo, 181–201. Paris: Institut Universitaire Varenne.

Williams, G., and D. Morris. 2000. *Language planning and language use: Welsh in a global age.* Cardiff: University of Wales Press.

Wyn Jones, Richard. 2005. In the shadow of the first-born: The colonial legacy in Welsh politics. In *Postcolonial Wales*, ed. Jane Aaron, and Chris Williams, 23–38. Cardiff: University of Wales Press.

Wyn Jones, Richard, and Roger Scully. 2008. The end of one-partyism? Party politics in Wales in the second decade of devolution. *Contemporary Wales* 21: 207–218.

Part 3

Welsh English

5

Variation and Change in the Grammar of Welsh English

Heli Paulasto

Mae'r bennod hon yn canolbwyntio ar newidiadau diweddar i forffo-gystrawen Saesneg Cymru, grŵp o dafodieithoedd Saesneg a ddylanwadwyd gan gyffyrddiad â'r Gymraeg. Rwyf yn cyflwyno dadansoddiad newydd o dair nodwedd a ddylanwadwyd gan gyffyrddiad—blaenu dibeniad cymal, defnydd estynedig o'r arddodiad with *a'r tagiau gofynnol* is it?/isn't it?. *Fe gymharir gwahanol ardaloedd yng Nghymru a siaradwyr gwahanol oedrannau. Mae rolau shifft ieithyddol, caffael iaith, cymuned a bri ieithyddol yn cydblethu â phatrymau o amrywio mewn ffyrdd cymhleth. Er bod y nodweddion mwyaf nodedig yn y tafodieithoedd yn cael eu lefelu, fe'u dylanwadir hefyd gan Saesneg Lloegr. Mae siaradwyr ifainc Saesneg Cymru, yn enwedig y rhai hynny o Dde Cymru, yn diweddaru eu tafodiaith tra eu bod hefyd yn cynnal agweddau rhanbarthol arni.*

H. Paulasto (✉)
University of Eastern Finland, Joensuu, Finland

© The Author(s) 2016
M. Durham, J. Morris (eds.), *Sociolinguistics in Wales*,
DOI 10.1057/978-1-137-52897-1_5

Introduction

In his comprehensive 1994 article, Alan Thomas predicts that 'Welsh English, as a distinct dialect, is a transitional phenomenon' (1994: 145). In this view, Welsh-induced grammatical transfer/substrate features will gradually disappear along with increasing English monolingualism and the continuing effect of Standard English (StE) in the formal registers and that of vernacular/dialectal English English (EngE) in the informal ones. Welsh English (WelE) will, thus, eventually be distinguished primarily by its accent and certain lexical and idiomatic features (op. cit.: 145–146). The starting point for the present chapter is to examine to what extent this morphosyntactic transitionality is evidenced in WelE dialect corpora and, hence, whether the above prediction seems to hold.

The structural features of WelE have been investigated extensively in the *Survey of Anglo-Welsh Dialects* (*SAWD*), published in three regional volumes (Parry 1977, 1979; Penhallurick 1991) and a compilation volume (Parry 1999). In addition to phonology and lexicon, the survey charts in detail the dialect grammar of conservative, Non-mobile Older Rural Male (and female; i.e. NORM) informants in all parts of Wales. Other studies give systematic descriptions of the morphosyntax of specific regional dialects (e.g. Lewis 1964; Coupland 1988; George 1990; Penhallurick 1994; and chapters in Coupland 1990), but they are limited in their quantitative and diachronic analyses. The synchronic bias is by no means unusual in research into the grammar of varieties of English, and it is only recently that linguists have begun to make forays into sociolinguistic variation and change in this field. The book *Grammatical Change in English World-Wide* (Collins, ed., 2015), for example, focuses specifically on this aspect of English linguistics, providing numerous innovative examples of methodology and corpora used in the diachronic study of the grammar of Postcolonial Englishes. The above title, then, constitutes the broader framework for the present chapter as well. The diachronic perspective into WelE is made possible through the use of a set of transcribed interview corpora from different parts of the country, representing speakers of varying ages (see section "Data and Methods").

The features studied in this chapter are focus fronting (FF), semantic extension of the preposition *with*, and invariant question tags *is it?/isn't it?*. These features are observed in *SAWD* and, varyingly, in general descriptions of WelE (e.g. Thomas 1984, 1994; Penhallurick 1993, 2004, 2007). Scholars are in agreement that each feature reflects the structure of a parallel Welsh construction and their regional distributions in *SAWD* indicate that they tend to occur in the Welsh-speaking north and west more frequently than in the historically English-speaking southern and eastern parts of the country. My previous studies (Paulasto 2006, 2013a, b) lend support to the proposed language contact origins and show, furthermore, that these features are all relatively frequent in Wales, which makes them suitable targets of corpus-based sociolinguistic research.[1]

Welsh English and Welsh Englishes

Within the wide range of Englishes in the world, termed the English Language Complex by Mesthrie and Bhatt (2008: 3), WelE can be characterised as a language-shift variety of British English (BrE; see also Trudgill 2009: 304). Crucial to its distinctiveness is the language contact influence of Welsh, both as a more or less stable substrate in L1 English speakers' dialect and as a source of transfer (intermingled with community-based dialect features) in L1 Welsh speakers' English. In Irish English, which is in many ways a sibling variety of WelE, further changes have already occurred: Mesthrie and Bhatt (2008: 6) note that Irish English has developed from a language-shift English, with L1 and L2 speakers interacting with each other, into a social dialect, having mainly L1 English speakers at present. In light of this view, WelE continues to be firmly at the shift variety stage due to the relatively large percentage of Welsh–English bilinguals. The heterogeneity and regional variation within WelE needs to be borne in mind however.

Whether an actual shift is still ongoing is another matter: as a result of vigorous language activism and determined language policy and planning, the percentages of Welsh speakers have not diminished a great deal since

---

[1] The results presented in this chapter are based my doctoral dissertation (Paulasto 2006), two previously unpublished conference papers (Paulasto 2013a, b) and fresh research on corpora from the southeast of Wales. Apart from the most recent findings, the results have been discussed in connection with two presentations, at the Amrywiaeth Ieithyddol yng Nghymru/Language Diversity in Wales conference in Aberystwyth, July 2014, and at the Seminar of the Language Research Centre in Swansea, May 2015. I would like to thank all discussants for their valuable comments and the editors of this volume for their feedback, suggestions, and care. Any remaining errors are my own. This research has been conducted with the support of the Research Council for Culture and Society, Academy of Finland (project no. 258999).

the census of 1971 (20.8%; Aitchison and Carter 2000: 51), being 19.0% according to the 2011 figures (Office for National Statistics[2]), L1 and L2 speakers combined. Although the traditional heartlands have continued to weaken over this period and the latest census shows a minor drop from 20.5% in 2001, one might describe the last 40 years in Wales as a period of language maintenance rather than language shift. Societal bilingualism is rarely stable, as the recent fluctuations demonstrate, but the position of the Welsh language is relatively secure in present-day Wales. It is therefore plausible that its L1 speakers continue to exert varying degrees of influence on the regional accents and dialects of English in Wales. However, with the higher levels of education and the widespread availability of standard BrE, morphosyntactic transfer is less likely to take place than a century ago: there is a vast difference in English language proficiency between the L1 Welsh NORM informants of the *SAWD*, in the Welsh heartlands in particular, and the present-day young L1 Welsh speakers (see below).

In the historical development of WelE, the language shift from Welsh to English is certainly a major factor. The Anglicization of Wales has nevertheless proceeded at a different pace in different parts of the country, leading to distinctive regional variation. Awbery (1997: 86–88) identifies three main varieties, one spoken in the longstanding English regions, one in the eastern conurbations, and one in Welsh Wales. The first two of these have a minor role in the present chapter: the longstanding English regions, encompassing southern Pembrokeshire, the Gower peninsula, and the eastern border region (e.g. Radnorshire) owe their historical dialects to late medieval settlers from the southwest of England and West Midlands. These are, in other words, transported dialects rather than shift varieties, and over the past century they have given way to more generally Welsh varieties of English or EngE. The urban dialects spoken in the Cardiff-Newport area and in the northeast near Liverpool, then, are independent developments arising from a diverse demography, with input from bordering EngE as well as WelE (see Coupland 1988: 24–51).

---

[2] 2011 Census: Key Statistics for Wales, March 2011, URL: http://www.ons.gov.uk/ons/rel/census/2011-census/key-statistics-for-unitary-authorities-in-wales/stb-2011-census-key-statistics-for-wales.html#tabDOUBLEHYPHEN-Proficiency-in-Welsh (last accessed 16 June 2015).

The third of Awbery's regions, Welsh Wales, is of central importance in this chapter. It can be furthermore divided into two phases of language shift: the industrial southeast and the rural Welsh heartlands. The southeast was Anglicised rapidly over the course of the nineteenth century as a result of industrialization and the work opportunities offered by the collieries and iron works of Glamorganshire. The coalfield also drew considerable numbers of Welsh-speaking workforce, making this area intensely bilingual, until monoglot English speakers became the majority at the turn of the twentieth century (Aitchison and Carter 2000: 42). The speed of the language shift and the informal means of acquiring English produced a variety which was initially highly Welsh in structure (see George 1990; Paulasto 2009), but which nevertheless also took on numerous characteristics of southwest and West Midland dialects (Lewis 1964). The percentages of Welsh speakers in the southeast vary between 8–15% today (Census 2011; Office for National Statistics). The northeast, especially Flintshire and Wrexham, also industrialised early, and culturally and demographically this area belongs to the Welsh borderland zone. It did not match the southeast in the speed and intensity of industrialization and urbanisation, however (Aitchison and Carter 2000: 119–120; Pryce 1998).

In the rural north and west of Wales (Carmarthen, Ceredigion, Gwynedd, and Anglesey), Welsh continues to be a central community language, although the percentages of Welsh speakers have fallen under 50% in the southwest. The change gained momentum with the infamous *Report of the Commissioners of Enquiry into the State of Education in Wales* in 1847, which contributed to the downgrading of the Welsh language even in the eyes of the Welsh speakers themselves (see Roberts 1998). It also contributed to the Education Act of 1870, providing all Welsh children free and compulsory schooling in the English language. The formal dissemination of English in the heartlands was accompanied by increasing in and out-migration and new social and occupational opportunities. As for the language shift and its outcomes, Ellis (1882: 189–205) provides evidence of non-dialectal 'book English' in Welsh-speaking localities along the Welsh–English border, resulting from formal education, and structurally distinctive 'Welsh English' in Merthyr Tydfil in the southeast, where English was spoken and acquired informally. Paulasto's (2009) results also indicate that the mode of acquisition, whether formal or informal, influenced the degree of Welsh language transfer, as some contact-induced features are highly frequent in the southeast in early twentieth century data. This does not mean that the impact of Welsh on English spoken in the heartlands can be downplayed: the *SAWD* data from the Welsh-speaking southwest (Parry 1979) and North Wales (Penhallurick 1991) is proof enough that English was very much a second language for a majority of the L1 Welsh NORM informants, and this shows in the structures and lexicon they use.[3]

Over the course of the twentieth century, the language-shift Englishes spoken in Welsh Wales have undergone further changes as a result of the increased impact of EngE. The development is inevitable, as Wales is firmly attached to the British political, economic, and cultural sphere in spite of the recent devolution and newly found significance of national identity. Furthermore, Penhallurick (1993: 31) observes that WelE does not have salient national significance in the country. In particular, it is not a marker of Welsh identity and affiliation for the L1 Welsh speakers; the Welsh language is (Paulasto 2014; see also Giles 1990: 265–266). For the monoglot English speakers in Wales, however, the situation is somewhat different, and the regional dialects of English are more easily seen as a source of pride and a covertly prestigious symbol of belonging in the community. Welsh dialects of English are typically not recognised as dialects, however, but rather in terms of accents.

These are, then, some of the central background factors for the following examination of diachronic changes in Welsh-induced grammar features. Of the previous studies, Paulasto (2006) gives a detailed account of regional variation and apparent-time changes in FF (and in extended uses of the progressive form, not examine here). The present chapter adds to these results with two more features, semantic extension of *with* and invariant question tags *is it?/isn't it?*, as well as a diachronic account of the three features in the grammar of the Rhondda, southeast Wales.

---

[3] The first languages of the *SAWD* informants and many other personal details are recorded in the original three volumes (Parry 1977, 1979; Penhallurick 1991). See Paulasto (2006) for previous research on the *SAWD* interview data at the Archive of Welsh English at Swansea University.

Data and Methods

The research data consist of four corpora, three of which I have collected during fieldwork trips in Wales: the Llandybie corpus (LC; collected in 1995–2000), the North Wales corpus (NWC; 2000), and the Tonypandy corpus (TC; 2012). Llandybie is situated in the south-eastern corner of Carmarthenshire, southwest Wales, and the North Wales corpus has been collected in four different localities (see Table 5.1). The fourth, Ceri George Corpus, consists of a small section of the interviews which were conducted by Ceri George for her doctoral dissertation in the Rhondda in 1981 (CGC; George 1990). Figure 5.1, below, puts the localities on the map in relation to the percentages of Welsh speakers in each area around the time of my fieldwork (Aitchison and Carter 2004), and in relation to the primary dialect areas of WelE, as defined by Garrett et al. (1999, 2003). The north–south distinction applies to the Welsh language as well as WelE, and other dialect

Table 5.1 Overview of the corpora used in this study

Corpus	Localities	Informants	Birth years of informants	No. of words
LC	Llandybie (Carm)	46 [35 L1 Welsh]	1915–1981	257,500
NWC	Pencaenewydd (Gwy) Llanuwchllyn (Gwy) Llwyngwril (Gwy) Ruthin (Denb)	23 [19 L1 Welsh]	1915–1984	120,000
TC	Tonypandy (RCT)	10 [monoglot English]	1927–1969	49,800
CGC	The Rhondda (RCT)[a]	5 [monoglot English][b]	1901–1920	30,050[c]

[a]Carm = Carmarthenshire; Gwy = Gwynedd; Denb = Denbighshire; RCT = Rhondda Cynon Taff. Ceri George conducted her interviews in several villages in the Rhondda valleys

[b]For the present purposes, I consider speakers to be monoglot English if they declare that they do not have conversational competence in Welsh even if they understand the language or have studied it at school. There are three such informants in LC along with eight L2 Welsh speakers. In NWC, all informants are by this definition bilingual

[c]Because the Ceri George corpus is only available as hand-written transcriptions, this word count is an estimation based on counting the informants' words on every fifth page of the transcriptions

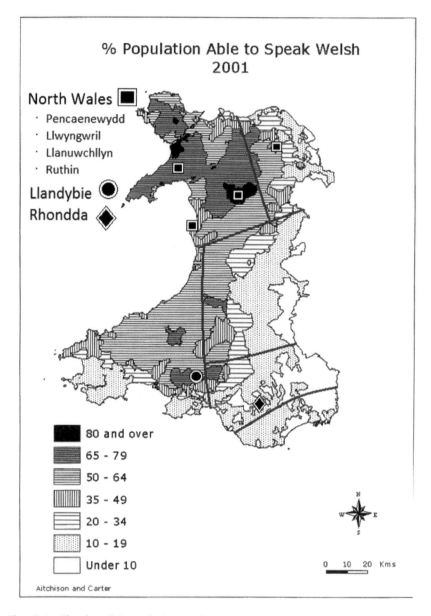

Fig. 5.1 The localities of the study, the percentages of Welsh language speakers in 2001 (Aitchison and Carter 2004: 52) and six main dialect areas of Welsh English (Garrett et al. 1999: 325) (Reproduced with permission from Aitchison and Carter)

divides largely coincide with the description in section "Welsh English and Welsh Englishes".

For a southern locality, Llandybie remains relatively strongly Welsh speaking (62.3% around the time of the interviews in 2001; Aitchison and Carter 2004: 151). It lies on the geographic and cultural border of the Anglicised, suburban south and the Welsh-speaking rural west, which means that while being bilingual, the village has a long history of English being spoken as a community language.

In the northern localities the levels of Welsh range from a little over 40% in Llwyngwril and Ruthin to 78% and 85% in Pencaenewydd and Llanuwchllyn, and the localities are quite a varied set in their demographic development (see Paulasto 2006: 147–148). NWC is only half the size of LC and it was designed as a comparison corpus, intended to represent northern WelE in general terms rather than with a specific geographic focus. As shown in Fig. 5.1, Ruthin belongs to the northeastern dialect area, distinct from the other localities. The generalised map masks a few details, however. Aitchison and Carter (2000: 120) place the surrounding district of Glyndŵr in the cultural transition zone, where Llandybie (in Dinefwr) belongs as well. Furthermore, Paulasto's (2006: 208, 264, 286–287) earlier results indicate that rather than geography, the use of Welsh-induced grammar features in the local dialects is influenced by the role of English as a community language: in NWC, the coastal Llwyngwril has more in common with Ruthin than with the other Gwynedd localities. There is thus no linguistic or regional justification for excluding Ruthin from the corpus.

Tonypandy, then, is situated in the Rhondda valleys in southeast Wales. In 2011, only 12.3% of the population in the county of Rhondda Cynon Taff were Welsh speaking (Office for National Statistics), and contrary to LC and NWC, all informants in TC are monoglot English speakers. In all three corpora, however, they were born and bred in the area or close by, or, in three cases in NWC, born in another part of North Wales but lived in the area most of their lives. For further information on LC, NWC, and their respective localities and informants, see Paulasto (2006: 141–148, 322–329).

All four corpora consist of sociolinguistic interviews dealing with, for example, the life histories of the informants and of the localities and their language situations. Ceri George had, furthermore, a lexical focus in her interviews with the aim of collecting local dialect words and lexicon related to the mining industry as part of SAWD data collection (George 1990: 47–50). Although her method is considerably less structured and formal than that of the questionnaire-based SAWD interviews in general, the lexical focus does produce some quantitative differences between the present corpora which are accounted for below. TC, too, contains a lexical questionnaire section, potentially with a similar impact on the results.

Diachronic changes in Llandybie, North Wales, and the Rhondda are approached using two methods, the first of which is the apparent-time method (see, e.g. Chambers 2009: 206–207). LC and NWC have been divided into age groups I–IV based on the decades of birth of the informants: I in 1910–20s, II in 1930–40s, III in 1950–60s, and IV in 1970–80s. LC is fairly large for a dialect corpus which has been collected in one locality, and the age groups are 52,000–85,000 words in size. For NWC, the age groups are smaller, 16,600–44,400 words, which is why the apparent-time results must be treated with some caution. NWC age group I is somewhat problematic, as four of the six informants in this group have college or university degrees and professional work histories; in LC, only 1 out of the 11 informants in group I has a college degree. The difference may influence some of the results below.

Changes in the Rhondda are examined through two corpora representing different informants and different time periods. The hypothesis of a stabilising sociolect which underlies the apparent-time method is relevant here, too, as the informants of CGC, born 1901–1920, are assumed to speak a dialect which predates that of TC. TC could, in theory, be divided into two age groups corresponding to II and III in LC and NWC, but as the corpus is relatively small, it will be considered as a whole.

The following sections will focus on the three specific dialect features and the changes and regional variation observed in the corpora.

Focus Fronting

FF (also termed focus preposing or predicate fronting) involves a word-order change, where a focused, normally postverbal (or verbal) item is moved initially, changing the canonical SVX word order and reversing the topic-comment information structure (e.g. Birner and Ward 1998). The subject and verb are 'given' information in the discourse context and inversion does not take place. In WelE, all major sentence elements can be fronted:

(1)	Object:	*Any sort of sports* I quite enjoy (NWC: SL)
(2)	Adverbial:	*Before the war* that was (LC: EA); *About seven miles* I go (NWC: AP)
(3)	Subj. pred.:	*Various news items* they are (LC: PD)
(4)	Obj. pred.:	*Pencae'r Eithin* they used to call it (LC: LW)
(5)	Verb phr.:	*Speaking English* he was (TC: AD)

FF appears to be quite widespread in varieties of English around the world, including EngE. Coupland (1988: 37), for example, calls for empirical comparisons between WelE and EngE to establish the 'Welshness' of FF. This is done in Paulasto (2006: 165ff.), where I conclude that FF is more frequent and syntactically and discourse-functionally less constrained in WelE than in traditional EngE dialects. Thus, FF is most likely a contact-induced feature in WelE, originating in the Welsh mixed sentence and identification sentence, where fronting the focused item is obligatory for contrast, emphasis, or informational salience (Fife and King 1991: 145; King 1993: 143–144).

Figure 5.2 illustrates the total use of FF in the corpora, LC and NWC are divided into four age groups and the frequencies normalised per

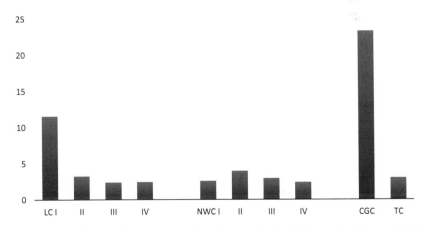

Fig. 5.2 Total use of FF constructions in Llandybie (LC), North Wales (NWC) and the Rhondda (CGC and TC; N/10,000 words)

10,000 words.[4] The frequencies are fairly level apart from two exceptions: LC I (oldest speaker group) and CGC. In Llandybie, there is a definite drop in the use of FF from LC I onwards, but the figure shows that the feature continues to be used by the youngest speakers, too. In NWC, the elderly speakers do not employ FF nearly to the same extent as in LC. This may partly be due to their higher level of education in comparison to the Llandybie informants, but also to the greater role of formal education in the acquisition of English. There are idiolectal differences between the youngest age groups in LC and NWC as well, the informants in LC IV using FF across the board, while in NWC IV, it occurs in the speech of one informant only. This implies that this feature may not be as well-established in present-day North Wales as in the southwest.

CGC is in a class of its own. This dialect feature in particular is influenced by the lexical orientation of the corpus, as in numerous instances the construction occurs in discussions over the name of a certain tool, workman, or other item. Methodological differences do not explain everything, however, as fronted objects and adverbials are also fairly common. In TC, the total frequency is similar to the other corpora, and so, some levelling has certainly taken place.

As for the fronted items, the only clear and statistically significant difference is between LC I and CGC, the former favouring fronted objects and adverbials and the latter predicatives ($\chi^2 \approx 21.4$, $p < 0.001$, with the omission of the category VP). Paulasto's (2006: 205–207) results indicate that predicatives are the foremost items in FF constructions in traditional EngE (represented by the Survey of English Dialects [SED] Spoken Corpus[5]; see Klemola and Jones 1999), and Filppula (1986: 221) confirms this: based on the assessment of educated BrE speakers, the front-

---

[4] There is no adequate means of circumscribing the variable context and quantifying the results more specifically, because assessing all contexts where FF would or would not be a possibility would be a highly impractical and subjective exercise.

[5] The *Survey of English Dialects* (*SED*) tape recordings comprise 479,000 words of guided informal interview data from 298 NORM informants born 1863–1909, covering 286 rural localities in England and the Isle of Man.

ing of predicatives is considered more acceptable than the fronting of objects and adverbials. It therefore seems that, despite being frequent, FF is syntactically more constrained and closer to EngE in the speech of elderly monoglot English speakers in the Rhondda than in the speech of L1 Welsh informants in Llandybie. As pointed out above, though, the reason for the difference may in part be methodological.

The numbers in most age groups are too low for statistical testing, but the main trend appears to be a shift in LC towards favouring the fronting of subject predicatives over objects and adverbials.

A change which the data show more clearly is discourse-functional narrowing. The discourse functions which FF appears in in WelE can be divided into six categories, based on orientation (information–speaker), textual incentive (explicit–implicit), and discourse effect (exclusive–affirmative–neutral–emotive; see Paulasto 2006: 179). The majority of functions are information oriented, apart from the emphatic function, and have an explicit textual incentive, apart from the specificational and emphatic functions.

(6)	Contrastive:	[There were some cats down there, weren't there?] Not on the face—*in the stables* they were. (CGC: EL)
(7)	Confirmatory:	[Do you speak Welsh here at home?] Oh yes, *only Welsh* we speak, yes. (LC: GV)
(8)	Reassertive:	Was it twister, was it? [...] Oh ye—I remember I had a game er [...] *Twister* I remember. (LC: BT)
(9)	Responsive:	...they'd been talking of doin' erm, twinning Tywyn with this town in Ireland. [Which one?] Erm, *Ennistymon* I think it was. (NWC: BJ)
(10)	Specificational (inferable):	...it was the main part of Zante. *Lagana* it's called. (TC: JBA)
(11)	Emphatic:	[What about washing?] Oh dear it was hard work, Ceri, *real hard work* that was. (CGC: DoJ)

The general discourse behaviour of FF entails that the focused item is in a textually/situationally salient 'partially ordered set relation' to the preceding context (Birner and Ward 1998: 35, 83–88). This relation corresponds in many ways to the category of 'inferable information' in Prince's taxonomy (1981: 236–237). The focused information is always either inferable or evoked, with the exception of the specificational function, which has no explicit incentive and can therefore be divided further into three types based on the newness of the focused item, whether brand-new, inferable, or evoked.

Table 5.2 gives percentages of the discourse functions of FF in the corpora. In comparison to traditional EngE, the contrastive function is most characteristic of WelE. This is particularly apparent in the LC corpus, but other WelE corpora used in Paulasto (2006: 189–196) support the finding. It is also noteworthy that the only brand-new fronted items occur in the speech of older speakers in LC and CGC. The most common function is specificational fronting conveying inferable information. The emphasis on this function is apparent in all present regional varieties, and the steep increase in LC IV is particularly telling of the recent developments in south-western WelE. The changes in LC and NWC are not statistically significant, however.

The corpora from the Rhondda are functionally very similar, both having sections with a lexical orientation. The functional distribution is, however, not significantly different from the south-western and northern corpora, and a slight increase in the specificational-inferable function can be witnessed here, as well. Considering that 60% of all instances in the SED corpus, too, belong in this category (Paulasto 2006: 210), one can consider the results as an indication of a functional alignment with common British usage. Further investigation of FF in present-day BrE is called for, however, to confirm this conclusion.

Table 5.2 Discourse functions of FF in Llandybie (LC), North Wales (NWC), and the Rhondda (CGC and TC; percentages)

	SP-NEW %	SP-INF %	SP-EV %	RESP %	CONF %	REASS %	CONTR %	EMPH %	Total n
LC I	7	37	11	4	2	4	29	7	56
II	7	29	18	7	11	14	14	0	28
III	0	27	7	7	0	13	40	7	15
IV	0	71	0	7	0	7	14	0	14
NWC I	0	75	12.5	12.5	0	0	0	0	8
II	0	61	0	8	0	8	23	0	13
III	0	69	0	23	0	0	8	0	13
IV	0	75	0	25	0	0	0	0	4
CGC	3	48	5	20	2	14	6	3	66
TC	0	57	0	21	0	14	7	0	14

Extended Possessive and Other Uses of *with*

Speakers of WelE are known to extend the preposition *with* to contexts indicating 'possession' in a broad sense (see Thomas 1994: 139; Parry 1999: 117–118). This feature, again, originates from the respective Welsh construction where possession is indicated with the verb *bod* 'be' plus preposition *(gy)da* (e.g. *Mae car 'da John* 'there is a car with John'; King 1993: 320). In North Welsh, *gan* (or *gyn*) is the possessive preposition equivalent to *with*, but it also has other uses both in the north and south, one of them corresponding to the English *by* in passive sentences (King 1993: 277). In WelE, this results in *with* being sometimes used in an agentive/means function (Parry 1999: 119). The *with* + NP construction in other words conveys a number of semantic relationships which in StE are indicated with *have* ('we have a field' in ex. 12), the genitive ('my English' in ex. 13b), a compound noun (e.g. *prices with the buses* for 'bus prices'), or other prepositional constructions.

  With is a preposition with a broad semantic range in English as it is. Quirk et al. (1985: 666, 679–711) mention it under eight different types of meanings, and Oxford English Dictionary (OED) Online[6] gives it as many as 40 meanings under three basic categories. Paulasto (2013a, Paulasto and Penhallurick forthcoming) examines the functions of *with* across five corpora of BrE and Irish English, dividing the observed functions into standard and vernacular types. The standard functions comprise ACCOMPANIMENT, 'HAVING', COMMUNICATION & CONDUCT, MEANS & INSTRUMENT, GENERAL RELATION, and OTHER (infrequent types), while the vernacular functions consist of the categories in examples (12–17) below and OTHER (miscellaneous types). Of these, IN ONE'S CASE, CAUSE & REASON and agentive use are mentioned in OED Online. IN ONE'S CASE is closely related to the INTEGRAL/PROXIMATE type, which in turn is an extension of the Welsh-induced possessive function.

---

[6] Oxford English Dictionary, URL: http://www.oed.com/view/Entry/229612 (last accessed 25 June 2015).

(12)	POSSESSIVE	There is a field at the top here *with us* which I own (LC: WD)
(13)	INTEGR./PROXIM.	a. Is there as much fuss at home *with you* about this Millennium thing? (LC: LL)
		b. I make myself understood but well, English is- is far stronger *with me*. (NWC: HD)
(14)	IN ONE'S CASE	I think that could be true, yeah, *with a lot of youngsters*. (LC: BT)
(15)	INSTITUTIONAL[7]	a. I was *with the motor van* that was taking the groceries around. (CGC: TS)
		b. all the regulations *with the milk marketing board* an' everything was becoming quite strict. (NWC: GN)
(16)	By (AGENT & MEANS)	I had this dreadful attack *with a dog*, [...] it attacked me (LC: EL)
(17)	CAUSE & REASON	a. They died *with a disease* what they call silicosis. (CGC: EL&KL)
		b. A: Edinburgh is a lovely city that is. B: [...] yeah, oh I've been up there loads of times *with the rugby* aye. (TC: AD)

Table 5.3 indicates that the vernacular functions are more common in the Welsh corpora than in either the West Midlands section of the SED corpus or in the Great Britain and Ireland components of the International Corpus of English (ICE-GB and ICE-Ire). The differences between all corpora are statistically highly significant ($\chi^2 \approx 74.697$, $p = 0.000$), but there is no significant difference between LC and NWC ($\chi^2 \approx 2.747$, $p = 0.0974$).

A closer examination of the functions shows that the distribution of vernacular usages in these corpora is different (Paulasto 2013a). Three of the functions (POSSESSIVE, INTEGRAL/PROXIMATE and AGENT & MEANS) are only recorded in WelE, while CAUSE & REASON occurs in all but is particularly characteristic of SED West and ICE-Ire. IN ONE'S CASE occurs to some extent in all corpora except SED West (being most common in WelE) and the INSTITUTIONAL function occurs in every corpus, especially WelE and ICE-GB (see Paulasto and Penhallurick forthcoming).

The total frequencies of vernacular functions in the present four corpora in Table 5.4 reveal some interesting differences from the earlier feature. In LC, the frequencies fall towards age group III but rise again in

---

[7] These involve institutional relationships with an employer, company, association, etc.

Table 5.3 Standard versus vernacular functions of *with* in corpora of British and Irish English

	Llandybie	North Wales	SED West	ICE-GB	ICE-IRE
Standard	852	492	373	435	453
Vernacular	120	51	15	13	11
Vernacular %	12.3	9.4	3.9	2.9	2.4
Total	972	543	388	448	464

Table 5.4 Categories and change in the use of vernacular functions of *with* in Llandybie (LC), North Wales (NWC), and the Rhondda (CGC and TC; raw figures and instances per 10,000 words, i.e. pttw)

	POSS	INTEGR	CASE	INSTIT	BY	CAUSE	OTHER	Total
	pttw	pttw	pttw	pttw	pttw	pttw	pttw	N (pttw)
LC I	0.77	2.31	0.77	1.15	0.58	0.58	1.35	39 (7.51)
II	0.24	1.06	0.47	1.41	0.94	0.12	0.71	42 (4.95)
III	0	0.63	0.16	0.63	0.16	0.32	0.32	14 (2.22)
IV	0	0.7	2.62	0.52	0.35	0	0	24 (4.19)
NWC I	0	1.29	0.32	0.96	0.32	0	0.64	11 (3.53)
II	0	0	0.36	2.15	0.36	1.08	0.72	13 (4.67)
III	0	1.13	0.23	1.58	0	0	0.23	14 (3.17)
IV	0	1.2	0.6	0.6	0	0	0	4 (2.40)
CGC	0	0.33	0	0.33	0	0.67	0	4 (1.33)
TC	0	0.2	0	0.2	0	0.6	0	5 (1.00)

IV. The main function causing the change is easy the pinpoint: In one's CASE picks up dramatically in young Llandybie informants' speech. The second major difference concerns CGC, where this feature is quite infrequent; only four instances in total. Thus, the change in TC is marginal at best.

In terms of the functional changes, it is noteworthy that the Possessive function closest to the Welsh construction is only used by the two oldest age groups in LC. The extended, Integral/proximate category dwindles as well, and there are very few instances indeed of these Welsh-induced types in the Rhondda corpora. NWC maintains the latter type to some extent, but it is clearly not in very common use.

In one's case, then, is a function found more generally in BrE, although it is quite infrequent in ICE-Ire and ICE-GB. The rise in the category implies that the *with*-construction continues to be relevant and productive among young speakers in the southwest but it approaches general BrE in functional terms. This is certainly a frequently heard feature in local English; it is also non-stigmatised and highly functional, which may go some way to explain its popularity. The apparent-time changes observed between the 'Welsh' and 'British-Irish' functions in LC are not quite statistically significant, but they are close (p = 0.0644).

NWC does not really differ functionally from LC, apart from a lack of the POSSESSIVE function and the somewhat anomalous age group II with its clear preference for general British vernacular functions. In CGC and TC, however, the majority of instances are of the 'non-Welsh' types, the Rhondda therefore grouping with BrE and Irish English rather than the bilingual Wales. With the high frequencies of FF (and habitual progressive form, see Paulasto 2006: 252) in CGC, the near-complete absence of Welsh-induced use of *with* is intriguing.

Invariant Question Tags *is it?* and *isn't it?*

The third feature examined here is the use of invariant question tags. Of these, the negative tag *isn't it?* has received more attention in the literature, but *is it?* is also discussed by, for example, B. M. Jones (1990: 199) and Williams (2003: 206). George (1990: 243), too, observes this feature in the Rhondda dialect and comments that the feature 'probably arises as a result of the influence of the Welsh generalised confirmatory interrogative *ydy fe?* "is it?" or the confirmatory negative *ontefe?* "isn't it?"'.[8] Following the classification in Algeo (1988), the negative *isn't it?* is mainly used in the confirmatory function in the present corpora, while *is it?* has an informational role (or 'surprise function' in some cases; see Andersen 2001: 102). Both tags are functionally varied, however.

The following examples illustrate both invariant and paradigmatic uses of the question tags. They can be used as question tags proper, as follow-up questions (18b) or in elliptical verbless clauses (20b). *Isn't it?* is frequently reduced in pronunciation into *isn' it?* or, especially in the south, *innit?*

---

[8] There is regional variation in the Welsh invariant question tags, though. Morris Jones (1990: 200) gives the positive variants *ie* (north) and *efe* (south) and negative ones *ynte* (north) and *yntefe* (south).

Positive tags:

(18)   Invariant   a. Our nephew you know he went to—to Stockholm, *is it?* (LC: CO)
b. [Well, you're just a year older than I am then.] *Is it?* (LC: EE)

(19)   Paradigmatic   …about six thousand. Which isn't very much as you say, *is it?* But it's—it's constant. (NWC: SE)

Negative tags:

(20)   Invariant   a. That depends on the individual really I suppose *isn' it?* (NWC: HD)
b. Ryan aye, well his—his son gin—with the ginger hair *innit?* (TC: AD)

(21)   Paradigmatic   the English language is an universal language, *isn't it?* (LC: EA)

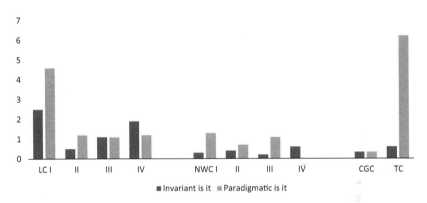

Fig. 5.3 Changes in the use of invariant (and paradigmatic) *is it?* in Llandybie (LC), North Wales (NWC) and the Rhondda (CGC and TC; N/10,000 words; see Appendix for the raw figures)

Figure 5.3 shows the invariant *is it?* to be more common in the south than in North Wales. There is again a drop in the frequencies in Llandybie in the middle age groups, but a rise in the youngest speakers. The distributional changes are not statistically significant, however. In NWC, a similar increase is not detected, the instances being very few.

In the Rhondda, paradigmatic *is it?* is used frequently, while the numbers for invariant *is it?* remain low. The increase from CGC is marked, but the low frequencies in CGC do not lend themselves to statistical analysis. The slightly different methods of data collection go some way to explain the vast change in paradigmatic use: CGC appears to consist of more traditional cultural history and dialect interviews, and the transcriptions contain little informal interaction between the interviewer and the informant(s). In TC, in contrast, the interview situations are perhaps more casual, the discussions sometimes involving several family members and questions also being directed to the interviewer. Informal interaction triggers question tag use more readily, and in the case of positive tags, this is mainly paradigmatic use. The frequent use is nevertheless also indicative of an actual change in discourse patterns in the Rhondda.

For the negative tag frequencies depicted in Fig. 5.4, the scale is completely different. In this case, too, the youngest speakers in LC display an increase in the use of invariant (and paradigmatic) question tags, the apparent-time changes being very nearly statistically significant ($\chi^2 \approx 7.8$, $p = 0.051$). In NWC, too, there is an increase in the use of paradigmatic *isn't it?*, while invariant tag use remains level. This time, the changes are statistically significant ($\chi^2 \approx 11.3$, $p < 0.05$). The differences between invariant *isn't it?* across the generations in LC and NWC also prove to be a significant ($\chi^2 \approx 12.1$, $p < 0.01$).

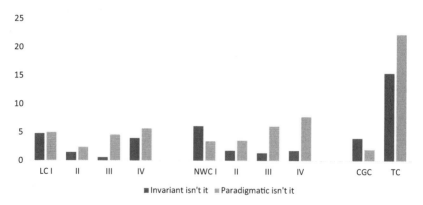

Fig. 5.4 Changes in the use of invariant (and paradigmatic) *isn't it?* in Llandybie (LC), North Wales (NWC), and the Rhondda (CGC and TC; N/10,000 words; see Appendix for the raw figures)

Although *isn't it?* is more common than *is it?* in LC and NWC, TC has far higher rates than the other communities. Of the three dialect features studied in this chapter, invariant *isn't it?* is clearly the favourite in present-day Rhondda. It is also the only one where the diachronic difference between CGC to TC indicates an increase in use, and the source for this increase is likely to be something other than Welsh substrate influence.[9]

In order to see what is happening, we must take a closer look at the functional changes. Williams (2003: 206–207) finds that early WelE usage reflects the focalising function of the Welsh invariant question tags. In light of Ceri George's interview data, he suggests that the question tag 'seems to be evolving towards an even greater invariability' (2003: 208).

A functional analysis is not given here in full, because only some of the functions are of interest in the WelE context. Broadly speaking, the findings in LC support the functional evolution proposed by Williams, although focusing tags feature not only in age group I (5 out of all 38 invariant tags) but also IV (3/34; see ex. 22). Most informational tags have a broad rather than a narrow focus (ex. 23). The vast majority of negative invariant question tags are confirmatory (ex. 24), but maximal invariability is found in so-called accord-building tags, which do not really concern the information of the main clause but the speaker–listener relationship (ex. 25; see also Williams 2003). They are similar in meaning to mainstream BrE *you know?* (cf. the narrative function described in Axelsson 2011: 54). This, then, is the majority function in the youngest generation's speech in Llandybie (52% of all negative invariant tags; cf. 12–15% in age groups I and II) and prominent in TC, too (27%). What is more, the majority of cases in the accord-building function appear in the form *innit?* in LC IV. In TC, too, *innit?* is the favoured variant of the tag, while making no appearances in CGC and very few in NWC or the older age groups of LC.

---

[9] The lexical questionnaire sections in TC provide a context for the occurrence of a number of instances: 57 of the total of 188, that is, 30.3%. This has no impact on the proportional difference between invariant and paradigmatic tags, however, and with the omission of the lexical sequences, the normalised frequencies would be even higher.

(22)	Informational (focusing)	a. A special school for the bank, you mean, *is it?* (LC: EE)
		b. Oh did you travel by car, *is it?* (LC: ML)
(23)	Informational	a. So you wouldn' have any sheep at all in Finland, *is it?* (NWC: EI)
		b. [I've met her too, I—I interviewed her mother.] *Is it?* (LC: BP)
(24)	Confirmatory	a. Yeah, they've got a lot of old funny sayings *innit?* (TC: AD)
		b. And if that canary dies, there's gas *isn't it.* (CGC: EL&KL)
(25)	Accord-building	a. I feel quite proud that they realise that I come from Wales, *isn't it?* (NWC: ME)
		b. ...we'd be walking round, you know West End sort of thing like *innit?* (TC: JBA)

The increased use of *isn't it?/innit?* in the southeast and in young southwestern speakers' English points heavily towards EngE superstrate influence, more specifically the London English question tag *innit?*, also used in speaker oriented and emotive, often somewhat negative contexts (see Algeo 1988: 180–187; Andersen 2001). Use of this tag is spreading in southern EngE. Its wide functional range is examined in a number of recent studies, and it is found in adults' as well as teenaged informants' speech (Krug 1998: 181, cited in Axelsson 2011: 101). Torgersen et al. (2011: 107, 113) show that among young London English speakers, *innit?* has become a common and established pragmatic marker, no longer attributable to any particular social group, although its roots are in non-Anglo communities. The frequencies for *innit?* in their London corpora (c. 16–17 per 10,000 words; op. cit.: 103) are surprisingly similar to invariant *isn't it?/innit?* in TC (Fig. 5.4).

The southern English invariant *innit?* is clearly distinct from the Welsh invariant *isn't it?*, but the present results indicate that the two have begun to merge. That the English superstrate affects the Rhondda and Llandybie dialects rather than North Wales may partly result from geography and partly from the more distinctive role of the invariant tags in southern than northern Welsh English. In Llandybie, the superstrate influence in negative tag use also seems to be feeding into to the Welsh-induced positive invariant tag, which is struggling in other regional varieties studied here.

Conclusion

The three Welsh-induced dialect features investigated in the present chapter all behave in somewhat different ways across the regional varieties and speaker age groups or corpora; yet they do share some common traits, too. The bilingual areas of the north and southwest appear remarkably similar in terms of the frequencies and functions of most dialect features, including the changes observed in apparent time. There are two exceptions to this: Firstly, two of the features (but not invariant *isn't it?*) are more common in elderly LC informants' speech than in any age group in the north. This is the outcome of several factors, including the disparate sampling of the informants, but it is also evidence of the impact of formal versus informal acquisition of English at the idiolectal level, and of the longer history and more prominent role of the regional dialect of English as a community language in Llandybie, especially in comparison to the highly Welsh localities in the north. Secondly, two features display an increase in frequency in the youngest age group in LC but not in NWC: extended *with* and invariant question tags. One of the central tenets of sociolinguistics is that a dialect or sociolect is transmitted to and maintained by the younger generations if it enjoys covert prestige (see, e.g. Chambers 2009: 234–240). Thus, the maintenance of (at least some of) the dialect features indicates that the regional variety is viewed positively in the community. Other social and linguistic factors may be involved as well, for example, the Welsh accent being considered more attractive today than a few decades ago,[10] or the possible interrelationship between code-switching and dialect grammar use, the former being more acceptable among younger than older Welsh bilinguals (Deuchar et al. 2016, this volume). It is difficult to say to what extent the situation is different from North Wales, however.

It is noteworthy that none of the three features has so far disappeared completely; they have simply become less common. Generally speaking, there is decreasing use in apparent time particularly when it comes to the most distinctly Welsh types and functions of use. However, all features also have semantic roles and functions which are more acceptable

---

[10] See, e.g. the YouGov poll from November 2014, where UK informants found the Welsh accent to be the third most attractive out of 15 British and Irish regional accents; URL: https://yougov.co.uk/news/2014/12/09/accent-map2/ (accessed 20 Jan 2016).

to the youngest speakers, and frequently, these functions are ones which approach features of EngE. In the case of FF, this applies to the fronting of predicatives and to the specificational-inferable function of FF, and as regards the semantic extension of *with*, the function IN ONE'S CASE appears in EngE and Irish English as well as being highly common in young LC informants' English. The negative invariant question tag *isn't it?*, then, is beginning to shift towards the London English tag *innit?* in form and function. The habitual progressive form studied in Paulasto (2006: 253–258) follows a similar trend, the standard progressive/delimited function remaining relatively frequent although the extended, non-delimited one is waning (see also Meriläinen et al. forthcoming).

The distribution of the features also indicates that there is a dialect divide between bilingual Wales and the predominantly English southeast: while FF and invariant (negative) question tags appear in all corpora, 'Welsh' functions of *with* (as well as extended habitual PF) occur in LC and NWC, but not in TC.[11] The comparison with CGC suggests that the situation was different in the Rhondda around the beginning of the century and that FF has since declined in use quite considerably. Possessive or related functions of *with* have never enjoyed great popularity in the southeast, however, and the resurgence of *isn't it?* is a fairly recent development influenced by EngE superstrate influence. (Note, however, that its high frequency in TC is unlikely to be matched by most southern EngE varieties, which makes it regionally distinctive of south-eastern WelE.) Cross-dialectal comparisons indicate that while invariant *isn't it?* and FF find a sounding board in vernacular BrE, this is not the case for the semantic extension of *with*. A more versatile investigation of TC in Paulasto and Penhallurick (forthcoming) shows that Tonypandy English aligns with vernacular EngE in its dialect morphology, too, while the bilingual north and west do not. It is undoubtedly the case that we can talk about 'Welsh Englishes' in the plural.

Based on the above results, it appears that Thomas (1994) was right in his assessment of the transitionality of Welsh English grammar: The most distinctive Welsh-induced features are fading out along with the elderly generations of speakers. However, they are not falling into obscurity, but the younger speakers are updating these features to align with vernacular EngE. Substrate

---

[11] Paulasto (2006: 287) notes the same distinction between FF and extended uses of PF in another corpus, the Urban SAWD interviews, where the former is used in all four localities (Caernarfon, Carmarthen, Wrexham and Grangetown in Cardiff) but the latter is restricted to the western, Welsh-speaking towns.

features are finding a new life with superstrate influence. From one stand-point, this may mean 'a general erosion of dialect differences in grammar' (Thomas 1994: 146), as the former Welsh-induced dialect features seem to become functionally engulfed by EngE and blend into the wallpaper of southern BrE. However, I believe that the question remains open to debate: In spite of the changes, these features continue to be regionally characteristic, at least *in combination with each other*, and cross-dialectally speaking quite frequent in Wales. It is certainly safe to conclude that dialect change is not a straightforward matter of certain features disappearing and others being picked up, but that the multiple factors of language and dialect contact at play may also coincide and combine in ways which lead to the maintenance of some degree of distinctiveness. The situation calls for future follow-up research.

Appendix

Table 5.5 Raw figures for invariant and paradigmatic *is it?* (POS) and *isn't it?* (NEG) in the four age groups of Llandybie (LC) and North Wales corpora (NWC) and in the Rhondda corpora (CGC and TC)

	Invar. POS N	Parad. POS N	Total POS N	Invar. NEG N	Parad. NEG N	Total NEG N
LC I	13	24	37	25	26	51
II	4	10	14	13	20	33
III	7	7	14	4	21	25
IV	11	7	18	23	33	56
NWC I	1	4	5	19	11	30
II	1	2	3	5	10	15
III	1	5	6	7	17	24
IV	1	0	1	3	13	16
CGC	1	1	2	12	6	18
TC	3	31	34	77	111	188

References

Aitchison, John, and Harold Carter. 2000. *Language, economy and society: The changing fortunes of the Welsh language in the twentieth century*. Cardiff: University of Wales Press.

———. 2004. *Spreading the word: The Welsh language 2001*. Talybont: Y Lolfa.

Algeo, John. 1988. The tag question in British English: It's different, i'n' it? *English World-Wide* 9(2): 171–191.

Andersen, Gisle. 2001. *Pragmatic markers and sociolinguistic variation. A relevance-theoretic approach to the language of adolescents.* Philadelphia: John Benjamins.

Awbery, Gwen. 1997. The English language in Wales. In *The Celtic Englishes*, ed. H.L.C. Tristram, 86–99. Heidelberg: Winter.

Axelsson, Karin. 2011. *Tag questions in fiction dialogue.* PhD dissertation at the University of Gothenburg, Sweden. E-publication available at: https://gupea.ub.gu.se/bitstream/2077/24047/1/gupea_2077_24047_1.pdf

Birner, Betty J., and Gregory Ward. 1998. *Information status and noncanonical word order in English.* Amsterdam/Philadelphia: John Benjamins.

Chambers, J. K. 2009. *Sociolinguistic theory: Linguistic variation and its social significance.* Revised edition. Oxford: Blackwell.

Collins, Peter (ed). 2015. *Grammatical change in English world-wide.* Amsterdam/Philadelphia: John Benjamins.

Coupland, Nikolas. 1988. *Dialect in use: Sociolinguistic variation in Cardiff English.* Cardiff: University of Wales Press (UWP).

Coupland, Nikolas (ed., in association with A. R. Thomas) 1990. *English in Wales: Diversity, conflict and change.* Clevedon: Multilingual Matters.

Deuchar, Margaret, Kevin Donnelly, and Caroline Piercy. 2016. Factors favouring the production of code-switching by Welsh–English bilingual speakers. In *Sociolinguistics in Wales*, ed. Mercedes Durham, and Jonathan Morris. Basingstoke: Palgrave Macmillan.

Ellis, Alexander J. 1882. On the delimitation of the English and Welsh languages. *Y Cymmrodor 4*: 173–208.

Fife, James, and Gareth King. 1991. Focus and the Welsh 'abnormal sentence': A cross-linguistic perspective. In *Studies in Brythonic word order*, ed. James Fife, and Erich Poppe, 81–153. Amsterdam: John Benjamins.

Filppula, Markku. 1986. *Some aspects of Hiberno-English in a functional sentence perspective.* Joensuu: University of Joensuu.

Garrett, Peter, Nikolas Coupland, and Angie Williams. 1999. Evaluating dialect in discourse: Teachers' and teenagers' responses to young English speakers in Wales. *Language in Society* 28: 321–354.

———. 2003. *Investigating language attitudes: Social meanings of dialect, ethnicity and performance.* Cardiff: University of Wales Press.

George, Ceri. 1990. *Community and coal: An investigation of the English-language dialect of the Rhondda Valleys, Mid Glamorgan.* Unpublished PhD thesis. Swansea: University College Swansea.

Giles, Howard. 1990. Social meanings of Welsh English. In *English in Wales: Diversity, conflict and change*, ed. Nikolas Coupland, 258–282. Clevedon: Multilingual Matters.

King, Gareth. 1993. *Modern Welsh: A comprehensive grammar*. London/New York: Routledge.

Klemola, Juhani, and Mark Jones. 1999. The Leeds Corpus of English Dialects B project. In *Dialectal variation in English: Proceedings of the Harold Orton Centenary conference 1998, Leeds studies in English*, ed. Clive Upton, and Katie Wales, 17–30. Leeds: University of Leeds, School of English.

Krug, Manfred. 1998. British English is developing a new discourse marker, *innit?* A study in lexicalisation based on social, regional and stylistic variation. *Arbeiten aus Anglistik und Amerikanistik* 23(2): 145–197.

Lewis, J. Windsor. 1964. Glamorgan Spoken English. Unpublished manuscript.

Meriläinen, Lea, Heli Paulasto, and Paula Rautionaho. forthcoming. Extended uses of the progressive form in inner, outer and expanding circle Englishes. In *Changing English: Global and local perspectives*, Topics in English Linguistics, ed. Markku Filppula, Juhani Klemola, Anna Mauranen, and Svetlana Vetchinnikova. Berlin: Mouton de Gruyter.

Mesthrie, Rajend, and Rakesh Bhatt. 2008. *World Englishes: The study of new linguistic varieties*. Cambridge: Cambridge University Press.

Morris Jones, Bob. 1990. Welsh influence on children's English. In *English in Wales: Diversity, conflict and change*, ed. Nikolas Coupland, 195–231. Clevedon: Multilingual Matters.

Parry, David. 1977. *The survey of Anglo-Welsh Dialects, Vol. 1: The South-East*. Swansea: David Parry, University College.

———. 1979. *The survey of Anglo-Welsh Dialects, Vol. 2: The South-West*. Swansea: David Parry, University College.

———. 1999. *A grammar and glossary of conservative Anglo-Welsh Dialects of rural Wales*. NATCECT. Occasional Publications, No. 8. Sheffield: University of Sheffield.

Paulasto, Heli. 2006. *Welsh English syntax: Contact and variation*. Joensuu: Joensuu University Press. Available at: http://epublications.uef.fi/pub/urn_ isbn_952-458-804-8/index_en.html

———. 2009. Regional effects of the mode of transmission in Welsh English. In *Language contacts meet English dialects: Studies in honour of Markku Filppula*, ed. Esa Penttilä and Heli Paulasto, 211–229. Newcastle-upon-Tyne: Cambridge Scholars Publishing.

———. 2013a. There's variation with *with* in Welsh English: A case of context extension. Paper presented at the CROSSLING Symposium: Language Contacts at the Crossroads of Disciplines, Joensuu, 28 Feb–1 Mar 2013.

———. 2013b. Invariant tags in Welsh English. Paper presented at IAWE 19, Tempe AZ, 16–18 Nov 2013.

————. 2014. Conceptions of Welsh English and the factors of time, space, and linguistic identity. Paper presented at Sociolinguistics Symposium 20, Jyväskylä, Finland, 15–18 June 2014.

Paulasto, Heli, and Rob Penhallurick. forthcoming. *Welsh English*. Boston/Berlin: De Gruyter Mouton.

Penhallurick, Rob. 1991. *The Anglo-Welsh Dialects of North Wales*. University of Bamberg Studies in English Linguistics, Vol. 27. Frankfurt am Main: Peter Lang.

————. 1993. Welsh English: A national language? *Dialectologia et Geolinguistica* 1: 28–46.

————. 1994. *Gowerland and its language*. University of Bamberg Studies in English Linguistics. Frankfurt am Main: Peter Lang.

————. 2004. Welsh English: Morphology and syntax. In *A handbook of varieties of English, Vol. 2: Morphology and syntax*, ed. Bernd Kortmann, Kate Burridge, Rajend Mesthrie, Edgar W. Schneider, and Clive Upton, 102–113. Berlin/New York: Mouton de Gruyter.

————. 2007. English in Wales. In *Language in the British Isles*, ed. David Britain, 152–170. Cambridge: Cambridge University Press.

Prince, Ellen F. 1981. Toward a taxonomy of given/new information. In *Radical pragmatics*, ed. Peter Cole, 223–255. New York: Academic Press.

Pryce, W.T.R. 1998. Language areas in north-east Wales *c.* 1800–1911. In *Language and community in the nineteenth century*, ed. Geraint H. Jenkins, 21–61. Cardiff: University of Wales Press.

Quirk, Randolph, Sidney Greenbaum, Geoffrey Leech, and Jan Svartvik. 1985. *A comprehensive grammar of the English language*. London: Longman.

Roberts, Gwyneth Tyson. 1998. *The language of the blue books: The perfect instrument of the empire*. Cardiff: University of Wales Press.

Thomas, Alan R. 1984. Welsh English. In *Languages in the British Isles*, ed. Peter Trudgill, 178–194. Cambridge: Cambridge University Press.

————. 1994. English in Wales. In *The Cambridge history of the English language, Vol. V: English in Britain and overseas: Origins and development*, ed. Robert Burchfield, 94–147. Cambridge: Cambridge University Press.

Torgersen, Eivind, Costas Gabrielatos, Sebastian Hoffmann, and Sue Fox. 2011. A corpus-based study of pragmatic markers in London English. *Corpus Linguistics and Linguistic Theory* 7(1): 93–118.

Trudgill, Peter. 2009. Vernacular universals and the sociolinguistic typology of English dialects. In *Vernacular universals and language contacts: Evidence from varieties of English and beyond*, ed. Markku Filppula, Juhani Klemola, and Heli Paulasto, 304–322. London/New York: Routledge.

Williams, Malcolm. 2003. Information packaging in Rhondda speech: A second look at the research of Ceri George. In *The Celtic Englishes III*, ed. Hildegard L.C. Tristram, 201–224. Heidelberg: C. Winter.

6

The Perceptual Dialectology of Wales from the Border

Chris Montgomery

Mae'r bennod hon yn cyflwyno gwaith tafodieitheg ganfyddiadol newydd ar ardaloedd y ffin rhwng Cymru a Lloegr. Fe ddaw'r data o bobl ifainc 16 a 17 mlwydd oed. Yn gyntaf, rhoddir adolygiad o'r llenyddiaeth flaenorol ar ganfyddiadau o ardaloedd tafodieithol Saesneg Cymru. Yn ail, cyflwynir canlyniadau newydd sydd yn dangos sut y mae siaradwyr yn canfod gwahanol ardaloedd tafodieithol. Yn ogystal â'r trosolwg hwn, dangosir bod gan siaradwyr ar ddwy ochr y ffin ganfyddiadau gwahanol o ardaloedd tafodieithol Saesneg Cymru. I gloi, trafodir gwerthusiadau o ardaloedd a roddwyd gan siaradwyr er mwyn dangos yr ardaloedd poblogaidd ac amhoblogaidd ymhlith siaradwyr ar y ffin.

Studying Perceptions of Dialect Variation

Investigating geographical perceptions of dialect variation (i.e. people's perceptions of the dialect landscape) has been an area of longstanding interest worldwide (Weijnen 1946; Sibata 1959; Hoenigswald 1966), and in more

C. Montgomery (✉)
University of Sheffield, Sheffield, UK

© The Author(s) 2016

151

M. Durham, J. Morris (eds.), *Sociolinguistics in Wales*,
DOI 10.1057/978-1-137-52897-1_6

recent decades a programme of perceptual dialectology has arisen. This programme has largely followed the work of Dennis Preston (e.g. Preston 1982, 1989, 1993, 1999a, 2002), and in general, has been viewed as a separate endeavour from research more generally in the field of language attitudes (e.g. Lambert et al. 1960; Giles 1970; Ryan and Giles 1982; Coupland and Bishop 2007). Indeed, Preston's motivation for designing early studies in perceptual dialectology was to address the shortcomings he perceived in language attitudes research, specifically, that this research did not ask respondents where they believed voice samples to be from (Preston 1989: 3). Despite these separate beginnings, as the methods and approaches of perceptual dialectology research developed Preston was able to state that 'any study of responses to regional speech is an integral part of the perceptual dialectology enterprise' (Preston 1999b: xxxviii). Thus, although Preston has preferred to discuss 'language regard' rather than 'language attitudes', dividing lines between the two fields have now become blurred (Preston 2010: 91), to the extent that Garrett (2010) includes a chapter on perceptual dialectology in his book on language attitudes.

Of course, this is not to claim that there is no difference between perceptual dialectology and language attitudes/regard research. Both fields deal with non-linguists' perceptions of language variation, but there is a specific focus in perceptual dialectology on respondents' geographical perceptions of language variation. In particular, perceptual dialectology is interested in non-linguists' 'mental maps' (Gould and White 1986) of language variation, including where respondents' concepts of dialect areas begin and end. Specifically, perceptual dialectology aims to answer five research questions:

(a) How different from (or similar to) their own do respondents find the speech of other areas?
(b) What [i.e. where] do respondents believe the dialect areas of a region to be?
(c) What do respondents believe about the characteristics of regional speech?
(d) Where do respondent believe taped voices to be from?
(e) What anecdotal evidence do respondents provide concerning their perceptions of language variation? (Preston 1988: 475–476).

Following these research questions, and the focus of mental constructs of place, the methods of perceptual dialectology are best known for their inclusion of a 'draw-a-map' task (Preston 1982) in which respondents draw lines on a blank or minimally detailed map indicating where they believe dialect areas to exist. It is this task that has seen the greatest amount of research worldwide (e.g. Inoue 1996; Long 1999a; Diercks 2002; Fought 2002; Bucholtz et al. 2007; Cramer 2010; Montgomery 2012; Cukor-Avila et al. 2012), and I will focus on the results of a such a task in this chapter. Other research elsewhere has also incorporated other task types such as rating regional speech areas on correctness and pleasantness scales (e.g. Preston 1999a; Montgomery 2007). In addition, research has also analysed data on respondents' perceptions of the characteristics of dialect areas (Long 1999b), investigated the placement of voice samples (e.g. Preston 1996; Plichta and Preston 2005; Montgomery 2011), and assessed qualitative interview data for anecdotal evidence of perceptions of dialect areas (e.g. Niedzielski and Preston 2003; Montgomery 2014).

Wales has not been neglected in the global perceptual dialectology project, and in the following section, I discuss research performed in the country within the last 20 years. This research demonstrates widespread interest in perceptions of dialect variation, and highlights the importance of Welsh perceptual dialectology.

Perceptual Dialectology in Wales

Wales has been particularly well-served in the study of non-linguists' perceptions of speech (see, for example Giles 1970, 1977; Giles and Bourhis 1975), and also saw a map-based perceptual dialectology study in the 1990s (reported in Coupland et al. 1994, 1999; Garrett et al. 1995; Williams et al. 1996). The focus of all of this research has been perceptions of Welsh English, and I am not aware of any research dealing with the perceptual dialectology of Welsh. The research presented in this chapter follows the previous research, and again focuses on perceptions of Welsh English. I will review the findings of these perceptual studies in below, after discussing the role of Wales in the perceptual dialectological landscape of Great Britain more generally.

The first national perceptual dialectology study of Britain was undertaken by Inoue in 1989. Focusing on the perception of English dialects across the country, Inoue collected data from students with the help of 'staff members of several universities in Great Britain' (Inoue 1996, 144). Inoue does not disclose which universities helped with the data collection, and therefore there is no data on the location of the students who added their data to the study. This is an important omission given the central role of proximity in the perceptual dialectology (see Montgomery 2012), which typically manifests itself in increased identification of near-to dialect areas at the expense of other areas (notwithstanding other important effects which modify proximity's role).[1] After a quantitative analysis of the lines his respondents had drawn, Inoue was able to calculate nine perceptual dialect areas, of which Wales was represented by only one area: 'Welsh'[2] (Inoue 1996: 149). Further research investigating the perceptions of England and Wales (Montgomery 2007), and Great Britain (Montgomery 2012) from the perspective of locations in northern England and southern Scotland demonstrated a similar perception of Wales as mono-dialectal, with respondents generally circling the country and labelling it 'Wales', or 'Welsh'.[3] Elsewhere, in relation to Scotland (Montgomery 2012, 2014), I have discussed such external perceptions of other, smaller, entities as generally 'other'. This finding highlights the need to investigate the perception of dialect variation from within the country of interest.

This is precisely what the perceptual dialectology research of the 1990s in Wales did, following a research project in which teachers in 32 schools across the country completed a questionnaire relating to their perceptions of dialects. The results of this questionnaire are reported in three papers, all of which include the members of the project team (Coupland et al. 1994; Garrett et al. 1995; Williams et al. 1996). The questionnaire had a number of sections, including a conceptual attitudes component (Garrett et al. 1995: 101) and a draw-a-map task in which respondents were asked to draw up to eight perceptual dialect regions (Williams et al. 1996: 179).

---

[1] It must however be assumed, given Inoue's then residence at the University of Essex, that the majority of students were based in and around this location.

[2] The other perceptual dialect areas were 'Scottish', 'Geordie', 'Scouse', 'York', 'Midland', 'Southern', 'Eastern', and 'Western'.

[3] By which respondents appear to mean 'Welsh English'.

The questionnaire was completed by respondents in multiple locations across the whole country resulting in a wide geographical spread (with the exception of Mid-Wales which was less well-represented (Coupland et al. 1994: 476)). Although this broad geographical sweep of the country contrasts with the data I will present in the next sections (which is drawn only from locations on the border of Wales and England), it is useful here to detail the main findings of the questionnaire in order to aid comparison.

I will discuss here only the results of the draw-a-map component of teachers' responses to the questionnaire, as this is most comparable with the data I present later. These draw-a-map data are most closely dealt with in Williams et al. (1996), where the labels used by map-drawers are discussed and prominent dialect areas examined. This analysis reveals that teachers were generally able to draw the maximum number of areas they were invited to,[4] with a mean of 7.72 areas drawn (Williams et al. 1996: 180). Although, as with all draw-a-map tasks, respondents were free to name and annotate their maps as they saw fit (resulting in many a varied labels for the areas added to the maps), labels fell 'fairly unambiguously into nine sets [i.e. perceptual dialect areas]' (Williams et al. 1996: 181). These nine perceptual dialect areas are listed below in Table 6.1.[5]

Table 6.1 Perceptual dialect areas and label types in perceptual dialectology of 1990s Wales (adapted from Williams et al. 1996: 181–183)

Perceptual dialect area	Label types used
Cardiff	Caardiff; City/Town
Liverpool	Liverpool; Scouse; Merseyside
Valleys	Valleys; Rhondda; Merthyr; Swansea
Pembrokeshire	Pembrokeshire
South West Wales	West Walian; Carmarthen; Cardigan; Dyfed
North Wales	North Wales; Gogledd
Mid-Wales/Borders	Mid-Wales; Central Wales; Borders
English	English; Little England; Anglicised
Welsh	Welsh

---

[4] Eight areas were asked for as this was the limit of the method of analysis employed by the researchers (Williams et al. 1996: 179).

[5] See Williams et al. (1996: 181–183) for a fuller list of labels used by respondents.

Although the numbers of respondents drawing each of the dialect areas is not considered in the report (in contrast to the way in which I discuss my data later in this chapter), the authors do examine some of the geographical factors associated with the areas. Areas are characterised as either 'sharp' or 'diffuse' in nature (i.e. possessing a clear 'centre of gravity', or not), and I have arranged Table 6.1 to reflect these classifications. Thus, Williams et al. (1996: 184) state that the Cardiff and Liverpool areas are sharply focused on the cities themselves, with Valleys and Pembrokeshire appearing to be reasonably so, despite each of these areas subsuming some variation (Williams et al. 1996: 184). The inclusion of an English city, Liverpool, in the perceptual dialectology of Wales might seem odd at first, but Williams, Garrett, and Coupland state that (its focused nature notwithstanding) respondents often 'mentioned specific areas of England with which they associated the "English" accents/dialects of Wales.' (Williams et al. 1996: 184). Thus, it is not the case that respondents considered Liverpool to be part of Wales, but that they perceived its influence to be felt on the dialect landscape. The South West Wales area occupied a middle ground between sharp and diffuse, with this area typically centring 'around Carmarthen but sometimes [including] Cardigan' (Williams et al. 1996: 184).

The other dialect areas are discussed as being much more diffuse, with the 'English' and 'Welsh' dialect areas highly diffuse. The 'English' area could refer to locations in 'the north-east (e.g., Wrexham/Merseyside, coastal, Clwyd, Scouse), the far southwest (Pembroke) and the borders (Shropshire, Newport/Gwent)' (Williams et al. 1996: 184). Further examination of some of the labels used for such highly diffuse areas reveal such labels as 'English sounding', 'Little England', 'Anglicised monotone', 'Soft Welsh', 'Very Welsh', 'Cultured Welsh', as well as mentions of specific areas 'with which they associated the "English" accents/dialects of Wales' (Williams et al. 1996: 184). It seems that these diffuse dialect areas reflect respondents' local experiences, and are less amenable to being thought of as "perceptual dialect *areas*" proper. This perhaps demonstrates a weakness of draw-a-map perceptual dialectology method in dealing with bilingual situations.

The research undertaken in the 1990s is valuable as it gives a point of comparison for the present study, and demonstrates the wide range of labelling techniques used by respondents. Research in England and Scotland has demonstrated both stability in certain perceptions as well as change in others (e.g. Montgomery 2012), and the situation in Wales can now be examined.

Borders and Boundaries

Border and boundaries are of particular importance in both the production and perception of language, and have attracted a good amount of attention in recent years (e.g. Watt and Llamas 2014b). Watt and Llamas state that 'in study after study, it is observed that language is central to how borderlanders portray themselves and perceive their neighbours' (Watt and Llamas 2014a: 1). Whether these borders are national borders (e.g. Llamas 2010) or other types of barrier (such as impassable terrain (e.g. Britain 2015)), or perceptual boundaries (e.g. Montgomery 2007), they have been shown to be important for the ways in which people use and perceive language.

Perceptually, borders are extremely important as they act as barriers to the flow of information. Notwithstanding the impact of large towns and cities and other perceptually prominent locations, it could be assumed that information would flow across space in a relatively interrupted fashion. Indeed, the 'first law of geography' (Tobler 1970) is that near things are more closely related than distant things. This simple understanding of the ways in which information flows between locations is complicated by borders and boundaries. One can imagine the role that physical features such as mountains and rivers have on the perception of entities on the 'other side' of them, and the same is true of political borders. Such borders are important for perception, as are other administrative or religious boundaries (e.g. Nomoto 1999; Montgomery and Stoeckle 2013).

The typical way in which borders have been theorised to affect information flows is that they will stop some information reaching the receiver, or delay it in some way, thus virtually increasing the distance between locations separated by a border or boundary (Gould and White 1986: 153). In my previous research on the perception of dialect areas by respondents on either side of the Scottish–English national border, this held for English respondents who were not able to draw a fine-grained perceptual map of Scottish dialect areas (Montgomery 2014). Scottish respondents, on the other hand, found no such problem in drawing the dialect areas of England in a comparable fashion to their English counterparts. I therefore found a unidirectional border effect, with respondents in the smaller country exhibiting detailed knowledge of both 'home' and 'other' dialect areas, but those in the larger entity only able to drawn detailed maps of their 'home' areas.

The Present Study and Respondents

The data presented here are the first set of results from a wider project considering the perception of dialect variation in Great Britain from the perspective of the Welsh–English border. Data were collected from four fieldwork sites, three of which are located in Wales, with a further site on the English side of the border. In total, there were 58 respondents, and full details can be found in Table 6.2. A map indicating survey locations and other places mentioned in this chapter can be found in Fig. 6.1.[6]

Respondents were all students attending schools and colleges in the survey locations, and were mostly studying for A-Level (post-16) qualifications, with the exception of the respondents in Presteigne, who were in the final year of their General Certificate of Secondary Education (GCSE)

Table 6.2 Respondent details

Location	Male	Female	Number	Mean age	Mean years resident	Travel experience	% of 3–15-year-old Welsh speakers in Local authority
Mold	14	7	21	16.7	14.9	2.8	32.49
Presteigne	4	12	16	15.9	12.3	2.6	39.91
Aberllynfi	5	5	10	17.5	14.1	2.9	39.91
Whitchurch	6	5	11	16.5	13.1	2.8	No data

[6] Elements of this work are based on data provided through www.VisionofBritain.org.uk and uses historical material which is copyright of the Great Britain Historical GIS Project and the University of Portsmouth. Boundary data contains Ordnance Survey data © Crown copyright and database right 2012, further boundary data contains National Statistics data © Crown copyright and database right 2012. Location data is ©Crown Copyright and Database Right 2015. Ordnance Survey (Digimap Licence).

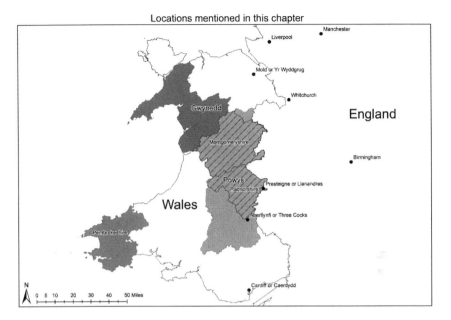

Fig. 6.1 Survey sites and other locations mentioned in this chapter

qualifications.[7] In order to gain some insight into the amount of time respondents had spent in the survey locations, they were asked to state how long they had lived there (shown in the 'Mean years resident' column), and to estimate their experience of travelling on a four-point scale (ranging from 'Lots of travel'=4, to 'No travel experience'=1), with the mean given in the 'Travel experience' column. The majority of respondents had been resident in the locations all their lives, and all had a reasonable estimation of their travel experience, although the (younger) respondents from Presteigne estimated that they had less than respondents in other sites. Welsh language competency was not controlled for in the fieldwork, although all survey locations were from the East of the country, outside of the main concentration of Welsh speakers in the West of Wales. All of the schools from which data were gathered in Wales were English-medium

---

[7] A-Level qualifications are taken by 18-year-olds in England and Wales. GCSE qualifications are taken by 16-year-olds in England and Wales, and represent the final set of compulsory qualifications in the two countries (although some further vocational or academic education is required until each student is 18).

schools, as defined by the Welsh Assembly Government (2007), which means that '1 or 2 subjects may be taught through the medium of Welsh as an option.' (Department for Children, Education, Lifelong Learning and Skills 2007: 15). This similar medium of instruction in each school, the similar levels of Welsh spoken amongst 3–15-year-olds in the local authority areas in which they sit, as well as catchment areas the lie within the Welsh border in all cases, means that the respondents from the three locations in Wales are broadly comparable.

The final column in Table 6.1 shows the percentage of people aged 3–15 who could speak Welsh at the date of the 2011 census, and Fig. 6.2 provides these figures in the country-wide context.[8]

As the only English location in the sample, I will give some further information about the school in Whitchurch. The school is located on the outskirts of the town, and draws its pupils from the immediate area, with none from across the border in Wales. In terms of the broader land-scape within which the school sits, commuting patterns from the 2011 census (Office for National Statistics 2011c) demonstrate connections with bordering locations in Wales. Figure 6.3 shows these interactions, and demonstrates commuting both to and from the statistical unit within which Whitchurch sits.[9] The figure reveals that Whitchurch is relatively well connected to the neighbouring Welsh area (Wrexham 18), with commuting both to and from this location. Further commuting takes place between Whitchurch and another area of Wrexham (Wrexham 20). Despite this, the majority of commuting takes place to and from English locations around the town.

Although it must of course be noted that these commuting data relate to the population above the age of 16 who are in full-time employment, and none of my respondents belong to this category, these data are none-theless indicative of the level of contact between locations. It is therefore likely that many of my respondents come into contact with people who commute regularly between England and Wales, although the majority

---

[8] Data extracted from the Office for National Statistics (2011a, b).

[9] See the Office for National Statistics guide to census data (Office for National Statistics 2011d) for more information about this classification.

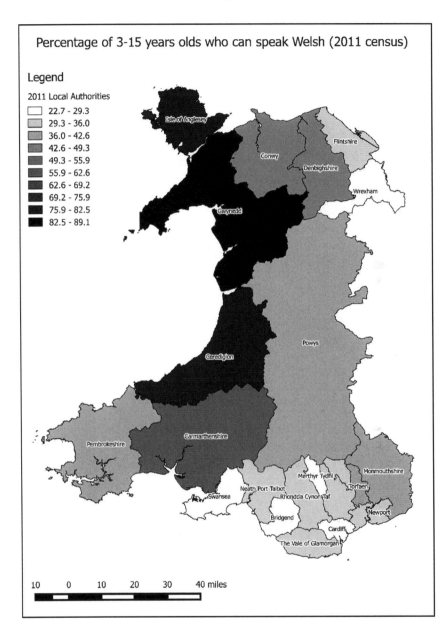

Fig. 6.2 Percentage of 3–15-year-olds who could speak Welsh on the date of the 2011 census, by local authority

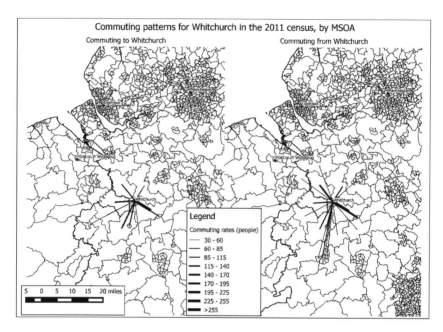

Fig. 6.3 Commuting to and from Whitchurch in the 2011 census, by Middle Super Output Area

of people working outside (or coming to work within) Whitchurch do so from English areas.

The data collection methodology was similar to other perceptual dialectology surveys carried out by myself (Montgomery 2007, 2012). Respondents were given a questionnaire pack, asked to fill in some biographical details, and were then directed to the draw-a-map task. Data collection was undertaken in a classroom, and after an introductory presentation explaining the purpose of the research and gaining consent for the data to be collected respondents were given ten minutes to complete the task. The base map used by the respondents was an outline map of Great Britain that was blank with the exception of some city location dots. For the first five minutes of the task, a location map showing major towns and cities in Great Britain was displayed in order to help orient respondents to the blank map. Respondents were asked to draw a North–South line (in England), and then to draw lines around dialect areas, to label the areas, and then (if they had time) to comment on the areas they had drawn. Having finished the draw-a-map task, respondents completed a listening task which involved them rating and placing voice samples on another blank map.

As discussed in the introduction, only the results from the draw-a-map task will be reported here. These data were processed by first performing an initial count of the lines drawn representing perceptual dialect areas on each respondents' map. These data, along with qualitative data, were tabulated in order to find the main trends in the data. Percentage recognition rates were calculated in order to compare perceptual prominence of areas across survey location. It is these numerical and qualitative data that I discuss below.

Perceptions of Welsh English Dialect Areas

It will not have escaped readers' notice that, unlike other perceptual dialectology studies undertaken in Wales (discussed above), one of the aims of the present piece of research was to gather perceptions dialects across the whole of Great Britain. Thus, although I will report specifically on the perceptions of Welsh English dialect areas below, it is useful to place these perceptions within the broader British perceptual landscape. Table 6.3 does this, showing the 20 most frequently drawn dialect areas across all four survey locations.

Table 6.3 reveals a familiar pattern of country-wide perception. There is a similar rank-order to the perceptual areas drawn by respondents in surveys over the last 30 years (Inoue 1996; Montgomery 2007, 2014), with 'Scouse', 'Brummie', and 'Geordie' the three most prominent dialect areas. The country-wide division, 'Scottish', is a typical boundary drawn by those in 'other' countries (cf. Montgomery 2014), which is something I return to below in my discussion of the Welsh–English border. Other prominent dialect areas are 'Manc' and 'Cockney', with the latter area demonstrating less recognition than in other studies (e.g. Montgomery 2012). Divisions of Wales can be found in the table, where the most prominent divisions are 'North Wales', 'South Wales', and 'Welsh', followed by a 'Valleys' area.

Table 6.3 The 20 most frequently drawn dialect areas

Perceptual area[a]	Lines drawn[b] (% recognition rate)
Scouse	49 (84.5)
Brummie	44 (75.9)
Scottish	38 (65.5)
Geordie	38 (65.5)
Cockney	29 (50.0)
Manc	28 (48.3)
North Wales	26 (44.8)
South Wales	25 (43.1)
Bristol	14 (24.1)
Welsh	13 (22.4)
Yorkshire	12 (20.7)
Glasgow	11 (19.0)
Valleys	11 (19.0)
Cornish	10 (17.2)
West Country	10 (17.2)
Farmer[c]	8 (14.0)
Essex	7 (12.1)
Posh	6 (10.3)
Shropshire	5 (8.6)

[a]The names given for each perceptual area follow the most frequently given name for the area by respondents, and refer to the following location (where the label is not transparent): *Scouse* = Liverpool; *Geordie* = Newcastle upon Tyne; *Manc* = Manchester; *Brummie* = Birmingham; *Valleys* = an area of South Wales
[b]The recognition rate was calculated by dividing the number of lines drawn by the number of respondents (58) and multiplying this figure by 100
[c]Labels such as 'Farmer' and 'Posh' were of the type described in the previous research on perceptions of Welsh dialects as 'diffuse'. Such labels have no focus on particular locations and reflect local perceptions of these categories

I now turn to the divisions of Wales by respondents from the four survey locations. Table 6.4 shows these divisions, along with the number of lines drawn and the percentage recognition rate.

Despite differences in processing techniques that make comparisons of numbers of lines and recognition rates impossible, a comparison of the areas listed in Table 6.4 with those in Table 6.1 from the study by Williams et al. (1996) reveals that all the areas listed as salient in their study remained so amongst my respondents. In addition to these areas, it is possible to add three further areas (Gwynedd, Radnor, and Montgomeryshire) that were not mentioned by respondents in Williams et al.'s (1996) research.

Table 6.4 Characteristics and evaluations of dialect areas by respondents from Welsh survey locations

	Mold	Presteigne	Aberllynfi
North Wales	Said to sound like Liverpool	Hard to understand (2); Farmers; Sheep; Scouse	Harsh accent [equated to Scouse]; Strong sounding; Proper Welsh; Gogs; Tuneful; Nice to hear
South Wales	Gentle and friendly; Spoken quite slowly; I like this accent; Cute; Patriotic; Friendly; Happy; Fun	'Presh'; 'But'; Slower speaking than North Wales; Sheep (2); Very patriotic	
Cardiff	Stronger Welsh accent; Taff; These people are farmers	Sheep	Harsh Welsh
Radnor		'Radnor Boh'; 'Radnor mun'; Farmers (4); THE BEST;	
Valleys	Very Welsh; Common	Legends; Welshies	Poorly educated in grammar; Often violent sounding; Chavvy
Welsh English			Normal; Wenglish; More English sounding
Welsh accent	[I] like the Welsh accent		Nice accent
Taff	Like it		

This table contains every example of dialect area characteristics given by respondents, multiple instances of the same label are given in parentheses

It is clear from the results from the three Welsh sites that North Wales is a prominent dialect area for all respondents. There was only one instance of a respondent labelling this region using the Welsh language term 'Gog', and no mentions of 'Gogland', as seen in Williams et al. (1996): 185. Instead, the most frequently used label (aside from 'North Wales') was 'North Walian'. This could suggest the potentially fleeting nature of some dialect area labels, especially those that are not centred on a specific location such as a town or city, or it could simply be an artefact of the different profiles of respondents in the two studies. The research undertaken by Williams et al. (1996) contained 46.9% Welsh speakers, which is quite different from my cohort of respondents, far fewer of whom are likely to be able to speak Welsh (and therefore less likely to use the Welsh-based name for the area). Regardless of the reasons for the different label, the northern region is clearly still salient. Also salient, at least for the two more northern Wales survey locations, is the South Wales dialect area, which is the top most recognised area for Mold and Presteigne respondents. Both the North–South divide amongst respondents' perceptions along with the high recognition rates for the two areas echoes the different reactions respondents had to dialect area labels in the previous perceptual research in Wales (Coupland et al. 1994: 483) and underlines the perceived differences between North and South Wales.

For the locations further south, Presteigne and Aberllynfi, there is an increasing awareness of variation in the south of the country. 'Valleys', Cardiff, and Pembrokeshire feature in the areas drawn for these locations. For the most southerly location, Aberllynfi, the high recognition rate for 'Valleys' (80%) shows a more nuanced picture of dialectal variation than for the most northerly of the locations, Mold, which simply includes all of the south in the 'South Wales' area. Such a proximity effect, mentioned above, has been found elsewhere in relation to similar studies in other parts of Great Britain (Montgomery 2012), and is demonstrated in other survey locations. For example, Presteigne is in the historic county of Radnorshire, whose name survives as 'Radnor' in the present administrative area of Powys. This area appears as perceptual dialect area in the Presteigne respondents' maps, which include the map in Fig. 6.4 proudly claiming the area as 'THE BEST', echoing Preston's Michigan respondents' mapping strategies in relation to their home state (Preston 1999a). Other typical mapping strategies can also be observed in Fig. 6.4, such as the lines drawn around a greater number of near-to perceptual areas (see further discussion of this below), and the use of dialect area labels for many of the areas drawn. Also evident, alongside a good amount of altitudinal data and comments about the areas drawn, is some use of the names of celebrities linked with the dialect areas. Although this was not typical of respondents in this fieldwork, this type of labelling was not uncommon in my previous research (cf. Montgomery 2012).

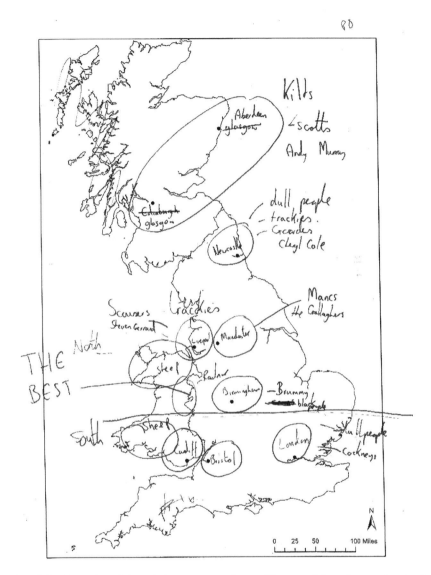

Fig. 6.4 Completed hand-drawn map by a 16-year-old male respondent from Presteigne

The use of evaluative dialect labels such as 'Strong Welsh', 'Harsh Welsh', and 'Soft Welsh' reflects different ways of completing the task by different participants. I will explore the evaluation of other areas and the extent to which these match with the areas drawn with primarily evaluative labels below. In the next subsection, I will discuss the perception of Welsh dialect areas from Whitchurch, and reflect on the role of the border in conditioning perceptions of dialect variation in the country.

The Role of the Border

Although proximity to dialect areas or their borders plays an important role in perceptions of these areas, it is not the only factor that influences how non-linguists view the dialect landscape, as I have discussed above. As noted, in the case of Scotland the border plays a large role in dialect perceptions (Montgomery 2014), and English respondents demonstrated little sensitivity to Scottish dialect variation (in contrast to their Scottish counterparts' perceptions of English areas). I will examine the Welsh–English border here.

Although a physical boundary between Wales and England was established by the creation of Offa's Dyke (Charles-Edwards 2013: 419) in the eighth century, the Welsh–English border as we understand it now was created after Wales' union with England in the 1530s (Davies 2007: 212). Although there has been legislation specific to Wales since the Acts of Union and prior to devolution in 1999, its legislative and institutional (county-based) structure was in effect merged with that of England. This entwined history with England means that the border between the two countries has for some centuries been no barrier to communication. A recent report assessing the impact of a fully independent Wales on the West of England states that

> The Welsh–English border is far more porous and economically connected than the Scottish–English border... Ninety per cent of the Welsh population lives within 50 miles of the English border, and there is a huge amount of connectivity, with 138 million journeys taken between the two countries each year. (Henderson et al. 2015: 3)

Such a high level of connectivity is also demonstrated in the 2011 census commuting data, which reveals statistically significant flows of population to and from England from each of the Welsh counties bordering England (Office for National Statistics 2014), as demonstrated in Figs. 6.3 and 6.5.

This level of cross-border activity, both historically and in the present day, might lead one to think that the border would be much less important in terms of perception for the respondents in this study than the Scottish–English border was in previous research, resulting in a more equal perception of the dialect variation in Wales amongst English respondents. Re-examination of Table 6.5 shows this not to be the case, however. A glance at the 'Sum' figures, indicating the total lines drawn indicating Welsh dialect areas and the percentage of the total lines drawn indicating Welsh areas shows that respondents in the English location drew fewer lines than those in the Welsh locations. Considering the areas

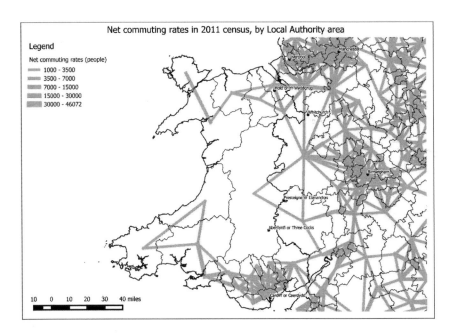

Fig. 6.5 Net commuting rates in the 2011 census, by local authority area (data from Office for National Statistics 2011b, c).

that were drawn by the Whitchurch respondents, it can be seen that there were only two 'Welsh' and 'Cardiff'. Figure 6.6 shows a typical map from Whitchurch.

To return to the perceptions of dialects, Fig. 6.6 reveals the general map drawing strategy for English respondents, which consists of a line drawn around Wales and the label 'Welsh'. This echoes my previous findings in relation to the Scottish–English border, with respondents from England ignoring the variation in the smaller entity. By contrast, as the data in Table 6.3 and the map in Fig. 6.4 shows, Welsh respondents had a similar perception of English dialect areas to their fellow participants in England, again echoing the results from the Scottish–English border, despite the Welsh–English border's quite different nature. In addition, it can be seen here that the map drawing strategy for the 'other' countries dialect areas are very similar, with the respondent simply drawing a block around each.

As both Figs. 6.4 and 6.6 reveal, the completed draw-a-map tasks not only contained dialect areas and their labels, but also a fair amount of evaluative and characteristic data, and I will deal with this in the next subsection for the major Welsh dialect areas.

Characteristics and Evaluations of Dialect Areas

Draw-a-map tasks are useful for gaining information relating to the characteristics and evaluations of dialect areas, although the free-form nature of the task means that varying strategies can be taken when adding such comments to the map. Table 6.4 shows the evaluative and characteristic labels that were added to the maps, by (Welsh) survey location.

Unsurprisingly, the most frequently drawn areas attract the greatest number of comments. Thus, North and South Wales were frequently labelled. For these areas (and others in the table), a general lack of agreement about the evaluation of the areas can be seen. There are often contradictory comments, especially for Aberllynfi respondents in relation to North Wales, with one comment stating that is a 'Harsh accent', and another claiming that it is 'Nice to hear'. This intra-location disagreement underlines the importance of gathering sufficient data in perceptual dialectology studies

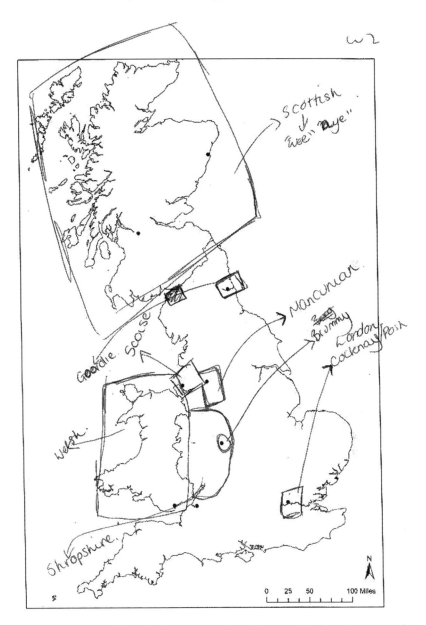

Fig. 6.6 Completed hand-drawn map by 17 year old female respondent from Whitchurch

Table 6.5 Welsh English dialect areas by survey location

	Mold (n = 21) Total lines drawn for all areas = 153		Presteigne (n = 16) Total lines drawn for all areas = 100		Aberllynfi (n = 10) Total lines drawn for all areas = 113		Whitchurch (n = 11) Total lines drawn for all areas = 79	
		N and % of respondents		N and % of respondents		N and % of respondents		N and % of respondents
South Wales	South Wales	13 (61.9)	South Wales	11 (68.8)	North Wales	9 (90)	Welsh	10 (90.9)
North Wales	North Wales	8 (38.1)	North Wales	9 (56.3)	Valleys	8 (80)	Cardiff	2 (18.2)
Taff	Taff	2 (9.5)	Radnor	5 (31.3)	Welsh English	4 (40)		
Strong Welsh	Strong Welsh	2 (9.5)	Valleys	3 (18.8)	Cardiff	2 (20)		
Welsh	Welsh	1 (4.8)	Welsh	1 (6.3)	Welsh accent	2 (20)		
Mid-Wales	Mid-Wales	1 (4.8)	Montgomeryshire	1 (6.3)	Welsh	1 (10)		
Gwynedd	Gwynedd	1 (4.8)			South Wales	1 (10)		
					Soft Welsh	1 (10)		
					Harsh Welsh	1 (10)		
					Pembrokeshire	1 (10)		
Sum of Welsh areas		28		30		30		12
% of Welsh areas		18.3ᵃ		30		26.5		15.2

ᵃThe percentage mean total areas drawn is calculated by summing the number of lines drawn indicating Welsh dialect areas and dividing these by the total lines drawn for all areas in each survey location to build up a general perceptual profile of an area, although individual comments are always invaluable to underscore important differences in perception and evaluation. Interestingly, despite the disagreement over the evaluation of the North Wales area, there is agreement that it perceived as being influenced by Liverpool. This is in contrast to the findings from the previous research discussed above that showed the perception of Liverpool as a separate dialect area, not an influence on North Wales.

From Table 6.5 it appears that of the two main divisions (North and South Wales) South Wales is largely preferred by the respondents in this study. The difference between northern and southern locations is again striking, with Mold-based respondents providing numerous comments for the South Wales dialect area but little by way of comment in relation to North Wales. The most southerly location, Aberllynfi, shows the opposite pattern, with no comments about South Wales but extensive comments in relation to the North Wales division. Presteigne respondents, by contrast, made comments about both areas. The North Wales area is characterised as 'Harsh', and equated to Scouse by respondents from all locations. Its 'Strong sounding' nature is mentioned, and it is said to be 'Hard to understand' by two respondents from Presteigne. By contrast, the South Wales dialect area is characterised as 'Gentle', 'Friendly', and is discussed as being spoken 'Slowly'. Interestingly, respondents from Mold and Presteigne state that the dialect is 'Patriotic'. This brings together the idea of accent with patriotism, and could suggest that these respondents consider this variety to be most strongly marked as embodying 'Welshness' to outsiders.

Other dialect areas attracted fewer comments, although the comments in relation Cardiff appear to support the 'city harsh' characterisation of the city noted in Garrett et al. (1995). The labelling of Cardiff as 'These people are farmers' was surprising, although there were other areas that attracted the label more frequently, chief amongst them the Radnor area. This area was only drawn by respondents from Presteigne, as noted above, and attracted four 'Farmer' labels. Although the area is largely rural, it is interesting that the farmer label can also be used for other dialect areas such as Cardiff which are characterised elsewhere as 'Strong' and 'Harsh'. The Radnor area also attracted two instances of linguistic forms: 'Radnor Boh' and 'Radnor mun'. The 'Valleys' dialect area was mostly negatively evaluated, and was variously characterised as 'Poorly educated', 'Common', 'Violent', and 'Chavvy'. This area also appeared to function as a Welsh heartland for some of the respondents, with speakers characterised as 'Very Welsh', and 'Welshies'. Indeed, data on Welsh-only identity from the 2011 census shows that this area is most likely to contain people who rejected other identity labels (such as 'British', or 'Welsh and British') (Harries et al. 2014: 3), supporting this 'Welsh Heartland' perception. The Welsh English area was only noted by the Aberllynfi respondents, and was drawn around their location, hence the label 'Normal'. The innovative label 'Wenglish' was also used to characterise the area. This label is not seen in previous research,[10] but has risen to prominence in recent years, with entries in Urban Dictionary[11] and Contemporary Humorous Localised Dialect Literature (CHLDL) (Honeybone and Watson 2013) publications in the 2000s (Edwards 2003; Lewis 2008).

Table 6.5 shows the numerous ways in which respondents characterised and evaluated the dialect areas they had drawn in Wales, and demonstrated the often contradictory nature of this type of labelling. It serves to underline one of the strengths of the perceptual dialectology method, and its ability to gain access to the full range of respondents' perceptions.

Summary and Conclusions

I have demonstrated in this short chapter that the perceptions of Welsh English dialect areas have remained rather static over the years from the perceptual dialectology research undertaken in the 1990s (Coupland et al. 1994; Garrett et al. 1995; Williams et al. 1996). Many of the same dialect areas were drawn by respondents in this study as in theirs, despite the differences in respondent groups (teachers vs. students).

The main dialect areas drawn by respondents in this study were North and South Wales, highlighting the importance of these two areas, and also the differences in perception from different locations

---

[10] Although see http://talktidy.com/<RefSource/>

[11] http://www.urbandictionary.com/define.php?term=Wenglish

in the country. These differences in perception according to location were also seen in the other areas respondents added to the map. The Radnor area, not mentioned in the previous research, is particularly significant for respondents from Presteigne, for example. Such proximity effects are extremely important in perceptual dialectology and speak to the need for national surveys to gather data from numerous locations.

Also important is the role of the Welsh–English border. As with previous research examining the Scottish–English border (Montgomery 2014), English respondents' perceptions of the smaller country (Wales) are generalised as 'other', with a large 'Welsh' area drawn by most respondents. The Welsh participants' perceptions were much more detailed and nuanced, with these perceptions extending over the border into England. This underlines the value of perceptual dialectology in understanding the perceptions of dialect areas from a number of perspectives, and the need to expose those outside smaller countries to the rich dialect landscape present within them.

References

Britain, David. 2015. Between north and south: The Fenland. In *Northern Englishes*, ed. Raymond Hickey, 417–426. Amsterdam: John Benjamins.

Bucholtz, Mary, Nancy Bermudez, Victor Fung, Lisa Edwards, and Rosalva Vargas. 2007. Hella Nor Cal or Totally So Cal? The perceptual dialectology of California. *Journal of English Linguistics* 35(4): 325–352.

Charles-Edwards, T.M. 2013. *Wales and the Britons, 350–1064*. Oxford: Oxford University Press.

Coupland, Nikolas, and Hywel Bishop. 2007. Ideologised values for British accents. *Journal of Sociolinguistics* 11(1): 74–103.

Coupland, Nikolas, Angie Williams, and Peter Garrett. 1994. The social meanings of Welsh English: Teachers' stereotyped judgements. *Journal of Multilingual and Multicultural Development* 15(6): 471–489. doi:10.1080/0 1434632.1994.9994585.

———. 1999. 'Welshness' and 'Englishness' as attitudinal dimensions of English language varieties in Wales. In *Handbook of perceptual dialectology*, vol 1, ed. Dennis R. Preston, 333–343. Amsterdam: John Benjamins.

Cramer, Jennifer. 2010. The effect of borders on the linguistic production and perception of regional identity in Louisville, Kentucky. Unpublished PhD thesis, Urbana: University of Illinois at Urbana-Champaign. https://www.ideals.illinois.edu/bitstream/handle/2142/18426/Cramer_Jennifer.pdf?sequence=1

Cukor-Avila, Patricia, Lisa Jeon, Patricia C. Rector, Chetan Tiwari and Zak Shelton. 2012. 'Texas – It's like a whole nuther country': Mapping Texans' perceptions of dialect variation in the Lone Star State. In *Proceedings of the Twentieth Annual Symposium About Language and Society*, 55: 10–19. Austin, TX.

Davies, John. 2007. *A history of Wales*. London: Penguin.

Department for Children, Education, Lifelong Learning and Skills. 2007. *Defining schools according to Welsh medium provision*. Cardiff: Welsh Assembly Government. http://gov.wales/topics/educationandskills/publications/guidance/defining-schools-welsh-medium/?lang=en

Diercks, Willy. 2002. Mental maps: Linguistic geographic concepts. In *Handbook of perceptual dialectology*, ed. Daniel Long, and Dennis R. Preston, 51–70. Amsterdam: John Benjamins.

Edwards, John. 2003. *"Talk Tidy": The art of speaking Wenglish*. Creigiau: Tidyprint Publications. (First published in 1985, Cowbridge: Brown Books).

Fought, Carmen. 2002. Californian students' perceptions of, you know, regions and dialects? In *Handbook of perceptual dialectology*, ed. Daniel Long, and Dennis R. Preston, 113–134. Amsterdam: John Benjamins.

Garrett, Peter. 2010. *Attitudes to language*, Key topics in sociolinguistics. Cambridge: Cambridge University Press.

Garrett, Peter, Nikolas Coupland, and Angie Williams. 1995. 'City Harsh' and 'the Welsh version of RP': Some ways in which teachers view dialects of Welsh English. *Language Awareness* 4(2): 99–107. doi:10.1080/09658416.1995.9959872.

Giles, Howard. 1970. Evaluative reactions to accents. *Educational Review* 22: 211–227.

———. 1977. *Language, ethnicity and intergroup relations*. London: Academic Press.

Giles, Howard, and Richard Bourhis. 1975. Linguistic assimilation: West Indians in Cardiff. *Language Sciences* 38: 9–12.

Gould, Peter, and Rodney White. 1986. *Mental maps*, 2nd edn. Boston: Allen & Unwin.

Harries, Bethan, Bridget Byrne and Kitty Lymperopoulou. 2014. *Who identifies as Welsh?: National identities and ethnicity in Wales. The dynamics of diversity: Evidence from the 2011 census.* Manchester: Centre on Dynamics of Ethnicity (CoDE).

Henderson, Graham, Guy Lodge, Guy Raikes and Alan Trench. 2015. *Borderland west: Assessing the implications of a stronger Wales for the west of England.* Manchester: Institute for Public Policy Research. http://www.ippr.org/files/publications/pdf/borderland-west_Wales_Feb2015.pdf?noredirect=1

Hoenigswald, Henry. 1966. A proposal for the study of folk linguistics. In *Sociolinguistics*, ed. William Bright, 16–26. The Hague: Mouton and Co.

Honeybone, Patrick, and Kevin Watson. 2013. Salience and the sociolinguistics of scouse spelling: Exploring the phonology of the contemporary humorous localised dialect literature of Liverpool. *English World-Wide* 34(3): 305–340.

Inoue, Fumio. 1996. Subjective dialect division in Great Britain. *American Speech* 71(2): 142–161.

Lambert, Wallace E., E.R. Hodgson, Robert C. Gardner, and Samuel Fillenbaum. 1960. Evaluational reactions to spoken languages. *Journal of Abnormal and Social Psychology* 60(1): 44–51.

Lewis, Robert. 2008. *Wenglish: The Dialect of the South Wales Valleys.* Tal-y-bont: Y Lolfa.

Llamas, Carmen. 2010. Convergence and divergence across a national border. In *Language and identities*, ed. Carmen Llamas, and Dominic Watt, 227–236. Edinburgh: Edinburgh University Press.

Long, Daniel. 1999a. Geographical perception of Japanese dialect regions. In *Handbook of perceptual dialectology*, ed. Dennis R. Preston, 177–198. Amsterdam: John Benjamins.

———. 1999b. Mapping nonlinguists' evaluations of Japanese language variation. In *Handbook of perceptual dialectology*, ed. Dennis R. Preston, 199–226. Amsterdam: John Benjamins.

Montgomery, Chris. 2007. Northern English dialects: A perceptual approach. Unpublished PhD thesis. Sheffield: University of Sheffield. http://etheses.whiterose.ac.uk/1203/

———. 2011. Starburst charts: Methods for investigating the geographical perception of and attitudes towards speech samples. *Studies in Variation, Contacts and Change in English* 7. http://www.helsinki.fi/varieng/journal/volumes/07/montgomery/index.html

———. 2012. The effect of proximity in perceptual dialectology. *Journal of Sociolinguistics* 16(5): 638–668. doi:10.1111/josl.12003.

―――. 2014. Perceptual ideology across the Scottish-English border. In *Language, borders and identities*, ed. Dominic Watt, and Carmen Llamas, 118–136. Edinburgh: Edinburgh University Press.

Montgomery, Chris, and Philipp Stoeckle. 2013. Geographic information systems and perceptual dialectology: A method for processing draw-a-map data. *Journal of Linguistic Geography* 1(1): 52–85.

Niedzielski, Nancy, and Dennis R. Preston. 2003. *Folk linguistics*. Berlin: Mouton de Gruyter.

Nomoto, Kikuo. 1999. Consciousness of linguistic boundaries and actual linguistic boundaries. In *Handbook of perceptual dialectology*, ed. Dennis R. Preston, 63–70. Amsterdam: Benjamins.

Office for National Statistics. 2011a. *2011 census: Aggregate data (England and Wales) [computer File]*. This information is licensed under the terms of the open government licence. http://www.nationalarchives.gov.uk/doc/open-Government-licence/version/2. UK Data Service Census Support. http://infuse.ukdataservice.ac.uk

―――. 2011b. *2011 census: Digitised boundary data (England and Wales) [computer File]*. UK Data Service Census Support. http://edina.ac.uk/census

―――. 2011c. *2011 census: Special workplace statistics (United Kingdom) [computer File]*. UK Data Service Census Support. https://wicid.ukdataservice.ac.uk.

―――. 2011d. *Super output area (SOA)*. Text. Office for National Statistics. December 8. http://www.ons.gov.uk/ons/guide-method/geography/beginner-s-guide/census/super-output-areas--soas-/index.html

―――. 2014. Commuting patterns in the United Kingdom, 2011 Census. http://www.neighbourhood.statistics.gov.uk/HTMLDocs/dvc193/index.html

Plichta, Bartlomiej, and Dennis Preston. 2005. The /ay/s have it: The perception of /ay/ as a north-south stereotype in United States English. *Acta Linguistica Hafniensia* 37(1): 107–130. doi:10.1080/03740463.2005.10416086.

Preston, Dennis R. 1982. Perceptual dialectology: Mental maps of United States dialects from a Hawaiian perspective. *Hawaii Working Papers in Linguistics* 14(2): 5–49.

―――. 1988. Change in the perception of language varieties. In *Historical dialectology: Regional and social*, ed. Jacek Fisiak, 475–504. Berlin: Mouton de Gruyter.

―――. 1989. *Perceptual dialectology: Non-linguists' view of aerial linguistics*. Dordrecht: Foris.

———. 1993. Folk dialectology. In *American dialect research*, ed. Dennis R. Preston, 333–377. Amsterdam: John Benjamins.

———. 1996. Where the worst English is spoken. In *Focus on the USA*, ed. Edgar W. Schneider, 297–360. Amsterdam: Benjamins.

———. 1999a. A language attitude approach to the perception of regional variety. In *Handbook of perceptual dialectology*, ed. Dennis R. Preston, 359–375. Amsterdam: John Benjamins.

———. 1999b. Introduction. In *Handbook of perceptual dialectology*, ed. Dennis R. Preston, xxiii–xxxix. Amsterdam: John Benjamins.

———. 2002. Language with an attitude. In *The handbook of language variation and change*, ed. J.K. Chambers, Peter Trudgill, and Natalie Schilling-Estes, 40–66. Oxford: Blackwell.

———. 2010. Language, people, salience, space: Perceptual dialectology and language regard. *Dialectologia* 5: 87–131.

Ryan, Ellen Bouchard, and Howard Giles. 1982. *Attitudes towards language variation: Social and applied contexts*. London: Hodder Arnold.

Sibata, Takesi. 1959. Hôgen Kyôkai No Ishiki. *Kenkyû* 36: 1–30.

Tobler, Waldo. 1970. A computer movie simulating urban growth in the Detroit region. *Economic Geography* 46(2): 234–240.

Watt, Dominic, and Carmen Llamas. 2014a. Introduction. In *Language, borders and identity*, 1–7. Edinburgh: Edinburgh University Press.

——— (ed). 2014b. *Language, borders and identity*. Edinburgh: Edinburgh University Press.

Weijnen, Antonius A. 1946. De grenzen tussen de Oost-Noordbrabantse dialecten onderling [The borders between the dialects of eastern North Brabant]. In *Oost-Noordbrabantse Dialectproblemen [Eastern North Brabant Dialect Problems]*, vol 8, ed. Antonius A. Weijnen, J.M. Renders, and Jac van Ginneken, 1–15 (Bijdragen En Mededelingen Der Dialectencommissie van de Koninklijke Nederlandse Akademie van Wetenschappen Te Amsterdam 8.) Amsterdam: Noord Hollandsche Uitgevers.

Williams, Angie, Peter Garrett, and Nikolas Coupland. 1996. Perceptual dialectology, folklinguistics, and regional stereotypes: Teachers' perceptions of variation in Welsh English. *Multilingua* 15(2): 171–199.

7

Changing Attitudes Towards the Welsh English Accent: A View from Twitter

Mae'r bennod hon yn cyflwyno dadansoddiad o drydariadau sydd yn cynnwys y termau Welsh *ac* accent. *Dadansoddwyd pob trydariad er mwyn ymchwilio i ymagweddau'r anfonwr tuag at acen Saesneg Cymru. Fe'u rhannwyd yn ôl tri chategori, sef positif, negyddol neu arall. Dangosodd 49% o'r trydariadau ymagweddau positif tuag at yr acen Gymreig o'i gymharu â 15% o drydariadau negyddol. Dywedodd y rhai positif fod yr acen Gymreig (a'i siaradwyr) yn ddeniadol. Dangosodd y canlyniadau fod pobl yn dueddol o feddwl am acen Cymoedd De Cymru wrth ystyried acen Gymreig. Rwyf yn honni bod nifer gynyddol yn gwerthfawrogi'r acen o achos dylanwad cyfresi teledu diweddar.*

Introduction

Our language is irrevocably linked to our sense of identity: whether it is the specific language(s) we speak or the accent(s) we speak them in. Other people's attitudes towards our language also affect how we see ourselves and whether we (try to) change the way we speak according to the situation. As

M. Durham (✉)
Cardiff University, Cardiff, UK

© The Author(s) 2016
M. Durham, J. Morris (eds.), *Sociolinguistics in Wales*,
DOI 10.1057/978-1-137-52897-1_7

has been discussed elsewhere in this volume, the use of the Welsh language is an essential marker of identity for some Welsh people (Welsh Language Board 1995), but it is clear that Welsh English accents and the attitudes towards them also play a part in national identity (Coupland 2009).

The most recent national census (ONS 2011) found that 80% of people in Wales report no ability in Welsh and related research has concluded that, of the people who do speak Welsh, all are fully bilingual (Jones 2012). Consequently, Welsh English is likely to also be an important part of the Welsh (linguistic) identity. What are the attitudes towards Welsh English accents and is the perception of these accents the same as in the past? What implications might a better (or worse) view of Welsh English accents than previously have for speakers of these varieties?

Recent online surveys (e.g. the Yougov one discussed in Wahlgreen 2014) show that the Welsh accent, as a single generic entity, is viewed much more favourably by people in Britain than in the past (compared to, e.g., Bourhis and Giles 1976; Coupland and Bishop 2007; Giles 1990; Williams et al. 1996). This chapter considers this issue by examining posts on *Twitter* containing the terms *Welsh* and *accent* appearing between September 2012 and May 2013 to establish what the main attitudes towards the accent are there. By comparing these findings to previous research on the attitudes towards the English accents of Wales, the chapter attempts to confirm whether a change in attitudes is underway as suggested by the Yougov survey. It also discusses what key elements come out of the tweets to establish what the main associations with the accent(s) are and how representative Twitter might be of British attitudes towards the accent more widely.

This chapter first presents some general facts about Welsh English accents (although see Chap. 1 of this volume for a more in-depth discussion) and findings of earlier studies of attitudes towards Welsh English. It will then discuss how Twitter can be a valuable tool for linguistic analysis, before presenting the data and the analysis.

Welsh English

English is one of the two main languages of Wales and has been spoken in some parts of the country since the thirteenth century (Jones 1993). In most areas, it remained a minority language (albeit a politically important one) for several centuries with Welsh being the language of the majority, but in other areas, such as in Gwent, it superseded Welsh almost completely much earlier. Today, as discussed in other chapters in this volume, English is the majority language in all but a few counties (Welsh Language Board 2004). The long-term contact between Welsh and English has meant that the Welsh dialects of English demonstrate a range of substratum features derived from Welsh (Wells 1982: 377).

The result of this is that the varieties of English spoken in Wales vary considerably from region to region, in part depending on how strong Welsh is (or was) in the areas and the extent to which it contains substratum features but also in terms of the extent of contact with English varieties. Many studies group Welsh English into three main categories: Northern, Southern 'heartland', and Anglicised varieties (such as Cardiff and Newport) (Awbery 1997; Coupland et al. 2005: 18). This reflects the key differences in terms of how long Welsh was maintained in each area as the main language, how much of a substratum effect there is in the varieties and the extent to which English accents and dialects have been in sustained contact with Welsh varieties. Nonetheless, there are a range of linguistic features which are seen to be distinctively or predominantly Welsh (Parry 1999; Paulasto 2006 and this volume, Penhallurick 2004).

What have the attitudes to this wide range of varieties been in the past and how might they be changing today?

Perceptual Dialectology and Attitudes Towards Welsh English

Research on language attitudes and perceptual dialectology, more generally, focusses on establishing laypeople's views of languages, dialects, accents, and linguistic features (Preston 2003). People's attitudes towards their own or other varieties can help us gain insight into which features are stigmatised or salient and which are below the level of consciousness. They can also help us uncover whether incoming forms are likely to gain ground quickly and whether older features (or language) have suffered a loss of prestige and may disappear.

The attitudes that we have towards accents can also influence our attitudes towards people with those accents and may cause us to judge them unfairly (Lippi-Green 1997). They may also demonstrate what associations we have with people who use those varieties more generally and many attitudinal studies orient their questions in order to gain insight into associations. For example, Zahn and Hopper (1985: 118) hypothesised that our attitudes fall into three main categories: attitudes related to superiority (e.g. education, class, and intelligence), those related to attractiveness (e.g. friendliness, kindness, warmth, and honesty), and those related to dynamism (e.g. strength, enthusiasm, and talkativeness). This means that our attitudes towards someone's language may make them seem more or less friendly, educated, confident, and so on.

Attitudes can be studied overtly, by asking people what they think of a specific variety, or, covertly, by asking people what they think of someone but without noting that language is the main focus of attention (see Preston 2003; Buchstaller 2006 for examples of these). These methods can yield different results as people may not always be willing to reveal their linguistic prejudices, or conversely might not be aware of them. By using Twitter, this chapter uses a slightly different method from the two above: unlike many studies, the attitudes here are completely unprompted by the researcher. I discuss the implications of this below.

Attitudes towards the Welsh accent have been studied since the 1970s with Bourhis and Giles (1976) examining how different accents affected people's perceptions of their ability to do a range of jobs. Giles (1970) also used a Welsh accent as one of the stimuli for his research on the persuasiveness of British accents. In these and other earlier studies (e.g. Coupland et al. 1994, 1999, 2005; Garrett et al. 1995; Williams et al. 1996), Welsh accents were rated lower than Standard British ones, mainly with respect to prestige, but in terms of attractiveness too. Some more recent research found that this may be changing, with Watson and Clark (2015) finding that the Cardiff accent is rated similarly to other accents in their study. They deliberately chose regionally marked varieties in their study, so it might not necessarily show an increase in prestige of the accent. Considering a wider range of varieties, Coupland and Bishop 2007 examined attitudes towards British accents in terms of attractiveness and intelligence. The Welsh accent, as well as the Cardiff accent, was included among other British and foreign accents. The responses were collected via a Yougov survey and asked people to give scores on the basis of the accents mentioned (i.e. it was not in response to actual accents, but to their general perception of them). They found that out of 34 options the Welsh accent came in 14th in terms of social attractiveness and 18th in terms of prestige. Cardiff and Swansea, the two Welsh locations sampled, are lower (24/25 for Cardiff and 25/27 for Swansea). In this survey and in others, many specific urban locations score lower than broader regional areas. Welsh and Scottish accents fare better than Cardiff and Glasgow and so on. Overall, however, the results show that Welsh accents score far lower than Standard English and far lower than many other regional accents (Southern Irish and Scottish accents were third and fourth, respectively). Other research on perceptual dialectology in Wales has focussed instead on what varieties people recognise, as well as what they think about them. Montgomery (this volume), for example, considers what linguistic regions schoolchildren in different parts of Wales (and nearby England) recognise. Overall, it seems that there has been a slight shift in perception of the Welsh accent and it is seen more favourably than before.

This increased social prestige of the Welsh accent is also evident in the results of another recent Yougov survey (Wahlgreen 2014). Respondents to this survey were asked which accents out of a set they found the most attractive. Here, the Welsh accent scored extremely highly, coming in third favourite behind Southern Irish and RP, but well ahead of Yorkshire and the West Country who were the next two highest and much higher than Liverpool, Manchester, and Birmingham which scored lowest. Here again, there is clearly a regional- versus city-specific divide, but for our purposes what matters is how well the Welsh accent fared. The current chapter examines whether the Welsh accent is spoken about positively on Twitter, but also looks more specifically what people are saying about it and tries to establish what may have triggered the current shift in attitudes to the dialect and what aspects of (perceived) Welsh accent or Welsh identity people might be responding to.

Twitter

Twitter was launched in 2006 as a social media platform on which people could post short status updates (of no more than 140 characters). The updates, called tweets (example 1), are visible to the poster's followers but crucially also to anyone who either views the poster's timeline or who searches for words that happen to be contained in it. The option to search for shared content is facilitated by the use of hashtags as clicking these allows people to see a list of all the tweets including them.

1. Wish I had a Welsh accent #lush[1]

Twitter has grown exponentially since its start and today more than 500 million tweets are sent daily (Internet Live Stats, n.d.). In practice, tweeters can make their timeline visible only to followers (there is an option to accept followers in this case, as opposed to an open account where they can add themselves automatically), but the majority of people on Twitter leave their tweets unprotected. The main aim of Twitter is to allow people to communicate and share information (and pictures and jokes), so having an account that is not visible makes this less possible.

Roughly speaking, tweets are of three types: standard, replies, and retweets (examples 2–4). A standard tweet is one which stands on its own (although they are often in response to external happenings). A reply is a tweet that answers someone else's tweet using the @username at the start (this category also included tweets which were directed at someone from the start). A retweet is a tweet that is copied from one timeline to another.

2. my welsh accent is terrible
3. @username I'd vote for him because you can't not love a welsh accent. He's lush ;)
4. RT @username: God, that Welsh accent is a bit annoying isn't it?

---

[1] In order to protect the identity of the tweeters, the examples used in this paper were slightly modified so that they cannot be as easily found in a search.

Often, retweets are used to show agreement or approval. Because retweets and replies are used differently than standard tweets, they were excluded from the current analysis. Despite this, it is clear that retweets of comments to do with the Welsh accent are useful as a gauge for how much agreement there is with the attitudes seen in the tweet. Figure 7.1 in the 'Methodology' section provides an idea of what the distribution of tweets to replies to retweets was.

Based on several studies, it appears that the tweeters tend to be slightly younger than the general population (Duggan et al. 2014). Its use with younger people is especially relevant given that, as will be demonstrated, many of the comments are linked to television shows which cater to younger audiences and which feature South East Wales or Valleys accents.

The high volume of messages sent on Twitter makes it a valuable tool for analysing such linguistic attitudes (Campbell-Kibler and Torelli 2012) as it offers opportunities to collect widespread attitudes quickly and across extended periods of time. Additionally, collecting tweets offers a spontaneous way of obtaining linguistic attitudes. In fact, it could be

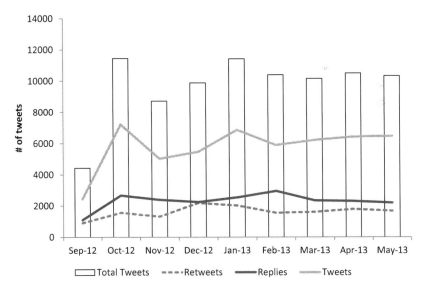

Fig. 7.1 Number of tweets containing the words *Welsh* and *accent* and proportion of different types of tweets (September 2012 to May 2013)

said to be a rather more indirect (and more subconscious) way of tapping into people's attitudes than many other methods used. Although tweeters are overtly discussing language, they have not been prompted to by researchers. This is quite different from studies in which respondents are asked about accents (whether they are told which ones they are listening to or not). This means that there is potential to gain insight into the more covert attitudes more quickly. Even the tweets which are in response to television shows and so not completely spontaneous, are clearly prompted by actual contact with the accent and not a researcher's question. By extracting and then coding tweets talking about a specific accent (or dialect), we can then attempt to gain insight into what the discourses and attitudes surrounding it might be, as well as gaining insight into how frequently it is discussed at all.

Tweets are marked for location in two ways: they can be geotagged and/ or the location of the tweeters can be gleaned from what is included in someone's profile. While geotagging is more accurate, it is problematic to rely solely on this for some kinds of research on Twitter, as most tweets do not have this feature enabled (Eisenstein 2015; Sloan and Morgan 2015). This means that only looking a geotagged tweets drastically reduces the number of tweets available and also is more likely to favour some types of tweeters over others (Sloan and Morgan 2015:12).

The current study does not attempt to pinpoint where the tweeters are from: because it is unlikely that the corpus contains more than a single tweet per person, it is simply not possible to try and recover information about each one. This means that also it does not consider the potential background of the tweeters in any way, beyond those that are clear from the tweets themselves (example 5, where the tweeter is unambiguously Welsh).

5. 'I would love to have a welsh accent' YOU CAN HAVE IT, I DON'T WANT IT!

This is not an issue for this analysis, as the main aim is to get an impression of what kinds of tweets are sent and not specifically to establish what kind of person was sending them. While having a clearer idea of the age, sex, and background of the tweeters would add to the overall picture, it is not strictly necessary in this instance as it is nonetheless possible to obtain an overall impression of the kinds of things that are said on Twitter. Further research might focus on tweet locations, but for the present purposes, all tweets relevant to the analysis were considered equally.

Methodology

This analysis aimed to obtain a snapshot of tweets discussing the Welsh accent sent over a period of nine months[2] (from September 2012 to May 2013). This was to ensure sufficient data and also to avoid the possibility that some events might have triggered attitudes unlike those found usually.

The data collection was accomplished by searching for all the tweets with the terms *Welsh* and *accent* using an online programme.[3] In the preliminary stages, other word combinations were examined (*Welsh + accents, Welsh + dialect* and *Welsh + dialects*), but they were all used substantially less frequently than the main search terms and are not included in this analysis. However, the first combination *Welsh + accents* was partially analysed and did reveal that the tweets were of a similar type (example 6). The two searches with *dialect*, on the other hand, tended not to be tweets about Welsh English, but instead to be about the Welsh language and the dialects found within it (example 7).

6. I love scottish and welsh accents
7. Parts of #Argentina are still Welsh speaking, and have their own dialects #travel

From Fig. 7.1, it is clear that the terms *Welsh* and *accent* appear frequently together. Over the nine months of data collection, 87,165 tweets with this combination were extracted. This underlines that the Welsh accent is often spoken about (on Twitter and elsewhere).

---

[2] The data collection is ongoing, but for the purposes of this analysis only tweet sent in the specific nine-month period will be considered.

[3] The first few months were collected using a now defunct site called http://searchhash.com and then with Martin Hawksey's google spreadsheet template (https://tags.hawksey.info/get-tags/).

Such a high volume of daily tweets meant that it was not possible to code all of them, even having excluded the retweets and replies. Instead, all the tweets sent on the same four days each month were coded. This allowed the analysis to remain unbiased (e.g. unlike selecting the most interesting tweets randomly) and yet manageable. Because data collection only began midway through September, only two days were coded for that month.

There was some variation in the number of tweets sent each month: for the eight months for which there is a full run, the number of tweets varies between 9000 to just under 12,000. This averages over 350 a day. The peaks are usually in response to television events: serendipitously for the data collection, the reality TV show *The Valleys* premiered in October 2012. This show presents a group of young people from the South Wales Valleys who move to Cardiff and live in a house together.

Having selected the days to be examined and excluded the retweets and replies as discussed above, each tweet was coded first of all for whether the attitudes in it were predominantly positive towards the Welsh accent, negative or if it showed other attitudes not clearly positive or negative (many demonstrated some kind of performance of the Welsh accent). Five separate categories were chosen:

- tweets where the main thrust of the content was to show love or appreciation for the Welsh accent;
- tweets where the main thrust was negative towards the Welsh accent;
- tweets which commented on the Welsh accent in some way, but were neither clearly positive or negative[4];
- tweets which contained a performance element to them (or a desired ability to be able to perform the accent);
- tweets which were about British dialects more generally.

Examples of each category are provided in Table 7.1 below.

As well as this general coding, a second run-through of the data was conducted. This was to code the tweets for more specific categories based on the perceived frequency of certain themes and key words in the first analysis of the data: these will be discussed following the presentation of the overall results. This secondary coding will make it possible to discuss

---

[4] These are categorised as metalinguistic, although all the tweets collected are metalinguistic in some way.

Table 7.1 Examples of the five main tweet categories

Love	If the Welsh accent was a person we'd be dating
	If you have a Welsh accent could you call and tell me a story?
	Welsh accents are the accent version of Jesus
Hate	It has come to my attention that this is not an impediment, merely a Welsh accent
	Dad said that if I ever pick up a Welsh accent I will be banished from the family
	Anyone with a Welsh accent I want to punch in the face
'Metalinguistic'	Mum's on the phone to her friend and all I can hear is her Welsh accent
	How does Siri manage to understand the Welsh accent
	Watching a show and I cringe at the way some girl is talking. Not the Welsh accent, just the way she talks... 'BEOWtifel'
Performance	Still can't do a Welsh accent to save my life
	Just found myself searching and following all the girls from #thevalleys and speaking in a Welsh accent in my head while writing this #ohgod
	Welsh accent 'you're well lush' ‚ô•___‚ô•
UK accents	What is a British accent? Is it Welsh, Scottish, and English mixed into one, because I have to say, I haven't heard an accent like that haha
	There is no such as a 'British accent' There is Scottish, Irish, Welsh, and English. Not British

the results more precisely in terms of how much the attitudes found in this study can be matched onto the categories suggested by Zahn and Hopper (1985).

Results

Nine months of tweets taken from the four selected days yielded 6232 instances to examine. While this represents a fraction of the tweets containing the words *Welsh* and *accent* sent over the period studied, it is nonetheless sufficient to gain an accurate overview of the attitudes of people towards the Welsh English accent and to be able to establish the main associations of the accent. Given that, except in a few cases, each tweeter is only represented in the dataset once, the large sample size makes the analysis likely to be fairly accurate in terms of what attitudes are found on Twitter.

Figure 7.2 provides the breakdown of tweets across the five categories.

The overall results make it clear that the majority of tweets are positive towards the Welsh accent (49%) and that the negative ones are more restricted (15%). This is in line with the Yougov survey which appeared shortly after these data were collected and together they support the sense that the Welsh English accent is viewed more positively in the UK now than in the past. The performance tweets (20%) have to do with people trying to put on a Welsh accent, so they also can be said to fall on the more positive side of the spectrum. They are seen as broadly positive, because, as will be discussed below, alongside the purely performance tweets, there is a subsection of the love tweets which are primarily about a desire for the accent (even if it is not being attempted), which also underlines the fact that some kind of prestige might be gained by having or performing a Welsh accent. The metalinguistic tweets (15%), as noted, are more difficult to classify in terms of positive or negative views and serve more to give a sense of the frequency with which the Welsh accent is mentioned.

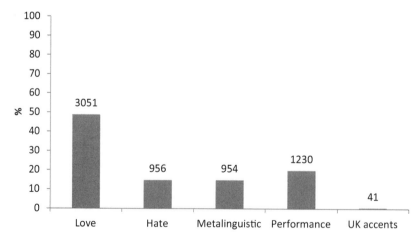

Fig. 7.2 Overall distribution of tweets by category (inc. totals of each category)

Because the tweets coded as 'UK accents' represent such a small fraction of the overall data (0.7%) and because they nearly all had to do with tweeters' annoyance at people talking about the British accents as if they were a monolithic entity, these will not be examined further, although it may be a venue of future research to confirm where the notion of a British accent comes from as the tweets imply it is mainly from the USA.

The overwhelming positivity of attitudes is particularly important in light of the fact that many researchers have found that the Internet in general and Twitter more specifically often demonstrate far more virulent critique than face-to-face interaction (Hardaker 2010, 2013). This is generally said to be due to the fact that anonymity gives people the ability to troll and to speak without thought of consequences. The fact that only a small portion of the tweets are negative about the Welsh accent underlines the extent to which it is viewed positively.

While useful in confirming that attitudes towards the Welsh accent are predominantly positive nowadays, this overall view can only provide limited insight into specifically what the attitudes are and a further breakdown of the results is necessary, which is why the second run-through of the data was conducted. The rest of this chapter focusses primarily on the content of the love and the hate tweets, but also aspects that come up throughout the tweets, such as aspects to do with television and *The Valleys* (the actual place and the television series). The metalinguistic tweets, as could be expected from a more general, hold-all category, were more difficult to group broadly.

The secondary coding was done in two ways. First of all, the word frequencies of each subset of tweets were examined and the most frequent content words were noted. Adjectives were focussed on particularly at this stage as they are the most easily comparable with Zahn and Hopper's categories. Secondly, categories that were noted as being potentially frequent and relevant when doing the first run-through the data were given an additional code.

It is worth noting that not all tweets could easily be grouped into one of these additional categories, in some cases because the subgrouping they would have fallen into was not frequent enough to warrant choosing it as a main subcategory. For example, 65% of the love tweets were not given an additional code.

The section below examines more precisely what was included in the tweets for the subsections of love and hate.

Love Tweets

Turning first to word frequencies to get an idea of what was discussed most often, Table 7.2 presents the content words that could be related to attitudes occurring more than 40 times across the love tweets. The table also includes two non-words that occurred frequently enough to warrant inclusion: the heart eyes emoji and the character combination that is

Table 7.2 Keywords (or symbols) in the love subset (3051 tweets in total)

	Number of occurrences	Percentage of total subset
love	1016	33.3
want	300	9.8
Irish	222	7.2
wish	199	6.5
like	167	5.4
<3	163	5.3
😍	137	4.4
Scottish	113	3.7
valleys (or thevalleys)	77	2.5
hot	76	2.5
omg	76	2.5
sexy	74	2.4
Geordie	66	2.2
please	66	2.2
best	65	2.1
amazing	63	2.1
nice	56	1.8
cute	50	1.6
attractive	49	1.6
favourite	45	1.5
marry	45	1.5
strong	44	1.5
Australian	43	1.4
good	42	1.4

commonly used to represent a heart online <3. The percentage of tweets within the total subset each keyword appeared in is given, although it is important to note that some tweets had several keywords.

Figure 7.3 provides a word cloud of the love subset of tweets to give a broader picture of the frequent (function and content) words. The programme removes common words by default (e.g. *a, the, I, is*) and the words *Welsh, accent,* and *love* were also removed from the figure as they were so frequent it would have been impossible to see the other frequent words otherwise. This closely matches what is shown in Table 7.2, although it is worth noting that the emoji and <3 are lost in the transfer to a word cloud.

Table 7.2 and Fig. 7.3 provide substantial insight into frequent associations with a positive view of the Welsh accent. The word *love* appears in a third of the tweets in this subcategory. Among other points, this subset underlines the frequency of tweets wanting or wishing for a Welsh accent, the numerous words used to underline the accent's attractiveness (*sexy, cute, nice, favourite, hot*), and the frequency to which the Welsh accent is mentioned along with other accents (*Irish, Scottish, Geordie*). I discuss the implications of each of these in turn below.

The desire tweets (i.e. those showing a desire for the accent) were given a separate code in the second run-through to make it possible to establish how many of the love tweets fell into this subcategory (examples 8–10).

Fig. 7.3 Word cloud of frequent items in the love subset

8. I want to be Welsh, can I have an accent transplant please?
9. I wish I had a welsh accent
10. Why can't I just have a Welsh accent :(

They were found to represent 24% ($N = 745$) of the love tweets and 12% of tweets overall. While it is unlikely that this is a genuine desire to have a Welsh accent permanently (although the tweeter asking for an accent transplant may well disagree), it is clear that something must be underlying these tweets. Having a Welsh accent would seem to provide a certain cachet to the speaker according to these tweeters. The desire for a Welsh accent in some cases is overtly explained; tweeters have a 'boring' accent and would like a more interesting one (example 11). The category of performance tweets is clearly related to these desire ones in terms of understanding what they show about attitudes towards the Welsh accent.

In the performance tweets, a high proportion (around 70%) is in fact people talking about their attempts to produce a Welsh accent (example 12) which further underlines the sense that a Welsh accent is desirable in some way. The smaller portion of performance tweets which are not related to desire consists of attempts to reproduce the Welsh accent in writing or noting which words and expressions are particularly pleasing (or entertaining) in a Welsh accent (example 13) (see Durham 2016 for a fuller discussion of the representation of the Welsh accent/dialect in the performance tweets).

11. I wish I had a good accent. A London one isn't that fun! I want a Welsh or Irish one!
12. Welsh is the one accent I can't do. I always end up sounding Indian.
13. 'Moussaka', as a word, sounds best in a welsh accent.

Taken together, this subsection of the love tweets and the performance tweets demonstrate that having a Welsh accent is seen to be something desirable. This sense is underlined when considering the adjectives frequently used in the love tweets.

The main adjectives used in the love tweets are, unsurprisingly, positive, and when considering what attributes they describe it is clear that it mainly has to do with the attractiveness dimension discussed by Zahn and Hopper (1985) and not the superiority and dynamism ones. Although many of tweets focus on a general kind of attractiveness, a large portion refer to how *sexy* or *hot* the accent is (examples 14–16), underlining that the elements mentioned on the social attractiveness dimension go beyond simply friendly aspects. This also helps to explain the high rate of the word *marry* found in the love tweets: they too represent an extreme version of the perceived attractiveness of the Welsh accent (example 17).

14. Anyone with a Welsh accent is automatically sexy.
15. If the Welsh accent were a person we'd be dating.
16. The Welsh accent makes me horny, Gavin and Stacey is like porn.
17. If you have a Welsh accent, I want to marry you.

Considering this, it bears thinking about what form the appreciation for the Welsh accent appears to have taken and what implications this may have. While the fact that the majority of the tweets refer to the attractiveness of the Welsh accent is undoubtedly an improvement on an accent being viewed negatively, there are numerous issues with this. If an accent is viewed solely in terms of its attractiveness, then it is not necessarily taken seriously.

This is further confirmed when examining the number of tweets which were coded as funny (meaning the accent was seen as funny) within the overall set. Most of these were in the metalinguistic category, but they were found in the other four main categories as well. There are 238 tweets coded this way, which represents 4% of the overall tweets. This is further evidence that the favour found in the tweets is primarily restricted to social category and may show that opinions about the intelligence, education, and so on of people with Welsh accents have not changed, although of course this must be assumed on the basis of absence of tweets related to these characteristics rather than clear evidence of attitudes about them. In fact, in some of the tweets there is almost what could be called an accent fetish (along the lines of language fetish discussed by Kelly-Holmes 2000) and tweets of that subtype bear further examination in future research as there is no space to fully discuss the potential issues and implications of this here.

Finally, there is the fact that in the love tweets the Welsh accent is frequently linked with other accents, primarily Irish and Scottish, but with Geordie and Australian as well (example 18). The co-occurrence of the Welsh accent with the Irish and the Scottish accents adds to the impression of a shift in people's perceptions of it since Coupland and Bishop's (2007) data collection. There, the Irish and Scottish accents were rated substantially higher than the Welsh one, whereas the results here imply that there may be a degree of cachet associated with all three Celtic Englishes now and not just with Irish and Scottish ones. It is difficult to establish at this stage whether the seeming inclusion of Welsh English in this group recently is due solely to a shift in perceptions of Welsh English or due to its being linked more in people's minds with Scottish and Irish varieties (rightly or wrongly) and there being a general trend that non-Southern British English varieties are seen as more different and therefore more attractive.

18. if you have a Canadian, American, Australian, Scottish, Irish or Welsh accent, marry me.

Hate Tweets

There are fewer hate tweets than love tweets, so there are also fewer words that occur more than 40 times in the subset. Those that do are presented in Table 7.3. Figure 7.4 gives the frequent words (again with the words *Welsh, accent* and very common words removed).

The word *hate* occurred 179 times in the subset, representing 19% overall. The second-most frequent word is *like,* which at a first glance is somewhat surprising. However, when examining the tweets, it is clear that they either occur with *don't* or are used as prepositions, conjunctions, or discourse markers (examples 19–20).

19. I really don't like the Welsh accent
20. Proper hate the Welsh accent, and Scottish actually! Like nails on a chalkboard.

The frequency of *like* in the hate subset underlines the importance of manually coding the tweets in a first instance. A sentiment analysis,

Table 7.3 Keywords in hate tweets (956 tweets in total)

	Number of occurrences	Percentage of total subset
hate	179	18.7
like	100	10.5
Valleys (or thevalleys)	93	9.7
annoying	86	9.0
fucking	56	5.9
worst	43	4.5

Fig. 7.4 Word cloud of most frequent items in the hate subset

which could have coded tweets automatically, would have been more likely to yield false positives in similar cases and rendered the analysis less accurate.

The remaining words are uniformly negative and focus primarily on the attractiveness dimension of attitudes, although it could be said that there are also a few examples of adjectives that are negative in terms of the superiority category (*stupid, difficult*). Here, it is important to look in more detail at the secondary coding as the broader groupings will provide insight into the attitudes even if the words used are not uniform. It was possible to further group around half of the tweets in this subset as shown in Table 7.4.

Table 7.4 Main groupings in hate subset (956 tweets in total)

	Number of occurrences	Percentage of total subset
annoying	140	14.6
extreme/worst	133	13.9
difficult	10	1.0
unattractive	38	4.0
Welsh	92	9.6

For the hate subset, the attitudes to do with the attractiveness dimension primarily focus on annoyingness and very extreme judgements (i.e. demonstrating very strong dislike of the accent) and only a portion on the supposed unattractiveness of the accent. The groupings also show that there is a relatively high portion of the hate tweets that seemingly were written by Welsh people themselves (example 21). It may be that earlier attitudes against the Welsh accent have made them linguistically insecure and they are uncomfortable with that perception of it.

21. I hate having a Welsh accent, when I speak English people don't understand me.

Discussion

To fully understand the tweets and what they show about attitudes towards the Welsh accent, two further, partly related, aspects need to be discussed. These are the apparent convergence of South East Wales (more specifically the South Wales Valleys) and the Welsh accent in the imagination of many and the degree to which television series appear to be a trigger for accent attitudes.

While previous research has noted that many British people consider Welsh English as if it were a single variety in their attitudes, the analysis of the tweets suggests that one accent in particular is most strongly associated with the Welsh accent. While many of the tweets analysed were indeed broad in their discussion of the Welsh accent, when a specific Welsh accent was mentioned it nearly always was the Valleys accent. A few tweets mentioned the Cardiff or the Swansea accent, but the Welsh accents of the North do not appear to exist in tweeters' minds beyond being part of a broad notion of a Welsh accent.

As can be seen in Tables 7.2 and 7.3, the Valleys are frequently mentioned both in the love and in the hate subsets and, across the whole dataset, they are mentioned in 349 tweets (11% of the total). These tweets discuss the geographical location and its accent, but also the reality TV show (whose speakers are from the South Wales Valleys themselves).

The accents found in the South Wales Valleys (i.e. some of the Southern 'heartland') are among the most distinct of the Welsh accents, partly due to the noticeable Welsh substratum in these varieties (Connolly 1981; Parry 1977; Walters 2003). Although the analysis here intended to focus on the Welsh accent generically, the frequent mention of the Valleys and of accent features associated with it is not anodyne. It demonstrates that while many people seemingly do not distinguish Welsh accents from each other, they nonetheless concentrate their attention on one particular one, that is, the Valleys accent. A tweet from a popular account about Welsh problems corroborates this impression (example 22), as one version of this tweet (the account often recycles popular tweets) was retweeted over a 100 times and favourited more than 200 times.

22. When someone says 'you don't sound Welsh' because you're not from the Valleys…

Beyond the substratum effects that make the Valleys accents distinctive in linguists' minds, it is worthwhile to consider non-linguistic factors that might explain the association of the Welsh accent with the Valleys (or the South East more generally), although an analysis of the performance tweets showed laypeople's abilities to recognise many subtle features of the accent (Durham 2016).

Nearly all the television shows mentioned in the tweets are focussed on the South East Wales and featured characters with Welsh Valleys or related accents: not only MTV's *The Valleys,* but also *Gavin and Stacey* and *Torchwood.* Other actors and television presenters who were mentioned also often had South East Wales accents.

As well as contributing to the association of the Welsh accent with a specific part of Wales, the television shows could be said to have more broadly influenced people's perceptions of the accent. The premiere of MTV's *The Valleys* show triggered an increase of tweets and a number of tweeters mentioned that they were rewatching *Gavin and Stacey* or *Torchwood*. Films with actors using Welsh accents (either natively or put on) also triggered tweets. *Gavin and Stacey*, even when not explicitly mentioned, appear to have provided many people with a set of purportedly Welsh expressions and words (or strengthened existing stereotypes they had) (examples 23–24).

23. I've perfected my 'alright Gav what's occurring' in a welsh accent
24. *Welsh accent* that's lush

Seemingly, the television shows provided examples of the Welsh accent to people who had not encountered them before. The consequence of television being the main source of 'models' might have for attitudes towards actual speakers will require closer examination. An example can be gleaned from the reaction to *The Valleys*. There are a number of tweets in which speakers comment that they had liked the accent until they watched the show (example 25).

25. Used to like the welsh accent till I heard it on the valleys

It seems likely then that at least some of the favour (and disfavour) for the Welsh accent today is directly related to its increased frequency in media. The wider attitudes towards the accent potentially come from a link between actors and their own language use and these attitudes are then transferred onto others with the same accent. This underlines that people may form their opinions about accents on just a few stereotypical models and it is likely to be these preconceived, and not necessarily accurate, models then provide us with our attitudinal reference point. This means that while the attitudes examined here are restricted to Twitter, they are likely to be indicative of the British population more broadly, or, more accurately, the section of the British population that watches the same shows.

Acknowledgements I would like to thank the Centre for Language and Communication Research at Cardiff University for a small research grant at the start of the project, as well as Dorottya Csenge Cserző for help with the initial analysis.

References

Awbery, Gwen. 1997. The English language in Wales. In *The Celtic Englishes*, ed. Hildegard L.C. Tristram, 86–99. Heidelberg: Winter.

Bourhis, Richard, and Howard Giles. 1976. The language of cooperation in Wales. A field study. *Language Sciences* 42: 13–16.

Buchstaller, Isabelle. 2006. Social stereotypes, personality traits and regional perceptions displaced: Attitudes towards the 'new' quotatives in the UK. *Journal of Sociolinguistics* 10(3): 362–381.

Campbell-Kibler, Kathryn and Amber Torelli. 2012. Tracking enregisterment through online social media. Paper presented at regional varieties, language shift and linguistic identities conference, Aston, Birmingham.

Connolly, John H. 1981. On the segmental phonology of a South Wales accent of English. *Journal of the International Phonetic Association* 11: 51–62.

Coupland, Nikolas. 2009. Dialect style, social class and metacultural performance: The pantomime dame. In *The new sociolinguistics reader*, ed. Nikolas Coupland, and Adam Jaworski, 311–325. Basingstoke/New York: Palgrave Macmillan.

Coupland, Nikolas, and Hywel Bishop. 2007. Ideologised values for British accents. *Journal of Sociolinguistics* 11(1): 74–103.

Coupland, Nikolas, Angie Williams, and Peter Garrett. 1994. The social meanings of Welsh English: Teachers' stereotyped judgements. *Journal of Multilingual and Multicultural Development* 15(6): 471–489. doi:10.1080/0 1434632.1994.9994585.

———. 1999. 'Welshness' and 'Englishness' as attitudinal dimensions of English language varieties in Wales. In *Handbook of perceptual dialectology*, vol 1, ed. Dennis R. Preston, 333–343. Amsterdam: John Benjamins.

Coupland, Nikolas, Hywel Bishop, Angie Williams, Betsy Evans, and Peter Garrett. 2005. Affiliation, engagement, language use and vitality: Secondary school students' subjective orientations to Welsh and Welshness. *International Journal of Bilingual Education and Bilingualism* 8(1): 1–24.

Duggan, Maeve, Nicole Ellison, Cliff Lampe, Amanda Lenhart and Mary Madden. 2014. Demographics of key social networking platforms. http://www.pewinternet.org/2015/01/09/social-media-update-2014/. Accessed 24 May 2016.

Durham, Mercedes. 2016. Representations of Welsh English online. What can tweets tell us about salience and enregisterment? Paper presented at New Ways of Analyzing Variation 44, Toronto.

Eisenstein, Jacob. 2015. Systematic patterning in phonologically- motivated orthographic variation. *Journal of Sociolinguistics* 19(2): 161–188.

Garrett, Peter, Nikolas Coupland, and Angie Williams. 1995. 'City Harsh' and 'the Welsh Version of RP': Some ways in which teachers view dialects of Welsh English. *Language Awareness* 4(2): 99–107.

Giles, Howard. 1970. Evaluative reactions to accents. *Educational Review* 22: 211–227.

———. 1990. Social meanings of Welsh English. In *English in Wales: Diversity, conflict, and change*, ed. Nikolas Coupland, 258–282. Clevedon: Multilingual Matters.

Hardaker, Claire. 2010. Trolling in asynchronous computer-mediated communication: From user discussions to theoretical concepts. *Journal of Politeness Research* 6(2): 215–242.

———. 2013. Uh.....not to be nitpicky,,,,,but...The past tense of drag is dragged, not drug.: An overview of trolling strategies. *Journal of Language Aggression and Conflict* 1(1): 57–86.

Internet Live Stats. (n.d.) Twitter Statistics. http://www.internetlivestats.com/twitter-statistics. Accessed 21 May 2016.

Jones, Robert Owen. 1993. The sociolinguistics of Welsh. In *The Celtic languages*, ed. Martin J. Ball, 536–605. London/New York: Routledge.

Jones, Hywel M. 2012. *A statistical overview of the Welsh language*. Cardiff: Welsh Language Board. http://www.comisiynyddygymraeg.cymru/Cymraeg/Rhestr%20Cyhoeddiadau/Darlun%20ystadegol%20Cymraeg.pdf. Accessed 23 May 2016.

Kelly-Holmes, Helen. 2000. Bier, parfum, kaas: Language fetish in European advertising. *European Journal of Cultural Studies* 3(1): 67–82.

Lippi-Green, Rosina. 1997. *English with an accent: Language, ideology and discrimination in the United States*. London: Routledge.

Office for National Statistics. (2011). Census: Aggregate data (England and Wales) UK data service census support. Available at: http://infuse.ukdataservice.ac.uk

Parry, David. 1977. *The survey of Anglo-Welsh dialects. Volume 1: The South-East*. Swansea: University College Swansea.

———. 1999. *A grammar and glossary of conservative Anglo-Welsh dialects of rural Wales.* NATCECT. Occasional Publications, No. 8. Sheffield: University of Sheffield.

Paulasto, Heli. 2006. *Welsh English syntax: Contact and variation.* Joensuu: Joensuu University Press http://epublications.uef.fi/pub/urn_isbn_952-458-804-8/index_en.html.

Penhallurick, Rob. 2004. Welsh English: Morphology and syntax. In *A handbook of varieties of english, Vol. 2: Morphology and syntax,* ed. Bernd Kortmann, Kate Burridge, Rajend Mesthrie, Edgar Schneider, and Clive Upton, 102–113. Berlin/New York: Mouton de Gruyter.

Preston, Dennis R. 2003. Language with an Attitude. In *The handbook of language variation and change,* ed. J.K. Chambers, Peter Trudgill, and Natalie Schilling-Estes, 40–66. Oxford: Blackwell.

Sloan, Luke and Jeffrey Morgan. 2015. Who tweets with their location? Understanding the relationship between demographic characteristics and the use of geoservices and geotagging on Twitter. *PLoS ONE* 10(11), e0142209.

Wahlgreen, Will. 2014. Brummie is the least attractive reference. (YouGov survey). https://yougov.co.uk/news/2014/12/09/accent-map2/. Accessed 21 May 2016.

Walters, J. Roderick. 2003. On the intonation of a South Wales 'Valleys accent' of English. *Journal of the International Phonetic Association* 33(2): 211–238.

Watson, Kevin, and Lynn Clark. 2015. Exploring listeners' real-time reactions to regional accents. *Language Awareness* 24(1): 38–59.

Wells, John. 1982. *Accents of English 2: The British Isles.* Cambridge: Cambridge University Press.

Welsh Language Board. 1995. Public attitudes to the Welsh language. Research report prepared by NOP Social and Political for the Central Office of Information and the Welsh Language Board. London: NOP Social and Political.

———. 2004. *2001 Census: Linguistic composition of Wales's households.* Cardiff: Welsh Language Board.

Williams, Angie, Peter Garrett, and Nikolas Coupland. 1996. Perceptual dialectology, Folklinguistics, and regional stereotypes: Teachers' perceptions of variation in Welsh English. *Multilingua* 15(2): 171–199.

Zahn, Christopher, and Robert Hopper. 1985. Measuring language attitudes: The speech evaluation instrument. *Journal of Language and Social Psychology* 4(2): 113–123.

Part 4

Bilingual and Multilingual Contact in Wales

8

'Mae pobl monolingual yn minority': Factors Favouring the Production of Code Switching by Welsh–English Bilingual Speakers

Margaret Deuchar, Kevin Donnelly, and Caroline Piercy

Mae'r bennod hon yn adrodd ar ganlyniadau dadansoddiad awtomatig o 67,515 o gymalau mewn corpws Cymraeg-Saesneg sy'n cynnwys 151 o siaradwyr. Nod yr ymchwil oedd canfod i ba raddau mae oedran, rhywedd, iaith gyntaf, iaith addysg a rhwydwaith gymdeithasol yn dylanwadu ar gyfnewid cod ac archwilio a oedd gwerthusiadau'r siaradwyr o'u hymddygiad ynglŷn â chyfnewid cod yn gywir. Astudiwyd cyfnewid cod o fewn cymalau a rhwng cymalau drwy ddefnyddio awtoglosydd ac fe ddadansoddwyd dylanwad ffactorau all-ieithyddol ar gynhyrchu cymalau dwyieithog neu uniaith drwy ddefnyddio modelau effeithiau cymysg. Dengys ein canlyniadau fod cyfnewid cod yn fwy

M. Deuchar (✉)
University of Cambridge, Cambridge, UK

K. Donnelly
Bangor, UK

C. Piercy
Google, London, UK

© The Author(s) 2016
M. Durham, J. Morris (eds.), *Sociolinguistics in Wales*,
DOI 10.1057/978-1-137-52897-1_8

209

cyffredin yn lleferydd siaradwyr ifainc ac ymhlith siaradwyr sydd wedi caffael y Gymraeg a'r Saesneg ar yr un pryd. Roedd y siaradwyr yn rhyfeddol o gywir ynghylch eu canfyddiadau o'u defnydd o gyfnewid cod.

Introduction

Although monolinguals constitute a minority in the world, English monolinguals make up the majority of speakers in the UK, and this has been the case in Wales too since early in the twentieth century. Welsh speakers in Wales appear to have been in the majority throughout the nineteenth century (see Jones 1993: 549), but the results of the 1901 census showed them to make up only half of the population of Wales, and their proportion dropped throughout the twentieth century. As Penhallurick (2007: 152) points out, by the 1960s not only had monolingualism in Welsh disappeared, but monolingualism in English had become characteristic of three quarters of the population (Penhallurick 2007: 152). According to the census in 2011, 19% of the population of Wales reported speaking Welsh, which means (given Penhallurick's observation and exposure to English in compulsory education) that 19% are bilingual in Welsh and English. There is considerable regional variation in this percentage, however, and Welsh speakers make up a higher proportion of the population in the north and west than in the south and east. Where the proportion of Welsh speakers is relatively high, Welsh is the primary language of communication for bilinguals. However, their competence in English means that code switching to English (as in the switches to 'monolingual' and 'minority' in the title of this chapter) is an option in informal communication, and varies from speaker to speaker. The study to be reported here investigates how patterns of bilingual acquisition affect the quantity of Welsh–English code switching by speakers, and how this may be changing over time. Our study relies on a naturalistic bilingual corpus collected from 151 speakers, most but not all residing in northwest Wales where the proportion of bilingual speakers in the population is over 40% in most places.

Mention of code switching in Wales can be found in publications from the 1980s onwards (see, for example, Thomas 1982a, b) but no systematic study on a reasonably large scale seems to have been conducted until the collection of the *Siarad* corpus (see Deuchar et al. 2014). However, our work builds on a well-established body of systematic research on other language pairs, especially Spanish and English. Poplack's (1980) landmark study of code switching among Puerto Rican Spanish-English speakers in New York City provided evidence that 'code-switching, rather than representing debasement of linguistic skill, is actually a sensitive indicator of bilingual ability' (Poplack 1980: 581). She found that those speakers who did the most intrasentential code switching (i.e. switching inside a sentence) had acquired both English and Spanish in early childhood and also rated themselves as 'bilingual' as opposed to dominant in Spanish or English.

Given the evidence that code switching appears to be facilitated by proficiency in the two languages, a question which has not yet been fully answered is how varying patterns of bilingual acquisition lead to a greater or lesser propensity to code switch. Meisel (2004), for example, distinguishes between simultaneous acquisition of two languages, child second-language acquisition, and adult second-language acquisition. He argues that the differing effects of these patterns of bilingual acquisition need to be determined 'in the light of empirical research investigating linguistic and neuropsychological aspects of bilingualism acquired during different age ranges' (Meisel 2004: 105). Indeed, in a study of structural plasticity in the bilingual brain, Mechelli et al. (2004) report on how the timing of bilingual acquisition and proficiency attained affect the density of grey matter and structural reorganisation in the brain. It seems likely, then, that similar factors may affect code-switching behaviour.

Poplack's (1980) study was not able to deal directly with the relation between patterns of acquisition and code switching, since only two of her 20 speakers were simultaneous bilinguals. However, since the time of her study, developments in corpus linguistics mean that we can now analyse much larger sets of data in a relatively short amount of time. These developments allow, among other things, the automatic extraction of data for analysis, as we shall demonstrate in our study of 148 Welsh–English bilinguals with varying patterns of bilingual acquisition.

Review of the Literature

In this section, we review some of the previous work which has investigated the relation between social and linguistic factors in the study of code switching, with special emphasis on the role of early bilingual acquisition. We also review relevant work on corpus linguistics and previous work specifically on Welsh–English data.

Relevant Studies on Code Switching

Poplack (1980) is one of the best known early studies on the multivariate analysis of code switching. Her data were collected in 'El Barrio', an area of New York City inhabited by a Puerto Rican community since the 1930s. Data were analysed from 20 speakers who differed from one another regarding their age of arrival in the USA. Eleven were male and nine female. Data were collected through interviews and 'natural' recordings by a member of the community, and speakers also completed a language attitude questionnaire. Sixty-six hours of recordings yielded 1835 instances of code switching, all of which were coded in terms of syntactic function. A broad distinction was drawn between intrasentential[1] and extrasentential switches,[2] and the relation between these categories and extralinguistic characteristics of the speakers was studied using VARBRUL 2 (Sankoff 1975), a tool for multivariate analysis. The results showed that the factors which were related to the production of intrasentential code switching were gender, age of arrival/L2 acquisition, language dominance, and work place. More intrasentential code switching was produced by women than men, by those who had been born in the USA or arrived in early childhood, by those who were balanced bilinguals rather than Spanish dominant, and by those who worked inside the community.

Almost all of Poplack's speakers had acquired English later than Spanish, albeit at different ages, and since the age of acquisition of English corresponded perfectly with the age of speakers' arrival in the USA, age of acquisition was not considered separately. Furthermore, since only two speakers had acquired English in early childhood, the effect of simultaneous versus successive acquisition could not be compared. Our study differs from Poplack's in that we are able to compare the effect of simul-

---

[1] An example from her data is *Why make Carol* **sentarse atrás pa' que** ('sit in the back so') *everybody has to move* **pa' que se salga** ('for her to get out').

[2] This included both 'sentential' (switches between sentences, also called 'intersentential') and 'tag' switches.

taneous and successive acquisition at different ages, and in that we are dealing with a fairly stable bilingual community which is not the result of the immigration of minority language speakers.

The study by Backus (1996) of Turkish-Dutch code switching provides some information about the effect of age of acquisition of the two languages in an immigrant context in the Netherlands. He classifies his speakers into three groups based on their age of arrival in the Netherlands. Those belonging to the 'first generation' arrived in the Netherlands and so were first exposed to Dutch when they were older than 12; the 'intermediate generation' arrived at between 5 and 12 years old, and the 'second generation' were either born in the Netherlands or were under 5 at the age of arrival. He found different patterns of code switching in the three groups. The first generation generally produced Dutch insertions within a Turkish morphosyntactic framework, while the intermediate generation produced frequent intersentential code switching as well as the same type of intrasentential code switching as the first generation. The second generation produced mostly intersentential code switching with infrequent intrasentential switching in which either language could provide the morphosyntactic frame. While the three groups doubtless differed from one another in their patterns of acquisition, we do not have sufficient detail about the bilingual acquisition of the second generation to determine whether they acquired Turkish in the home first and Dutch later, or whether they acquired both Turkish and Dutch simultaneously from birth.

Treffers-Daller (1992) reports on a study of Dutch-French code switching in Brussels which might be considered more similar to the community in our own study in that the community is not the result of recent migration. Of the factors that Treffers-Daller expected to contribute to intrasentential code switching, she found that local background, language of education, self-rated proficiency in each language, and degree of puristic attitudes were all significant predictors, although there was some interaction between local background and language of education. Treffers-Daller (1994) includes details of the background questionnaire administered to participants, but information about their patterns of language acquisition in childhood is not elicited, and so we cannot determine how this might be linked to their code-switching patterns. However, she did investigate the effect of age on the production of code switching. The code switching of speakers over the age of 60 was compared with those under 60, and though no significant difference was found, Treffers-Daller reports a 'trend that older informants switch more within sentences than younger informants' (Treffers-Daller 1992: 148) She suggests that intra-sentential code switching is actually disappearing in Brussels owing to the influence of purism in Dutch.

In studies of language variation, the age of the speaker is of course an important independent variable because of the possibilities of the 'apparent time paradigm' (cf. Bailey 2002), according to which the speech of younger speakers may be indicative of language change. Thus, the extent of code switching by younger speakers compared with older speakers may provide an indication of whether code switching is decreasing or increasing. Poplack (1980) found that the age of the speaker was not a significant variable in predicting the type of code switching. However, this may be because of the relatively small number (20) of her speakers and the fact that 75% of them were between the ages of 20 and 40. The age of our 148 speakers ranged from 10 to 89 and we shall show how age is a key variable in our study.

As mentioned above, Poplack (1980) found that gender was a sig-nificant variable and that women produced more intrasentential switch-ing than men. In fact, over half of their switches were intrasentential compared with only one-third of men's switches. Given what are often considered robust findings regarding the differences between male and female monolingual speech in English, termed 'the sociolinguistic gen-der pattern' by Cheshire and Gardner-Chloros (1998), these authors set out to investigate whether 'other factors being equal, the general pattern appeared to hold, with women code-switching less than men in order to conform with a more purist or socially acceptable speech style' (Cheshire and Gardner-Chloros 1998: 14). They were able to find little evidence for this 'general pattern', reporting, for example, that Treffers-Daller (1992) had found no significant difference between men's and women's use of intrasentential switching and that Gardner-Chloros (1992) had found no significant difference in the switching rates of male and female Greek Cypriot-English bilingual speakers. Overall, they conclude that 'although a consistent pattern of sex differentiation is assumed to exist in [language use in] monolingual communities, there is no evidence of any consistent patterning of this kind in bilingual communities' (Cheshire and Gardner-Chloros 1998: 28).

Previous Studies of Welsh–English Code Switching

Our study on the factors influencing the code-switching patterns of Welsh–English also builds on previous work we have done in this area. Deuchar (2005) used pilot conversational data to demonstrate that code switching was more likely to occur where there was both paradigmatic and syntagmatic congruence between the grammatical categories of Welsh and English. Deuchar (2006) used a small sample of conversational data to argue that Welsh–English code switching was conducive to analysis by the Matrix Language Frame (MLF) approach in that a matrix language (ML) (usually Welsh) could clearly be identified in bilingual clauses. Similar results were reported by Davies and Deuchar (2010) in a paper which argued that there was very little evidence that the speech of bilinguals was leading to convergence between Welsh and English. Similarly, Deuchar and Davies (2009) argued that although some of the clauses (16%) of a sample of speakers were bilingual in that they contained both Welsh and English words, the morphosyntactic frame of the clauses was almost always Welsh, justifying confidence in the stability of the Welsh language.

Lloyd (2008) conducted a study using some of the same data as ours in order to determine which external variables affected the percentage of English words used in otherwise Welsh conversations. She analysed the speech of 121 speakers from our *Siarad* corpus who had been brought up in North Wales. Using background information from our questionnaire, she found that the age of the speaker, the language of their education, and parental input were all important factors. However, she did not examine the effect of pattern of bilingual acquisition, a key variable in our study. Her results showed that older speakers used a smaller percentage of English words on average than younger speakers. In particular, that speakers aged under 30 used a significantly greater proportion of English words than speakers in their 1960s. Regarding language of education, Lloyd found that speakers who had received both their primary and their secondary education through the medium of Welsh tended to insert more English than those who had had their education in both Welsh and English. This result was contrary to her predictions in that she had expected the latter category to use more English words. However, there was a confound with age in that those who had received their education in both Welsh and English tended to be older. Regarding home language, Lloyd found that speakers who had heard Welsh from at least one parent had a (statistically non-significant) tendency to use more English than those who had heard only English. She suggests that those speakers who have heard more Welsh at home may be more likely to be balanced bilinguals because of the large amount of English input in society at large. This argument might also help to explain her results relating to the language of education and are in line with Gathercole and Thomas (2009)'s findings that enhanced input in Welsh is necessary for command of Welsh to equal command of English in Wales.

Carter, Deuchar, Davies, and Parafita Couto (2011) reported on a comparative analysis of the factors influencing code-switching patterns in a sample of speakers from three bilingual corpora.[3] One of these was the Welsh–English corpus analysed here, and the other two were collected in Miami (USA) and Patagonia (Argentina). They compared the proportion of bilingual versus monolingual clauses in each sample and identified the matrix language or morphosyntactic frame of each clause. The highest proportion of bilingual clauses (19%) was found in the Welsh–English sample collected in Wales, while the lowest proportion (3%) was found in the Welsh-Spanish sample collected in Patagonia. Regarding the matrix language of the bilingual clauses, this was found to be most uniform in the sample from Wales, where 100% of the clauses had Welsh as the matrix language. The Patagonia sample was almost as uniform, with 93% of the bilingual clauses having Welsh as a matrix language, but the Miami data showed more variability with 66% of the Spanish-English bilingual clauses having a Spanish ML and the remaining 34% having English as a matrix language. Carter et al. (2011) noted that there was uniformity in the choice of ML when the language pair had contrasting word orders, as in VSO (Welsh) versus SVO (English and Spanish) in Wales and Patagonia. They then sought to account for the specific choice of the ML in terms of external factors. Self-reported proficiency in both languages turned out to be relatively high in both Wales and Miami, and it seems that this may have favoured the production of bilingual clauses in those two samples, whereas the lower proportion of fluent bilinguals in Patagonia may account for the smaller proportion of bilingual clauses there. Regarding the choice of the matrix language, Carter et al. predicted

---

[3] See www.bangortalk.org.uk.

that the most common language of the social network would also be the most common matrix language. This prediction was fulfilled in Wales, where speakers' mainly Welsh-speaking social network could be linked to their overwhelming choice of Welsh as a matrix language. Similarly, the tendency of Spanish-English speakers in Miami to have a more bilingual social network was arguably reflected in the more diverse choice of both Spanish and English as matrix languages. In Patagonia, the relation between social networks and matrix language was unclear, partly because of the small number of Welsh speakers in that community.

Parafita Couto et al. (2014) report on the first multivariate analysis of our Spanish-English data, in which we attempted to find a relation between external factors and the choice of Spanish versus English as matrix language in our Miami data. An analysis of 2611 clauses extracted manually from three transcripts of conversations, using the Goldvarb X program, revealed no significant relationship between the choice of matrix language and external factors, but this may have been because of the small amount of data. In the study to be reported here, we were able to analyse 67,515 clauses as a result of computer-assisted glossing and clause segmentation.

Our study is therefore set against a body of previous work in code switching, in the development of corpora and tools for analysing variation, and in our own previous work specifically on Welsh–English code switching. In the next sections, we describe how we addressed the following research questions:

1. What is the extent of intraclausal code switching (switching within clauses) in the *Siarad* corpus?
2. Do speaker characteristics such as age and pattern of bilingual acquisition predict the observed code switching?

Data Collection and Transcription

In collecting our corpus, we were able to build on the example of other corpora containing code switching which have been available in the public domain since about 2000 (see e.g. Talkbank.org/BilingBank and the appendix to Gardner-Chloros 2009 on the LIDES project). For example, one of the first corpora on the Talkbank website to be extensively analysed is the Eppler corpus of German-English conversation by Austrian immigrants in London, described in a monograph by Duran Eppler (2010). Duran Eppler used the CHAT system from Talkbank (MacWhinney 2000) for the transcription of her data, which means that she could also use the Talkbank CLAN programs for its analysis. She used the CLAN programs to generate quantitative analyses of her data, for example, on the frequency of code switching, but her syntactic analysis was done manually. She uses CLAN to report on the distribution of languages per speaker, but did not otherwise study code-switching patterns in relation to speakers or speaker characteristics.

In collecting the *Siarad* Welsh–English corpus, we obtained 40 hours of spontaneous data based on 69 half-hour informal conversations between pairs of bilingual speakers. Most of the data were collected over a two-year period (2005–2007) and came from 151 speakers. On average, the corpus contains about 3000 words per speaker.

Our aim was to recruit a wide range of bilingual speakers, the main criterion being that participants considered themselves to be bilingual in Welsh and English. We were based in Bangor, NW Wales, and recruited mostly but not exclusively in that area. We aimed to record both men and women, of a wide range of ages (but mostly adults), with varying proficiency in the two languages. Proficiency was self-assessed[4] as part of questionnaires administered after the recordings. We also gathered information on a wide range of other external variables which included age, gender, area of upbringing,[5] occupation, age of acquisition of the two languages, language input in the family, social networks, and self-report on the extent of participants' code switching. Our method of recruitment was to send letters to bilingual speakers known to our research team or their contacts and also to place advertisements in the university and in public places. Our researchers were themselves Welsh–English bilinguals who could draw to some extent on their own social networks. The proj-

---

[4] Participants were asked to rate their ability to speak Welsh and English. For each language, there were four possible responses: (i) only know some words and expressions, (ii) confident in basic conversations, (iii) fairly confident in extended conversations, and (iv) confident in extended conversations.

[5] Details of the areas where individual participants were brought up (NW, NE, Mid, SW, and SE Wales) are provided in the *Siarad* 'questionnaire data' file available at www.bangortalk.org.uk.

ect was described as concerning bilingual communication, and the letter mentioned that we wanted to make recordings of informal conversation between bilingual people. We invited letter recipients to choose a bilingual family or friend with whom they would be willing to be recorded. Recipients were invited to choose the place of recording, whether at home or work, for example. While this freedom of choice meant that we could not control the environmental sound in the recordings, it helped to ensure informality.

Once appointments had been made with participants, they were met by one of the researchers and given a short briefing about the project: they were told that we were studying how bilinguals communicate with each other, although no mention was made of mixing languages or code switching, and that we would record them having a conversation for 35–40 minutes. Before the recording, it was explained that their anonymity would be protected by using pseudonyms for them and anyone they mentioned in the course of the conversation, and that they would be able to ask for anything they said to be deleted if they subsequently changed their mind. The recording equipment used for most recordings was a Marantz hard disk recorder, while a small number were recorded with a portable Sony minidisk recorder. Several steps were taken to reduce as much as possible any effect of the Observer's Paradox. The speakers were recorded with partners whom they already knew, in most cases very well. Audio recording without video was used so as to intrude less on the conversation. Wherever possible, the researcher left the room or house so that their presence would not influence the language choices made by the participants or inhibit code switching because of any self-consciousness. The pair was also left to talk for several minutes longer than the length that would become the final edited version in the corpus. This was so that the first five minutes of each recording could be removed in case the participants' speech might have been affected while they became accustomed to the recording equipment. These precautions proved to be highly successful in eliciting the naturalistic data sought. It is noticeable from the relaxed way in which the speakers interact, and the potentially sensitive topics that they discuss, that they did not seem to feel observed.

The transcription system selected was CHAT, and its associated CLAN software CLAN (see MacWhinney (2000) and http://childes.psy.cmu.

edu/manuals/CHAT.pdf) since it was to be made available on *Talkbank*, where CHAT is the standard software system. The fundamental features of CHAT notation are that utterances are placed on tiers: minimally, a main tier that consists of an orthographic representation of the words in the utterance. There are also optional tiers which may contain phonological and/or phonetic representations, word-by-word glosses of non-English material, a translation of the utterance, discourse level markup, comments, and so on. We decided that each transcribed utterance would minimally have a main tier, a gloss tier, and a tier with translation into English. These tiers are illustrated in example (1) below from stammers2. The first (line 91) is the main tier, the second (line 93) a gloss tier, and the third (94) is the translation tier.

91	*JAQ:	mi ges i heddiw # crackers@s:cym&eng # a # egg@s:eng mayonnaise@s:cym&eng .
93	%gls:	PRT get.1S.PAST PRON.1S today crackers and egg mayonnaise
94	%eng:	I had today crackers and egg mayonnaise

The main tier contains the actual words of the speaker's utterance, and also shows the source language of each word. Following the current norms in CHAT, words belonging to the ('default') language, which has the most words in the transcript, are not marked for language, but words from other languages are so marked. In *Siarad*, Welsh is always the default language, and English words are marked with the tag '@s:eng' as in the English word 'egg@s:eng' in the above example. There are also a large number of words (often loans from English into Welsh) which are marked with the tag '@s:cym&eng' indicating 'undetermined language'. Words such as 'mayonnaise@s:cym&eng' in the example above are originally English words but are found in Welsh dictionaries and often pronounced as in English. Words of this kind are spelled with English orthography but marked as undetermined. Similar neutral language marking was also used with place names and some interactional markers that we considered to belong to both language systems, for example, 'ah@s:cym&eng'.

The glossing of the main tier (resulting in the words in the gloss tier (marked with '%gls')) was initially done manually, but was later augmented by adding a further tier (%aut) containing glosses generated automatically by computer (Donnelly and Deuchar 2011), and it is these glosses which were used for the analysis reported in this paper. The

location	surface	auto	langid
1	mi	PRT.AFF	cym
2	ges	get.V.1S.PAST+SM	cym
3	i	I.PRON.1S	cym
4	heddiw	today.ADV	cym
5	crackers	cracker.N.SG+PL	cym&eng
6	a	and.CONJ	cym
7	egg	egg.N.SG	eng
8	mayonnaise	mayonnaise.N.SG	cym&eng
9	.	NULL	999

Fig. 8.1 Example of utterance with automatic glosses

automatic system splits the transcribed utterances into words, looks up the words in open source dictionaries, adds glosses to each word, uses constraint grammar[6] to disambiguate multiple glosses, and writes the final glosses into the CHAT file. It is calculated to be 97–98% accurate. Figure 8.1 shows the utterance from example (1) as stored in the database: the spoken words are in the column labelled 'surface', the automatic glosses in the 'auto' column, and the language origin of each word ('cym' for Welsh, 'eng' for English) is in the last column.

Example (1) can then be expanded with more detailed glossing information as (1a) below:

(1a)
---
*JAQ: mi ges i heddiw # crackers@s:cym&eng # a # egg@s:eng mayonnaise@s:cym&eng.
%gls: PRT get.1S.PAST PRON.1S today crackers and egg mayonnaise
%aut: PRT.AFF get.V.1S.PAST+AM I.PRON.1S today.ADV cracker.N.SG+PL and.CONJ egg.N.SG mayonnaise.N.SG
%eng: I had today crackers and egg mayonnaise

---

[6] Constraint grammar contains rules which help to identify which gloss is correct in dictionary entries containing more than one possible gloss. For example, *i* in Welsh could be either a first person singular pronoun or a preposition. Constraint grammar identifies it as a first person singular pronoun if it follows a first person verb form.

The automatic glosses in the '%aut' tier allow the analysis to be performed. We shall see how this works in our data analysis, to which we now turn.

Data Analysis

Our unit of analysis was the clause, and our measure of the extent of intraclausal code switching was the proportion of clauses containing code switching compared with the proportion that did not.

Intraclausal versus Interclausal Code Switching

The terms *intraclausal* and *interclausal* correspond roughly to what are called *intrasentential* and *intersentential* code switching elsewhere but are more precise. Deuchar (2012) argues that the term *intrasentential* can be ambiguous between *intraclausal* and *interclausal* when *intrasentential* refers to switching between two clauses in the same sentence. Intraclausal code switching (as understood in our study) is illustrated by example (2) [7] below and interclausal code switching by example (3):

(2)	[maen	nhw	(y)n	rhoi	e
	be.V.3S.PRES	they.PRON.3P	PRT	give.V.INFIN	he.PRON.M.3S
	yn	y	STEAM	ROOM	[dw
	in.PREP	the.DET.DEF	steam.N.SG	room.N.SG	be.V.1S.PRES
	i	mynd	yn]]	.	
	I.PRON.1S	go.V.INFIN	in.PREP		

'They put it in the steam-room I go to.'[fusser27: 139[8]]

---

[7] Words in lower case bold are Welsh, in upper case English, and bold italics are used for words belonging to both languages. The glosses have been aligned with the words for the ease of reading and are explained in the *Siarad* documentation file to be found at www.bangortalk.org.uk.

[8] Examples (2)–(10) are referenced by giving the name of the file they come from, followed by the number of the utterance (called the 'main tier' in CLAN).

(3)	[*so*	*bosib*	*hwnna*	*(y)dy*	*o*]
	so.ADV	possible.ADJ+SM	that.PRON. DEM.M.SG	be.V.3S.PRES	he.PRON.M.3S
	[I	DON'T	KNOW]	.	
	I.PRON. SUB.1S	do.V.1S.PRES+NEG	know.V.INFIN		

'So possibly that's it, I don't know' [fusser25: 1073].

In example (2), there is a switch within the clause to the English phrase *steam room,* whereas in example (3) there is a switch from an entire Welsh clause to the English clause *I don't know.* This can be verified by noting the position of the clause boundaries, marked with square brackets.

Our analysis focused on intraclausal code switching, which was much more frequent in our data than interclausal code switching. For the purposes of the analysis, intraclausal code switching was considered to be manifest in clauses coded as bilingual rather than monolingual. Example (2) above would be coded as bilingual because it contains words from both English and Welsh. Example (3), however, would be considered to consist of two monolingual clauses, one in Welsh and the other in English. Words which could belong to either Welsh or English (on the grounds that they were found in dictionaries of both languages) were ignored in the process of coding. Thus, English loanwords in Welsh were distinguished from switches. The extent of intraclausal code switching was measured in terms of the number of bilingual clauses produced as a proportion of the total number of clauses.

Data Preparation

Because of our focus on the clause as a unit of analysis, all utterances from the corpus had to be split into clauses. In fact, only 24% of the utterances in the corpus were longer than one clause and therefore required this. Welsh is the predominant language of the corpus (only 4% of words are unambiguously English), but since no parser is as yet available for Welsh, we used a relatively unsophisticated method to segment these utterances. (A similar approach was used for English and mixed utterances.) This involved (i) using the autogloss to mark all finite verbs, (ii) moving the marker leftwards as required onto conjunctions, relatives or interrogatives where these preceded the verb, and (iii) dividing the utterance at the marker.[9]

To test the accuracy of the segmentation of clauses in Welsh, the predominant language, 1318 Welsh-only utterances which had been split into four or more clauses were collected, and every tenth one was examined to check whether the clauses were correctly segmented. In the 528 clauses in the sample, there were 35 errors (7%). There were 30 instances of a split where none was required, four of a required split not being made, and one where a clause had been marked as finite when it contained no verb. Although utterances consisting of four clauses or more (as in the test) make up only 2.4% of the corpus, they make a particularly rigorous test sample because their length increases the number of possible places for segmentation errors to occur. Thus, the error rate for these longer utterances is likely to be an upper limit on the overall error rate, and one would expect the error rate to be lower overall. This expectation was tested manually using a sample from stammers4. The first 200 utterances of the transcript of stammers4 were split by hand and compared to the output from the clause splitter. In these 277 clauses, there was only one error (a split where none was required)—an error rate of less than 1%.

Statistical Analysis

For our analysis, we used Rbrul (Johnson 2009), a new version of the variable rule program originally developed by Sankoff (1975). Johnson (2009) describes the variable rule program as 'one of the predominant data analysis tools used in sociolinguistics, employed successfully for over three decades to quantitatively assess the influence of multiple factors on linguistic variables'. The various versions of the program allow sociolinguists to calculate the effects of multiple factors (both linguistic and extralinguistic) on linguistic choices between variants, broadly alternative ways of saying the same thing. Johnson argues that Rbrul is less idiosyncratic than Goldvarb when compared with other statistical packages

[9] For more information about how the corpus was segmented, see section 4.2 of an earlier version of this paper at http://www.ling.cam.ac.uk/COPIL/.

in common use, although its results can be presented in a similar format to that of Goldvarb if desired. One of the advantages of Rbrul over Goldvarb is that it uses mixed-effects modelling which allows the investigator to take into account random effects such as those introduced by individual speakers (cf. Baayen et al. 2008). On comparing Rbrul with Goldvarb, Johnson notes that the latter treats each token as if it were independent, even though this is not the case: the tokens are not independent, since they occur in groups produced by individual speakers. There is therefore a danger of Goldvarb overestimating external effects such as gender and age. However, mixed-effects models can distinguish between 'fixed effects' such as gender and age and 'random effects' such as the effects of individual speakers. Drager and Hay (2012: 60) argue that an increase in statistical robustness is the main reason that this model should be adopted by sociolinguists, and point out that the model allows the simultaneous study of both group and individual variation.

Data Coding and Sample

The coding of each clause for linguality (monolingual vs. bilingual, as described above) allowed us to quantify the amount of code switching by speakers in terms of its presence (in bilingual clauses) versus absence (in monolingual clauses). The categories 'bilingual clause' versus 'monolingual clause' were treated as variants of the dependent variable which we label 'linguality'. Table 8.1 illustrates the automatic coding of the linguality of each clause, whether bilingual ('biling'), monolingual Welsh

Table 8.1 Illustration of how linguality of extracted clauses was coded

File name	Utterance ID	Speaker	Clause	Verblg	Linguality
fusser17	1257	AET	oedd o yn dechrau diflannu	cym	monoW
fusser25	148	HUN	because they're leaving	eng	monoE
robert2	267	RIS	achos mae gynna chdi spellchecker Cymraeg arno fo	cym	biling
lloyd1	720	GRG	in Cymru we recycle	eng	biling

(monoW), or monolingual English (monoE). Clauses coded as monolingual contain only words from one language (whether Welsh or English), whereas bilingual clauses contain one or more words from both languages. In addition, the language of the verb ('verblg'), whether Welsh ('cym') or English ('eng'), as well as the name of the file for the recording, the utterance ID, and the pseudonym of the speaker were all automatically coded.

The data comprised 80,352 clauses from the 151[10] speakers in the *Siarad* corpus. The speakers were distributed by age and gender as shown[11] in Table 8.2. The effect of speaker gender turned out not to be significant unlike that of age, on which we report below.

Before the analysis of intraclausal code switching could begin, clauses consisting of only one word were removed from the data set. This is because we considered it necessary for there to be at least two words within a clause to provide an opportunity for intraclausal code switching to take place.[12] In total, 11,601 clauses of only one word were removed leaving 67,515 clauses in the data set distributed as shown in Table 8.3.

Table 8.3 shows that the majority of clauses (88%) are monolingual Welsh and only a tiny fraction (2%) are monolingual English. However,

Table 8.2 The speaker sample by age and gender

	Overall	Male	Female
N	148	70	78
Average age	42	43	40
Youngest	10	12	10
Oldest	89	86	89
%	100	47	43

---

[10] For this analysis, we removed two speakers EVA and GLA who had learned Dutch as their first language, because we wished to focus on the role of Welsh and English acquisition in early childhood as a predictor of code switching. It was also necessary to remove a further speaker, ARD, since the data on first language acquired were missing. Removing these three speakers gives a large data set for the analysis of 148 speakers and 79,116 clauses.

[11] More detailed information about each speaker's age and gender is available in the documentation file at http://www.bangortalk.org.uk/speakers.php?c=siarad.

[12] Word-internal code switching can occur in Welsh when an English verb is given a verbal suffix, for example, concentrate-io. There were 333 instances of this in the 11,061 clauses that we removed and thus these instances were not included in our analysis of intraclausal code switching.

Table 8.3 Distribution of clauses consisting of more than word by language and speaker

Distribution of clauses	N	%
Total clauses	67,515	100
Of which:	59,152	88
Monolingual Welsh		
Monolingual English	1656	2
Bilingual (Welsh and English)	6707	10
Mean per speaker	456	
Minimum per speaker	47	
Maximum per speaker	1106	

bilingual clauses (those containing intraclausal code switches) make up 10% of all clauses. The morphosyntactic frame of the bilingual clauses is almost always Welsh: bilingual clauses with an English grammatical frame are very rare, and none at all were found in the sample analysed by Deuchar and Davies 2009 (see also Parafita Couto et al. 2014: 127–128). One hundred and forty-seven of the 148 speakers in the analysis to be reported here used a majority of Welsh monolingual clauses (range 61.7–99.7% per speaker). Contrast this with the use of English: here, the range of use, excepting speaker GRG (81.8% solely English clauses), was 0–28% monolingual English clauses; indeed, this analysis shows that 21 speakers used no monolingual English clauses at all. All but one speaker, DER, produced intraclausal code switches to varying degrees; the range per speaker is 0–31.1% intraclausal code switches per speaker.

The bilingual clauses listed in Table 8.3 are evidence of intraclausal code switching. The aim of our study was to examine to what extent speaker attributes were correlated with the use of intraclausal code switching. The *Siarad* questionnaire responses provided a rich and diverse set of social data to analyse. However, many of the questionnaire responses were designed to elicit related information, and answers to these questions were therefore often correlated. For example, speakers were asked to assess their own ability in Welsh and English and also about when they learned both languages. In order to ensure the independence of external factors in the multivariate model, we chose to focus in the analysis to be reported here on how diverse patterns of bilingual acquisition and the age of the speaker influenced the production of code-switching. Age was treated as a continuous variable, while the factor group 'pattern of bilingual acquisition' included five factors: (1) Welsh and English were acquired simultaneously from birth, (2) the second language (L2, whether Welsh or English) was being acquired by age four, (3) L2 was acquired at primary school, (4) L2 was acquired at secondary school, and (5) L2 was acquired in adulthood. Information about participants' age of acquisition was obtained from their answers to the questionnaire items 'Since when have you been able to speak Welsh?' and 'Since when have you been able to speak English?' They were asked to indicate one of the following categories in relation to each language: (a) since 2 years old or younger, (b) since 4 years old or younger, (c) since primary school, (d) since secondary school, and (e) since becoming an adult. The answers in relation to the two languages were combined to yield the five categories outlined above, where the term 'L2' is used for convenience to indicate the timing of sequential acquisition in categories (2)–(4).

Results

The multivariate analysis was conducted in R using Rbrul (Johnson 2009). The dependent variable was the linguality of each clause: bilingual versus monolingual Welsh or English. The analysis used a mixed-effects model with speaker included as a random intercept. This approach has the advantage of compensating for the effects of idiosyncratic linguistic behaviour by particular speakers. The results of our analysis are shown in Table 8.4. Table 8.4 shows that the age and pattern of bilingual acquisition are related to the number of intraclausal code switches a speaker produces.

Regarding age, the analysis shows that as age increases the presence of bilingual clauses decreases. Details of the relation between age and code switching are shown in Fig. 8.2.

Table 8.4 also shows that speakers who learned Welsh and English simultaneously were more likely to produce intraclausal code switches than speakers who learnt one language later than the other.

Table 8.4 Mixed effects logistic regression predicting bilingual clauses with speaker as a random effect

	Log-odds	Number of clauses	% of bilingual clauses	Centred factor weight
Age	−0.02	67,515		
Pattern of bilingual acquisition				
Both Welsh and English from birth	0.407	15,572	14.7	0.6
L2 by age four	−0.053	19,006	10.3	0.487
L2 at primary school	−0.087	26,501	7.8	0.478
L2 at secondary school	−0.059	3710	6.6	0.485
L2 in adulthood	−0.209	2726	5.6	0.448

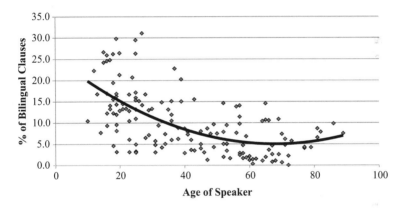

Fig. 8.2 Percentage of bilingual clauses by speaker age

The analysis of intraclausal code switching reported so far has been quantitative, but we also considered whether simultaneous acquisition of two languages in infancy would lead to qualitative as well as quantitative differences in code switching. Although not working with simultaneous bilinguals, Finlayson et al. (1998) found that multilinguals with a higher level of English proficiency produced more switched English phrases than those with a lower level of proficiency, who tended to switch single English words. Treffers-Daller (1992: 144) reports excluding single-word switches from her analysis of French-Dutch code switching in case they might be borrowings. In our study, we excluded borrowings (described above as loans marked in our transcription as '@s:cym&eng') from our analysis of code switching, but decided to investigate whether simultaneous bilinguals produced more switched phrases (as opposed to switched single words) than those who had acquired one language later than the other.

To do this, we classified the bilingual clauses into two types: single-word insertions and multi-word insertions. Single-word insertions were defined as being single words in otherwise monolingual Welsh clauses as seen in (4). Or they could be multiple incidences of single-word insertions within an otherwise Welsh clause as seen in (5).

(4)	ti	(e)rioed	yn	SERIOUS
	you.PRON.2S	never.ADV	PRT	serious.ADJ

'You're never serious.' [davies6: 494]

(5)	*well*	APPARENTLY	*well*	APPARENTLY	*mae*
	well.ADV	apparently.ADV	well.ADV	apparently.ADV	be.V.3S.PRES
	MONOLINGUAL	pobl	MONOLINGUAL	yn	MINORITY
	monolingual.ADJ	people.N.F.SG	monolingual.ADJ	PRT	minority.N.SG
	bach	yn	y	byd	.
	small.ADJ	in.PREP	the.DET.DEF	world.N.M.SG	

'Well, apparently monolingual people are a small minority in the world' [stammers3: 339].

Multi-word insertions are those that have longer structures of the switched language. Example (6) shows a multi-word insertion of English into a clause with a Welsh-inflected verb and (7) shows a multi-word insertion of Welsh into a clause with an English-inflected verb.

(6)	dylet	ti	fod	yn	gallu
	ought_to.V.2S.IMPERF	you.PRON.2S	be.V.INFIN+SM	PRT	be_able.V.INFIN
	gwrando	(ar)no	fe	TOP	TO
	listen.V.INFIN	on_him.PREP+PRON.M.3S	he.PRON.M.3S	top.N.SG	to.PREP
	BOTTOM	AND	ENJOY	THE	WHOLE
	bottom.N.SG	and.CONJ	enjoy.V.INFIN	the.DET.DEF	whole.ADJ
	THING	.			
	thing.N.SG				

'You should be able to listen to it top to bottom and enjoy the whole thing' [davies9: 183].

(7)	YOU	KNOW	DOING	USUAL	a
	you.PRON. SUB.2SP	know.V.2SP. PRES	do.V.PRESPART	usual. ADJ	and.CONJ
	siarad talk.V.INFIN	**dros** over.PREP+SM	**popeth** everything.N.M.SG	.	

'You know, doing the usual and talking across everything' [davies12: 3380].

Table 8.5 shows that in our data the majority of code switches were single-word insertions.

In this analysis, we divided our speakers into three groups: those who acquired English and Welsh simultaneously, those who acquired English first, and those who acquired Welsh first. Figure 8.3 shows the percentage of single-word versus multi-word insertions produced by each group. It can be seen that single-word insertions are used more

Table 8.5 Distribution of single-word versus multi-word insertions

	No. of bilingual clauses	% of bilingual clauses
Total	6707	100
Of which single-word insertions	4772	71
Of which multi-word insertions	1935	29

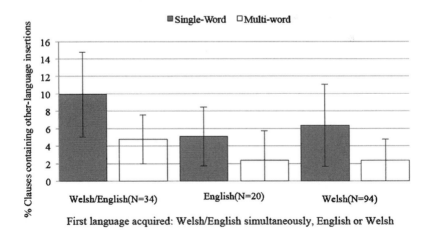

Fig. 8.3 Single-word versus multi-word insertions by first language acquired

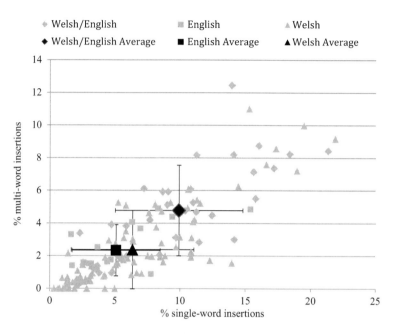

Fig. 8.4 Correlation between single-word and multi-word insertions
Note: Error bars show one standard deviation.

frequently than multi-word insertions by all groups, but that the speakers who learnt both English and Welsh simultaneously use more of both.

Two-tailed *t*-tests showed that the groups who had learnt English or Welsh first were not significantly different from each other in their production of either single-word insertions ($p = 0.26$) or multi-word clauses ($p = 0.94$). Furthermore, single-word insertions and multi-word insertions were positively correlated ($r = 0.83$, $p = <0.0001$), as shown in Fig. 8.4. This means that speakers who use more single-word insertions also use more multi-word insertions. Thus in our data at least we do not yet have evidence for the pattern of bilingual acquisition affecting the size of insertions in code switching.

Discussion

In the 'Introduction' section, we pointed out that although ideas about the relation between code switching and proficiency have been familiar since Poplack's (1980) work, little has previously been known about the impact of patterns of bilingual acquisition on adult bilinguals' speech production. In particular, we have not known how these patterns are related to speakers' choice to code switch within clauses or not to switch. Our results as reported in Table 8.4 show that those speakers who had acquired both Welsh and English from birth were significantly more likely to produce intraclausal code switching than all other categories of speaker, including those who had acquired their second language as young as age four. Although the overall percentage of bilingual clauses in our data is 10%, the bilingual clauses of speakers who were simultaneous bilinguals as infants make up 15% of their output. This percentage drops to 6% for those who acquired their second language as adults.

It is well known that achieving native-like competence in a language or languages is very rarely possible unless the languages are acquired at a young age, but there is debate about what exactly this cut-off age is. Meisel (2010) found that sequential German-French bilinguals who had begun acquiring French at age three in Hamburg produced errors in the production of French finite verb forms even after 6 years of exposure to the language, whereas errors of this type where virtually never produced by simultaneous German-French bilinguals. Meisel suggests that these differences may be explained by neural maturation, with some important changes occurring in the fourth year of life. He refers to neuroscientific studies which support his conclusion. Our results suggest that it may make a difference whether bilingual acquisition is simultaneous or successive even when the second language is acquired very early but not simultaneously with the first.

In the 'Introduction' section, we referred to the study by Mechelli et al. (2004) which showed how the timing of bilingual acquisition affected the density of grey matter in the brain. Specifically, they found that grey matter density in the inferior parietal cortex was negatively correlated with the age of acquisition in the second language. In other words, simultaneous bilinguals had the greatest density of grey matter in this area, followed by those who had acquired their second language early, followed by those who had acquired it later. Furthermore, the authors point out that 'the inferior parietal region that is associated with second-language acquisition corresponds exactly to an area that has been shown by functional imaging to become activated during verbal-fluency tasks' (Mechelli et al. 2004: 757). We suggest that intraclausal code switching is the type of activity to be particularly favoured by verbal fluency. Another relevant study is that by Weber-Fox and Neville (1999) who explore how the age of acquisition of a second language affects the neural subsystems involved in language processing. The participants in their study were Chinese-English bilinguals who had acquired English at five different age categories similar to those used in our study. ERPs elicited by phrase structure violations showed 'increased bilateral distribution with increased second language immersion' (Weber-Fox and Neville 1999: 30). These and some behavioural results showing slower syntactic processing with increased age of second language acquisition led them to conclude that 'the development of at least some neural subsystems for language processing is constrained by maturational changes, even in early childhood' (Weber-Fox and Neville 1999: 36). This conclusion suggests to us that the timing of bilingual acquisition may indeed affect that facility with which speakers switch back and forth between two languages with different syntactic structures, and thus the frequency with which they will choose to code switch.

Although our results show a relation between simultaneous acquisition of the two languages and the more frequent production of code switching, this does not mean that such a relationship will be found in all bilingual communities, since community norms doubtless play a role. While our own observations in Wales and the evidence of the *Siarad* corpus demonstrate that code switching is a community norm in informal conversations between Welsh–English bilinguals, not all bilingual communities use code switching. For example, it is not common in Patagonia, Argentina, where we collected a Welsh-Spanish corpus; see the Patagonia corpus at www.bangortalk.org.uk and Carter et al. (2011). However, we do predict a similar finding to ours in an analysis of our Spanish-English corpus from Miami (see www.bangortalk.org.uk and Parafita Couto et al. (2014)).

Our results showed that the other important external factor was age. Figure 8.2 shows a negative correlation between age and code switching, such that the older the speaker, the less frequent the proportion of bilingual clauses. A similar result was found by Lloyd (2008) who used some of the same speaker data as us but measured the proportion of English words rather than the proportion of bilingual clauses used by speakers. We may interpret our and Lloyd's results within the 'apparent time' paradigm, inferring that there is an ongoing change in language norms and that code switching is becoming more common and acceptable, at least in informal contexts. This interpretation is supported by Lloyd's additional finding that younger people showed more positive attitudes to code switching than older people. Both Lloyd's and our results show a slight upturn in the quantity of code switching used by the most elderly people, and though the numbers are small it may be possible to interpret their usage in terms of 'age-grading' or the idea that people's usage may change over their lifespan, for example, because of the relaxation of 'marketplace pressure' (cf. Wagner 2012: 378).

Our results have methodological as well as theoretical implications. Although our methods of automatic parsing and analysis can be improved further, we have shown that it is possible to extract large amounts of data with a low level of error. Using automatic glossing and data extraction methods has made it possible to deal with data from a larger number of speakers than has previously been possible in code-switching studies. This means that we can also be more confident in the validity of our results.

Finally, we can consider the implications of our results for the future of bilingualism in Wales. Our findings suggest that early exposure to both languages has a good chance of leading to fluent bilingualism, which will include code switching. Given the minority status of Welsh and the conclusions of Gathercole and Thomas (2009) reported above, parents making decisions about which language to use with their children may need to pay special attention to the role of Welsh. Furthermore, the connection we have demonstrated between code switching and fluency should help to persuade those who still associate code switching with inadequate command of Welsh to rethink their positions.

Conclusion

Our multivariate analysis of 67,515 bilingual and monolingual clauses from 40 hours of Welsh–English conversational data collected from 148 speakers showed that intraclausal code switching was produced more frequently by those who had acquired Welsh and English in infancy than those who had acquired the two languages sequentially. We speculated that this difference could be due to the timing of different patterns of bilingual acquisition in relation to neural maturation. We also found a tendency for younger speakers to code-switch more than for older speakers, and suggested that there is a change in progress related to more permissive attitudes to code switching. Finally, we suggest that the large size of our corpus and our automatic data extraction methods allow considerable confidence in our results.

Acknowledgements We are grateful for the financial support of the AHRC and ESRC in the collection and analysis of the data, and for the contribution of all those who provided, collected, and transcribed data.

References

Baayen, R. Harald, Douglas J. Davidson, and Douglas M. Bates. 2008. Mixed-effects modeling with crossed random effects for subjects and items. *Journal of Memory and Language* 59(4): 390–412.

Backus, Ad. 1996. *Two in one. Bilingual speech of Turkish immigrants in the Netherlands*. Tilburg: Tilburg University Press.

Bailey, Guy. 2002. Real and apparent time. In *The handbook of language variation and change*, ed. J.K. Chambers, Peter Trudgill, and Natalie Schilling-Estes, 312–332. Oxford: Blackwell.

Carter, Diana, Margaret Deuchar, Peredur Davies, and María del Carmen Parafita Couto. 2011. A systematic comparison of factors affecting the choice of matrix language in three bilingual communities. *Journal of Language Contact* 4: 153–183.

Cheshire, Jenny, and Penelope Gardner-Chloros. 1998. Code-switching and the sociolinguistic gender pattern. *International Journal of the Sociology of Language* 129(1): 5–34.

Davies, Peredur, and Margaret Deuchar. 2010. Using the Matrix Language Frame model to measure the extent of word-order convergence in Welsh–English bilingual speech. In *Continuity and change in grammar*, ed. Anne Breitbarth, Christopher Lucas, Sheila Watts, and David Willis. Amsterdam/Philadelphia: John Benjamins Publishing.

Deuchar, Margaret. 2005. Congruence and Welsh–English code-switching. *Bilingualism: Language and Cognition* 8(3): 255–269.

———. 2006. Welsh–English code-switching and the Matrix Language Frame model. *Lingua* 116(11): 1986–2011.

———. 2012. Code-switching. In *Encyclopedia of applied linguistics*, ed. Carol A. Chapelle, 657–664. New York: Wiley.

Deuchar, Margaret, and Peredur Davies. 2009. Code switching and the future of the Welsh language. *International Journal of the Sociology of Language* 2009(195): 15–38.

Deuchar, Margaret, Peredur Davies, Jon Russell Herring, M. Carmen Parafita Couto, and Diana Carter. 2014. Building bilingual corpora. In *Advances in the study of Bilingualism*, ed. Enlli Môn Thomas, and Ineke Mennen, 93–110. Bristol: Multilingual Matters.

Donnelly, Kevin, and Margaret Deuchar. 2011. Using constraint grammar in the Bangor Autoglosser to disambiguate multilingual spoken text. In *Proceedings of the NODALIDA 2011 workshop constraint grammar applications, NEALT proceedings series 14*, eds. Eckhard Bick, Kristin Hagen, Kaili Müürisep, Trond Trosterud, 17–25. http://hdl.handle.net/10062/19298

Drager, Katie, and Jennifer Hay. 2012. Exploiting random intercepts: Two case studies in sociophonetics. *Language Variation and Change* 24(1): 59–78.

Duran Eppler, Eva. 2010. *Emigranto: The syntax of German/English code-switching*. Vienna: Braumüller.

Finlayson, Rosalie, Karen Calteaux, and Carol Myers-Scotton. 1998. Orderly mixing and accommodation in South African codeswitching. *Journal of Sociolinguistics* 2(3): 395–420.

Gardner-Chloros, Penelope. 1992. The sociolinguistics of the Greek-Cypriot community in London. In Plurilinguismes: Sociolinguistique du grec et de la Grèce, ed. Marilena Karyolemou, 4, 112–136. Paris: CERPL.

———. 2009. *Code-switching*. Cambridge: Cambridge University Press.

Gathercole, Virginia C.M., and Enlli Môn Thomas. 2009. Bilingual first-language development: Dominant language takeover, threatened minority language take-up. *Bilingualism: Language and Cognition* 12(2): 213–237.

Johnson, Daniel E. 2009. Getting off the GoldVarb standard: Introducing Rbrul for mixed-effects variable rule analysis. *Language and Linguistics Compass* 3(1): 359–383.

Jones, Robert O. 1993. The sociolinguistics of Welsh. In *The Celtic languages*, ed. Martin J. Ball, and James Fife, 536–604. London: Routledge.

Lloyd, Siân W. 2008. Variables that affect English language use within Welsh conversations in North Wales, Unpublished Master's thesis, Bangor University.

MacWhinney, Brian. 2000. *The CHILDES project: Tools for analyzing talk.* Mahwah: Lawrence Erlbaum Associates.

Mechelli, Andrea, Jenny T. Crinion, Uta Noppeney, John O'Doherty, John Ashburner, Richard S. Frackowiak, and Cathy J. Price. 2004. Neurolinguistics: Structural plasticity in the bilingual brain. *Nature* 431(7010): 757.

Meisel, Jürgen M. 2004. The bilingual child. In *The handbook of Bilingualism*, ed. Tej K. Bhatia, and William C. Ritchie, 91–113. Oxford: Blackwell.

———. 2010. Age of onset in successive acquisition of bilingualism: Effects on grammatical development. In *Language acquisition across linguistic and cognitive systems*, ed. Michèle Kail, and Maya Hickmann, 225–248. Amsterdam: John Benjamins.

Parafita Couto, M. Carmen, Peredur Davies, Diana Carter, and Margaret Deuchar. 2014. Factors influencing code-switching. In *Advances in the study of Bilingualism*, ed. Enlli Môn Thomas and Ineke Mennen, 111–138. Bristol: Multilingual Matters.

Penhallurick, Robert. 2007. English in Wales. In *Language in the British Isles*, ed. David Britain, 152–170. Cambridge: Cambridge University Press.

Poplack, Shana. 1980. Sometimes I'll start a sentence in Spanish Y TERMINO EN ESPAÑOL: Toward a typology of code-switching. *Linguistics* 18(7–8): 581–618.

Sankoff, David. 1975. VARBRUL 2. Unpublished program and documentation.

Thomas, Alan. 1982a. Change and decay in language. In *Linguistic controversies: Essays in linguistic theory and practice in honour of F. R. Palmer*, ed. David Crystal, 209–19. London: Edward Arnold.

Thomas, Ceinwen H. 1982b. Registers in Welsh. *International Journal of the Sociology of Language* 35: 87–115.

Treffers-Daller, Jeanine. 1992. French-Dutch codeswitching in Brussels: Social factors explaining its disappearance. *Journal of Multilingual and Multicultural Development* 13(1–2): 143–156.

————. 1994. *Mixing two languages: French-Dutch contact in a comparative perspective*. Berlin/New York: Mouton de Gruyter.

Wagner, Suzanne Evans. 2012. Age grading in sociolinguistic theory. *Language and Linguistics Compass* 6(6): 371–382.

Weber-Fox, Christine, and Helen Neville. 1999. Functional neural subsystems are differentially affected by delays in second language immersion: ERP and behavioral evidence in bilinguals. In *Second language acquisition and the critical period hypothesis*, ed. David Birdsong, 23–38. Mahwah: Lawrence Erlbaum Associates.

9

The Role of Linguistic Background on Sound Variation in Welsh and Welsh English

Jonathan Morris, Robert Mayr, and Ineke Mennen

Yn y bennod hon, rydym yn ymchwilio i amrywio seinegol a ffonolegol yn lleferydd siaradwyr dwyieithog Cymraeg-Saesneg rhwng 16 a 18 mlwydd oed. Rydym yn gofyn a yw cefndir ieithyddol yn dylanwadu ar amrywio yn y ddwy iaith ac i ba raddau y mae'r nodweddion dan sylw yn debyg yn y ddwy iaith. Yn gyntaf, cyflwynir astudiaeth o lafariaid a gynhyrchwyd gan siaradwyr o Rydaman (Sir Gaerfyrddin) er mwyn canfod a oes amrywio seinegol o fewn yr ieithoedd a rhyngddynt. Yn ail, rydym yn dadansoddi /r/ yn lleferydd pobl ifainc o'r Wyddgrug (Sir y Fflint) er mwyn ymchwilio i drosglwyddo ffonolegol. Yn drydydd, rydym yn ystyried i ba raddau y gall ffactorau megis defnydd o'r Gymraeg yn y gymuned a chyffyrddiad iaith hirdymor esbonio'r patrymau a gafwyd.

J. Morris (✉)
Cardiff University, Cardiff, UK

R. Mayr
Cardiff Metropolitan University, Cardiff, UK

I. Mennen
University of Graz, Graz, Austria

© The Author(s) 2016
M. Durham, J. Morris (eds.), *Sociolinguistics in Wales*,
DOI 10.1057/978-1-137-52897-1_9

Introduction

It is well established that there is an interaction between the two languages in a bilingual speaker's repertoire (Paradis 2001; Grosjean 2001). In the case of sound production, bilingual speakers have been shown to often produce phonemes differently to their monolingual peers due to either unidirectional or bidirectional *cross-linguistic phonetic interactions* between the phonetic subsystems of their two languages (e.g. Guion et al. 2000; Kehoe et al. 2004; Mennen 2004; Elordieta and Calleja 2005; Fowler et al. 2008; Simonet 2010). Similarly, *phonological transfer* describes the appearance of phonological features from one of the speaker's language in the other (see Flege 1995 for an overview) and has been shown to occur in segments, phonotactic patterns, prosody, and post-lexical phonological rules (Simon 2010: 63–64).

Both phonetic interactions and phonological transfer can be influenced by a number of extra-linguistic factors including age of acquisition, use of the two languages, social networks, and speech context (e.g. Piske et al. 2001; Grosjean 2001). They have therefore become increasingly relevant to variationist sociolinguistic work on non-monolingual speech and migrant communities (see Treffers-Daller and Mougeon 2005). Many studies have considered the transfer of phonological features from heritage languages to English (e.g. Mendoza-Denton 1996; Fought 1999) and found that transferred material can become a marker of ethnic identity and feature in the speech of subsequent generations of monolinguals (Holmes 1996; Sharma and Sankaran 2011). More recently, more fine-grained phonetic interactions have been found in studies of both minority ethnic groups (e.g. Alam and Stuart-Smith 2011) and minority language contexts (Nance 2014, 2015).

In the case of Welsh–English bilingualism, the role of linguistic background (often conceptualised as home language or age of acquisition) on sound variation has largely been ignored despite being found to be significant in a number of studies examining bilingual language acquisition of Welsh and English (e.g. Munro et al. 2005; Gathercole and Thomas 2009; Rhys and Thomas 2013; Mayr et al. 2014, 2015). It is therefore unknown the extent to which linguistic background influences variation in both Welsh and Welsh–English despite many communities in Wales comprising bilinguals who have either (1) acquired Welsh via parental transmission or (2) acquired the language via Welsh-medium or bilingual education, as well as English monolinguals with little functional ability in Welsh.

Phonological similarities exist in the vowel systems of southern varieties of Welsh and Welsh English and comparisons of previous work suggest that there is a large degree of overlap (Wells 1982; Jones 1984). Such changes may be due to similarities in the phonological systems prior to contact or be due to contact-induced change (Thomason and Kaufman 1988; Silva-Corvalán 2000; Thomason 2001). Similarly, a number of phonological features differ between the two languages with the Welsh variant being noted in the English of Welsh-dominant areas as a transfer effect. Descriptive accounts of Welsh, for instance, claim that the voiced alveolar trill [r] is expected in word-initial and word-medial intervocalic positions (the voiced alveolar tap [ɾ] is also common in intervocalic position in the North West; Jones 1984: 49–50). In English, the voiced alveolar approximant [ɹ] is expected although [r] is noted in Welsh-dominant areas and as a feature of Welsh–English bilinguals' speech (Wells 1982: 390).

In the case of phonologically identical features, it is not known whether there are cross-linguistic phonetic influences affecting the speech of bilinguals as has been found in previous studies. In the case where segments which differ between the two languages, the extent to which transfer occurs between the two languages has also not been quantified. More generally, and in the context of long-term bilingualism and language contact, it remains to be seen whether home language influences variation and how we account for differences between these two types of interaction in bilingual speech.

The aim of this chapter is therefore to (1) examine the influence of home language on cross-linguistic phonetic interactions and on phonological transfer and (2) compare potential differences between this influence on these two processes. In order to achieve these aims, we ask the following research questions:

1. Is there evidence for cross-linguistic phonetic interaction in the production of monophthongs and phonological transfer in the production of /r/ in Welsh–English bilingual speech?
2. To what extent does linguistic background influence variation with regard to these features?
3. How can the results be explained in light of community dynamics, long-term language contact, and synchronic Welsh–English bilingualism?

We present data from Welsh–English bilinguals aged 16–18 in Ammanford (Carmarthenshire) and Mold (Flintshire). Although these data sets come from two different areas, they do allow us to examine two different types of features. Firstly, we compare intra-linguistic and cross-linguistic variation in the production of monophthongs in Ammanford in order to ascertain whether there are fine-grained phonetic interactions. Secondly, we present an analysis of the phonological transfer of /r/ in both the Welsh and English of bilinguals in Mold. Taken together, these analyses present an overview of how (or if) long-term language contact and synchronic bilingualism affect variation in the speech of Welsh–English bilinguals.

The remainder of the chapter is structured as follows. Firstly, we provide more information on the communities and speakers studied. Secondly, we present the analysis of monophthongs in Ammanford (using data from Mayr et al. 2015). Thirdly, we examine phonological transfer of /r/ in Mold. Finally, we compare the results of the two studies in light of the research questions and highlight avenues for future research.

Communities and Speakers

The study of monophthongs is based on data from Ammanford (Mayr et al. 2015) and our analysis of /r/ variation is based on data from Mold. Both data sets include speakers of the same age who, at the time of recording, were attending a Welsh-medium or a bilingual school.

Communities

The town of Ammanford (*Rhydaman*, pop.: 5411, Office for National Statistics 2011a) is located in the county of Carmarthenshire (*Sir Gaerfyrddin*). Carmarthenshire is one of the counties where the Welsh language is most widely spoken (Jones 2012: 6), although the vitality of the language in the county has been questioned recently following a −6.4% point change in speaker numbers between 2001 and 2011 (Welsh Language Commissioner 2013). Data from the 2011 census indicate that 43.9% of the county's population are able to speak Welsh (Carmarthenshire County Council 2013). Ammanford itself has seen a

9.9% decrease in the number of Welsh speakers from 61.4% in 2001 to 51.5% in 2011 (Welsh Language Commissioner 2013).

The second data set comprises speakers from the town of Mold (*Yr Wyddgrug*, pop.: 10,058 Office for National Statistics 2011b) in Flintshire (*Sir y Fflint*). Welsh–English language contact has been more sustained in Flintshire than in Ammanford, with English place names being attested in the area prior to 1750 (Aitchison and Carter 1994). 22.7% of the population in Mold report being able to speak Welsh (Office for National Statistics 2011c).

The two areas under investigation differ clearly in the extent to which Welsh is spoken by the wider population. Despite these differences, however, further analysis of individual speakers' language use based on questionnaire data showed that in both areas English is the dominant language of interaction between peer groups with Welsh being used in families (where parents speak Welsh) and amongst smaller friendship groups. It is to the individual speakers that we now turn.

Speakers

The Ammanford data set comprises 30 male speakers. The school attended by the participants is designated as a 'Category 2C' bilingual school, meaning that pupils are able to either follow the curriculum wholly in English (with the exception of Welsh as a second language), or are able to receive the majority of their teaching through the medium of Welsh (see Welsh Assembly Government 2007: 12). Despite attending the same school, pupils on the Welsh-medium pathway typically study for statutory examinations in Welsh as a first language and have either acquired Welsh via parental transmission and/or have attended Welsh-medium primary education. Pupils on the English–medium pathway study Welsh as a second language until the age of 16 and generally have little functional knowledge of Welsh. According to the Estyn (Welsh Schools' Inspectorate) report for the school, around 49% of the school's pupils follow the Welsh-language pathway with the majority of these students coming from Welsh-speaking homes.

This data set contains both Welsh-English bilinguals from different home-language backgrounds (who had followed the Welsh-medium pathway at school) and English monolinguals (who had followed the English–medium pathway). The decision to include monolingual speak-

Table 9.1 Summary of speakers in the Ammanford data set

	Welsh–English bilinguals		English monolinguals	Total
	Welsh at home	English at home		
N (all male speakers)	10	10	10	30

ers was made, firstly, in order to make comparisons between the role of bilingual ability on speech production. Secondly, the inclusion of monolingual speakers for comparison was possible due to the nature of the school (see above) where speakers were all part of the same peer group (being part of a small Sixth-Form unit) but attended different classes. Table 9.1, summarises the Ammanford data set.

As Table 9.1 shows, a distinction was made between (1) those from Welsh-speaking homes (where both parents spoke Welsh), (2) those who had acquired Welsh solely via education and spoke English at home, and (3) those who came from monolingual English backgrounds.[1]

The Mold data set contains 16 male and female Welsh-English bilinguals. Monolingual speakers were not included in this data set as the focus of this analysis is on phonological transfer between the two languages of bilinguals. Furthermore, English monolinguals did not attend the school studied in Mold and were not part of the immediate peer group. Table 9.2 summarises the Mold sample.

The school in Mold is a Welsh-medium secondary school where all subjects apart from English are taught in Welsh to all pupils (Welsh Assembly Government 2007). Similar to the school in Ammanford, the majority of speakers in the school acquire Welsh either via caregiver transmission or solely via immersion education.[2] The school has around

---

[1] Despite having studied towards compulsory examinations in Welsh as a second language at the age of 16 (see above), the English monolinguals reported being unable to hold sustained and unrehearsed conversations and did not have any receptive exposure to Welsh apart from 'incidental Welsh' used in school. This is not surprising in light of recent concerns over the efficacy of Welsh Second Language courses in creating at least semi-proficient speakers in Welsh (Welsh Government 2013).

[2] An intense immersion course is available for pupils who have attended English-medium primary schools and would like to complete secondary education in Welsh. These are not included in the study.

Table 9.2 Summary of speakers in the Mold data set

	Women		Men		Total
	Welsh at home	English at home	Welsh at home	English at home	
N	4	4	4	4	16

549 pupils and 70 students in the Sixth Form. Reflecting the dominance of English in the wider community, 90% of students come from homes where Welsh is not the main language.

All bilingual speakers completed a language attitude and use questionnaire (see Morris 2014 for an analysis of this data in Mold; Mayr et al. 2015). This questionnaire elicited information on participants' use of Welsh in the family (in order to correctly stratify the sample), use of Welsh outside of the classroom when partaking in various activities (e.g. watching television), use of Welsh with friends, and attitudes towards Welsh.

The questionnaire data suggest similarities in the way in which the two communities of speakers use both languages. In both areas, the take-up of Welsh-language media was extremely low and pupils' leisure activities were conducted mostly through English. Despite this, there was a slight tendency for Welsh to be used more frequently by those from Welsh-speaking homes (excluding in the classroom and family language use). This supports findings from previous research, which suggest that Welsh is used more frequently amongst those who have acquired the language via caregiver transmission (Jones 2008). Peer-group interactions are also similar in both areas. English was noted as being the language used exclusively with peers at school and larger friendship groups and use of Welsh does not appear to be normalised unlike in more Welsh home-language communities (see Morris 2014: 82). Some participants from Welsh-speaking families noted that they use Welsh with smaller groups of friends from similar backgrounds outside of school.

Having outlined the communities and speakers under discussion in this chapter, we now turn to the analysis of phonetic variation in the production of monophthongs.

Monophthongs

In this section, we investigate the influence of linguistic background on the production of monophthongs in Welsh–English bilingual speech in Ammanford. We compare these data with English monolingual speakers in order to ascertain whether there are differences between bilingual and monolingual speakers living in the same community.

Procedure and Analysis

Speakers were recorded individually in a quiet room on school premises. For bilingual speakers, individual languages were recorded during separate sessions held on different days. The first author, a Welsh–English bilingual from North East Wales, recorded the sessions. The first recording session was always held in English with no Welsh spoken by the researcher. The sessions held with monolingual speakers were, naturally, held entirely in English.

As we are examining differences between and within Welsh and Welsh English and evaluating the role of home language on differences at the level of phonetics, it was necessary to create a uniform task which controlled for phonetic context and (situational) setting. In other words, we attempted to isolate all other possible influences on variation in order to concentrate on the influence of home language on both languages and cross-linguistic variation.

The target vowels were presented in a hVd frame (each target vowel was presented after [h] and before [d]) in order to control for phonetic context, and primed with two real words which use those vowels (see Mayr and Davies 2011). Speakers read the two real words aloud before moving on to the target word (either a nonce or a real word) which was presented in the carrier phrase *Dweda… 'Say…'*. The carrier phrase was produced three times for each vowel. Table 9.3 shows the target words and the International Phonetic Alphabet (IPA) representation of the vowels for both Southern Welsh[3] and Welsh English. A list of the real-word primes is given in Appendix A.

---

[3] Northern Welsh contains two additional central vowel categories which were represented by the words hûd and hud. These were included in order to ascertain whether speakers produced these vowels (for instance, because of family connections to North Wales). However, hîd and hûd as well

Table 9.3 Target words and corresponding IPA symbols used in the study of monophthongs

Welsh		English		
Target word	IPA	Target word	Standard lexical set	IPA
had	/a/	had	TRAP	/a/
hâd	/ɑ/	hard	PALM	/ɑ/ ~ /ɑ:/
hed	/ɛ/	head	DRESS	/ɛ/
hêd	/e/	hared	SQUARE	/ɛ:/
hid/hud	/ɪ/	hid	KIT	/ɪ/
hîd/hûd	/i/	heed	FLEECE	/i:/
hod	/ɔ/	hod	LOT	/ɒ/ ~ /ɔ/
hôd	/o/	hoard	THOUGHT	/o:/
hwd	/ʊ/	hood	FOOT	/ʊ/
hŵd	/u/	who'd	GOOSE	/u:/
hyd	/ə/	hud	STRUT	/ʌ/ ~ /ə/
		herd	NURSE	/ə:/ ~ /œ:/

A total of 39 tokens were collected in Welsh and 36 tokens in English per participant which yielded 767 Welsh tokens (39 × 20 participants with 13 tokens excluded due to poor quality) and 1073 English tokens (36 × 30 participants with seven tokens excluded due to poor quality).

Individual vowels were segmented using Praat (Boersma and Weenink 2015). The $F1$ and $F2$ values were taken from the midpoint of each vowel using Praat's formant tracker based on a frequency maximum of 5500 Hz with a dynamic range of 35 dB. Any incorrect automatic measurements as a result of mistracking were hand-corrected. Durational data were collected using an automatic script. The duration of eight tokens per speaker was manually checked and no errors were found. Raw Hertz values were converted into Bark (Traunmüller 1990) to correspond to an auditory measure of frequency.

Mixed-effects modelling using the lme4 package in R (Bates et al. 2015; R Core Team 2015) was conducted in order to ascertain whether there is a statistically significant relationship between linguistic background and $F1$ (Bark), $F2$ (Bark), and duration.

---

as hid and hud were homophonous for all participants, and consistently produced as /i:/ and /ɪ/, respectively. As a result, the two sets of categories were merged.

Results

Three sets of analyses were carried out. In what follows, we first present a comparison of the monolingual and bilingual participants' English vowel productions. Subsequently, the bilingual participants' realisations of the Welsh vowels will be discussed. The purpose of these analyses was to determine the effects of individual linguistic experience on vowel production. Finally, in order to determine the extent of phonetic overlap between English and Welsh vowels, the results of a cross-linguistic comparative analysis will be presented.

English Vowels

Figure 9.1 presents the mean $F1$ and $F2$ values (in Bark), and Fig. 9.2 the durations of the English vowels produced by the Welsh home-language

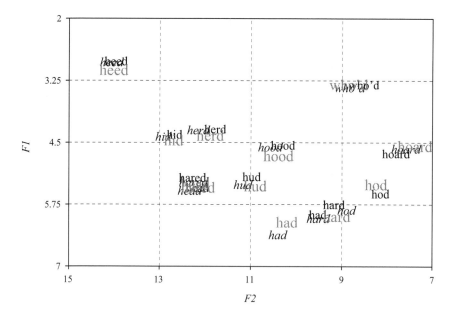

Fig. 9.1 $F1$–$F2$ plot (Bark) of the English vowels produced by the Welsh home-language bilinguals (black), the English home-language bilinguals (italics), and the English monolinguals (grey)

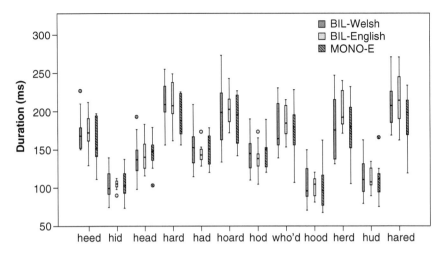

Fig. 9.2 Boxplot of the duration (in ms) of the English vowels produced by the Welsh–English bilinguals from Welsh-speaking homes, the Welsh–English bilinguals from English-speaking homes, and the English monolinguals

bilinguals, the English home-language bilinguals, and the English monolinguals.

Mixed-effects models were run separately for the three dependent variables of $F1$ (Bark), $F2$ (Bark), and duration. In each model, the aim was to ascertain whether the vowel categories were produced differently (as would be expected) and whether the linguistic background of the speaker influenced variation. *English vowel* and *language group* were entered as fixed factors (including interaction) and *speaker* as a random factor with random intercepts for *speaker* and random slopes for *English vowel* (see Mayr et al. 2015: 10 for further details).

Table 9.4, below, shows the results of the three models. As expected, *English vowel* is significant on the three dependent variables meaning that all vowels are produced with different acoustic values. The table shows that *language group* is not a significant predictor and therefore speakers from different linguistic backgrounds do not differ in how they produce vowels in English.

Table 9.4 Results of the mixed-effects models for English *F*1 (Bark), *F*2 (Bark), and duration (ms)

Model		β	SE	t	p
English *F*1	Intercept	4.83	0.05	104.64	<0.001
(Bark)	English vowel	0.26	0.01	31.31	<0.001
	Language group	−0.04	0.06	−0.72	0.479
	English vowel × Language group	0.00	0.01	0.09	0.932
English *F*2	Intercept	10.71	0.05	202.81	<0.001
(Bark)	English vowel	0.53	0.01	44.80	<0.001
	Language group	−0.02	0.06	−0.36	0.720
	English vowel × Language group	−0.00	0.01	0.01	0.990
English	Intercept	157.16	4.05	38.83	<0.001
duration (ms)	English vowel	10.28	0.44	23.33	<0.001
	Language group	3.72	4.96	0.75	0.459
	English vowel × Language group	0.81	0.54	1.50	0.146

Welsh Vowels

Figure 9.3 presents the mean *F*1 and *F*2 values (in Bark), and Fig. 9.4 the duration of the Welsh vowels produced by the Welsh home-language bilinguals and the English home-language bilinguals.

The statistical modelling applied to this subset mirrors that which was applied to English data (see above). The results are displayed in Table 9.5. As expected, there were main effects of *Welsh vowel* on the three dependent variables meaning that the vowels are produced differently. Similar to the English subset, *language group* was not a significant predictor which suggests that the linguistic background of Welsh–English bilinguals does not affect how they produce monophthongs in Welsh.

Cross-linguistic Comparison

In order to establish the extent to which the monophthongs in both languages are phonetically identical, we followed previous studies in conducting a Linear Discriminant Analysis (e.g. Williams and Escudero 2014). In the absence of monolingual Welsh speakers (as normally comparisons

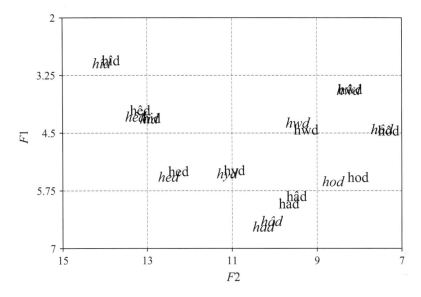

Fig. 9.3 *F1–F2* plot (in Bark) of the Welsh vowels realised by the Welsh home-language bilinguals (black) and the English home-language bilinguals (grey)

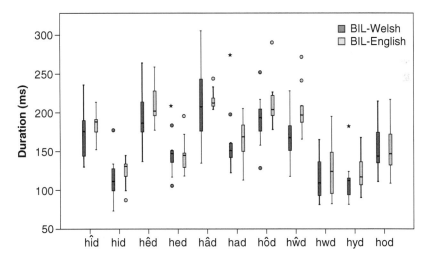

Fig. 9.4 Boxplot of the duration (in ms) of the Welsh vowels produced by the Welsh–English bilinguals from Welsh-speaking homes and the Welsh–English bilinguals from English-speaking homes

Table 9.5 Results of the mixed-effects models for Welsh *F*1 (Bark), *F*2 (Bark), and duration (ms)

Model		β	SE	*t*	*p*
Welsh *F*1 (Bark)	Intercept	4.75	0.06	75.55	<0.001
	Welsh vowel	0.32	0.01	26.33	<0.001
	Language group	0.14	0.13	1.08	0.295
	Welsh vowel × Language group	0.04	0.02	1.52	0.145
Welsh *F*2 (Bark)	Intercept	10.60	0.08	128.32	<0.001
	Welsh vowel	0.68	0.02	36.48	<0.001
	Language group	0.25	0.17	1.49	0.155
	Welsh vowel × Language group	0.02	0.04	−0.46	0.651
Welsh duration (ms)	Intercept	163.31	5.39	30.29	<0.001
	Welsh vowel	10.48	0.55	19.09	<0.001
	Language group	9.60	10.78	0.89	0.385
	Welsh vowel × Language group	1.17	1.10	1.06	0.301

would involve groups of monolingual speakers, cf. Meyerhoff 2009), and on the basis of the language use data, it was decided to compare the Welsh data from the bilinguals from Welsh-speaking homes with the data from English monolinguals. In short, the analysis shows the number of times a Welsh monophthong produced by the Welsh home-language bilinguals could be categorised as an English monophthong produced by the monolingual speakers based on *F*1 (Bark), *F*2 (Bark), and durational values and this is presented as a percentage. Table 9.6 shows the percentage classification of Welsh vowel categories in terms of English vowel categories.

The results in bold in Table 9.6 show the instances where over 50% of the vowels produced could be classified within a single phonological category. In the case of the *hid–hid*, *hîd–heed*, and *hôd–hoard* vowel pairs, there was a cross-linguistic match in over 90% of cases which suggests near-total phonetic convergence. A number of other vowel pairs were cross-linguistically matched in 60–80% of cases. Interestingly, the Welsh target *hêd* was matched with the English target *herd* in 70% of cases. This is somewhat surprising, considering different vowels would be expected (see Table 9.3), but does provide evidence for some phonetic overlap. Conversely, the had–had vowel pair was only cross-linguistically matched in 50% of instances.

Table 9.6 Percentage classification of Welsh vowel categories (Welsh–English bilinguals from Welsh-speaking homes) in terms of English vowel categories (English monolinguals)

	had	hâd	hed	hêd	hid	hîd	hod	Hôd	hwd	hŵd	hyd
had	**50**	10	0	0	0	0	0	0	10	0	0
hard	30	**80**	0	0	0	0	20	10	0	0	0
hared	0	0	20	10	0	0	0	0	0	0	10
head	0	0	**70**	0	10	0	0	0	0	0	0
heed	0	0	0	10	0	**100**	0	0	0	0	0
herd	0	0	10	**70**	0	0	0	0	0	0	0
hid	0	0	0	10	**90**	0	0	0	0	0	0
hoard	0	0	0	0	0	0	20	**90**	0	20	0
hod	10	10	0	0	0	0	**60**	0	20	0	0
hood	0	0	0	0	0	0	0	0	**60**	0	20
hud	10	0	0	0	0	0	0	0	0	0	**70**
who'd	0	0	0	0	0	0	0	0	10	**80**	0
Total	100	100	100	100	100	100	100	100	100	100	100

Modal classifications are in bold

On the basis of the Linear Discriminant Analysis, we were able to pair vowels from English and Welsh in order to compare their phonetic differences in more detail using mixed-effects modelling. The only category which was not classified as closest to any other category was English *hared*. The remaining vowel pairs are *hid–hid*, *hîd–heed*, *hod–hod*, *hôd–hoard*, *had–had*, *had–hâd*, *hed–head*, *hêd–herd*, *hwd–hood*, *hŵd–who'd*, and *hyd–hud*. Figure 9.5 shows the mean *F*1–*F*2 values in Bark for these vowels and Fig. 9.6 shows the average duration.

To determine cross-linguistic differences in vowel realisation, three further mixed-effects models were run separately for *F*1 (Bark), *F*2 (Bark), and the duration on the English tokens produced by English monolinguals and the Welsh tokens produced by the Welsh home-language bilinguals. The fixed factors (with interaction among them) were *vowel pair* and *language group* and *speaker* was included in the model as a random factor.

The results are depicted in Table 9.7. They reveal main effects of vowel pair on the three measures. Interestingly, there were no significant main effects or interactions involving *language group* on almost all measures, suggesting a high degree of phonetic overlap between English and Welsh vowels. However, there was a significant *vowel pair × language group* interaction on *F*2 (Bark), which suggests that the two groups produced some vowels differently on this measure.

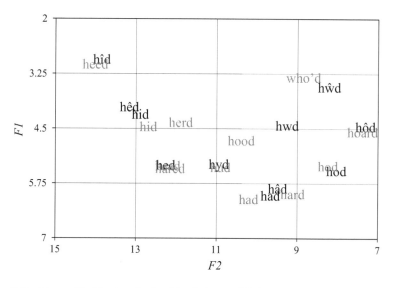

Fig. 9.5 Mean *F1–F2* plot (in Bark) of the Welsh home-language bilinguals' productions of the Welsh vowels (black) and the English monolinguals' productions of the English vowels (grey)

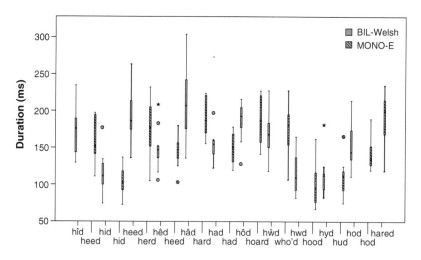

Fig. 9.6 Boxplot of the duration (in ms) of the Welsh vowels produced by the Welsh–English bilinguals from Welsh-speaking homes and the English vowels produced by the English monolinguals

Table 9.7 Results of the mixed-effects models for vowel pair *F*1 (Bark), *F*2 (Bark), and duration (ms)

Model		β	SE	*t*	*p*
Mixed *F*1 (Bark)	Intercept	4.74	0.06	85.99	<0.001
	Vowel pair	0.29	0.01	55.34	<0.001
	Language group	−0.−12	0.11	−1.05	0.308
	Vowel pair × Language group	−0.01	0.01	1.30	0.195
Mixed *F*2 (Bark)	Intercept	10.48	0.05	190.86	<0.001
	Vowel pair	0.64	0.01	80.10	<0.001
	Language group	0.09	0.11	0.82	0.424
	Vowel pair × Language group	−0.06	0.02	−3.59	<0.001
Mixed duration (ms)	Intercept	153.44	6.05	25.37	<0.001
	Vowel pair	9.64	0.30	32.55	<0.001
	Language group	−10.22	12.09	0.85	0.409
	Vowel pair × Language group	−0.32	0.59	0.54	0.592

Table 9.8 Significant predictor of language group in vowel pair *F*2 (Bark) mixed-effects models

Model		β	SE	*t*	*p*
hêd–herd *F*2 (Bark)	Intercept	12.52	0.6	215.60	<0.001
	Language group	−1.28	0.12	−11.00	<0.001
hwd–hood *F*2 (Bark)	Intercept	9.81	0.20	48.08	<0.001
	Language group	1.14	0.41	2.80	0.012

To examine the *vowel pair × language group* interaction on *F*2 (Bark), we ran separate regression models for each *vowel pair* with *language group* as a fixed factor and *speaker* as a random factor. Table 9.8 shows the results of these models.

Of the 11 vowel pairs, *language group* proved to be a significant predictor of *F*2 (Bark) only for *hêd–herd* and *hwd–hood*. As shown in Table 9.8, the *F*2 of *herd* of is on average 1.28 Bark lower than that of *hêd*, and the *F*2 of *hood* is on average 1.14 Bark higher than that of *hwd*.

Summary

To summarise, the analysis of the production of English and Welsh monophthongs showed no differences in $F2$–$F1$ and duration for speakers from differing language backgrounds. Cross-linguistically, we found a high degree of phonetic overlap between the vowel systems of the two languages. However, no cross-linguistic match was found for English *hared*, and significant differences were found not only between $F1$ and $F2$ for the *hêd–herd* pair (where different phonological vowel categories are expected) but also, more surprisingly, between $F2$ values for the *hwd–hood* vowel pair.

/r/ in Prevocalic and Intervocalic Positions

This section presents the results of the analysis of /r/ in prevocalic and intervocalic positions in Mold. Here, we are interested in the appearance of variants traditionally associated with Welsh in English and vice versa, and the extent to which this is influenced by home language.

In word-initial prevocalic and word-medial intervocalic positions, the voiced alveolar trill [r] is reported as being the most commonly produced variant of /r/ in Welsh. The voiced alveolar tap [ɾ] is often used in word-medial intervocalic position in the North West (e.g. Jones 1984: 49–50). The approximant is noted as being a dialectal feature for eastern areas of Powys (an area in Mid-Wales which borders England; Davies 1971).

The trilled and tapped variants of /r/ are cited as being a feature of English for Welsh–English bilinguals, and in particular in the speech of those living in the North West. It is otherwise assumed that it is the approximant which tends to occur in Welsh–English (Penhallurick 1991: 132).

There have been no quantitative studies which examine the phonological transfer of /r/ in bilinguals' speech and which examine the role of home language on this variation. The Mold data set comprises Welsh and English speech from bilinguals obtained via sociolinguistic interview and wordlist (e.g. Labov 1972). This allows us to examine the extent to which there are differences in the rate of transfer between contextual styles.

The Mold data set also allows us to examine the influence of home language in light of this chapter's aims. In order to do this, however, it is necessary to consider the influence of other factors which may be significant predictors of variation. The remainder of the section expands on this further and provides more information on data collection and analysis. We then present the results of the English and Welsh data.

Procedure and Analysis

Similar to the Ammanford data set, speakers were recorded individually with separate sessions for each language on different days. The sessions also took place with the first author.

The tokens included in the analysis of /r/ in prevocalic and intervocalic positions are confined to word-medial intervocalic contexts (V_V) and word-initial tokens which follow a pause (#_V). All instances of /r/ in these positions after the initial ten minutes of each interview were transcribed in ELAN (Sloetjes and Wittenburg 2008). The extraction of tokens was in temporal order, but only the first three instances of the same word were coded. This yielded a total number of 181 interview tokens and 272 wordlist tokens (*n* = 453) in Welsh. In English, 157 interview tokens and 384 wordlist tokens were analysed in English (*n* = 541).

Tokens were analysed auditorily and checked acoustically in Praat (following Chand 2010). Each token was categorised as approximant, tap, trill, uvular, or zero realisation. The voiced uvular trill [ʀ] and voiced uvular fricative [ʁ] have been attested in the town of Bala in North Wales (Jones 1984: 50) and were found in the repertoire of one speaker whose grandfather came from the area.

Linear mixed-effects models were fitted to predict the realisation of the alveolar approximant in both languages. *Speaker* and *word* were included as random factors. The independent variables included in the modelling were *language group*, *speaker sex*, *speech context* (interview or wordlist), *syllable stress*, and *phonological context*. Non-significant factors were removed from the models until the best-fitting model was found (Nance 2014: 5; Baayen 2008: 205).

Results

Separate analyses were conducted on the English and Welsh data. Due to the large differences in variation between the two languages, no cross-linguistic statistical analyses were conducted.

English

Of instances of /r/, 99.4% were produced as the alveolar approximant [ɹ] (*n* = 538) and the remaining 0.6% of instances (*n* = 3) were zero realisations. This shows that this variant is near-categorical regardless of speaker background and that no transfer occurs from Welsh to English in Mold Welsh regardless of the home language of the speaker.

Welsh

More variability was found in the Welsh data. Surprisingly, 79.7% of tokens contained the alveolar approximant [ɹ] (*n* = 361) despite the voiced alveolar trill [r] being expected. Table 9.9 shows the percentage and number of tokens for each variant:

Table 9.9 Percentage and number of /r/ variants in Mold Welsh

Variant	%	N
Approximant	79.7	361
Trill	3.1	14
Tap	11.9	54
Uvular	4.9	22
Zero	0.4	2
Total		453

The results of the statistical model (shown in Table 9.10) indicate that not only is [ɹ] present in the Welsh speech of Welsh–English bilinguals in Mold but that, interestingly, it is subject to extra-linguistic constraints.

Language group is the strongest predictor of [ɹ] production in this data set but *speech context* is also significant, with [ɹ] being more likely in informal speech style. To exemplify this further, Fig. 9.7 shows the pro-

Table 9.10 Regression model predicting the realisation of the voiced alveolar approximant in Mold Welsh with *word* and *speaker* as random factors

	β	SE	t	p
Intercept	−3.63	0.89	−4.0	<0.001
Language group (Welsh home language)	2.28	0.93	2.45	0.01
Context (wordlist)	1.04	0.41	2.53	0.01
Syllable stress (unstressed)	0.34	0.45	0.72	0.47
Sex (males)	−0.98	0.93	−1.06	0.30

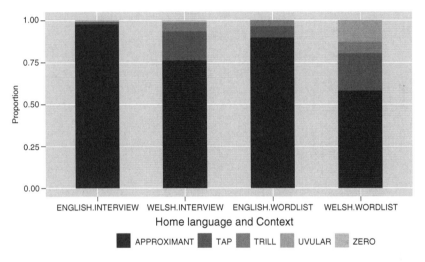

Fig. 9.7 Proportion of /r/ variants produced in the Welsh speech of Welsh–English bilinguals in Mold by context (wordlist/interview) and home language (Welsh/English)

portion of variants in the Welsh data set stratified by speakers' home language and context.

An analysis of the proportions for each language group and context suggests that [ɹ] is the most common variant in the repertoires of these speakers despite not being expected in Welsh. In the speech of those from Welsh-speaking homes, it appears in 76% (*n* = 57) of interview tokens and 58.1% (*n* = 79) of wordlist tokens. In the speech of those from English-speaking homes, it appears in 97.2% (*n* = 103) of interview tokens and 89.7% (*n* = 122) of wordlist tokens.

Summary

The data from Mold have shown that the transfer of /r/ variants appears to be unidirectional and from English to Welsh. In English, [ɹ] is produced universally by speakers regardless of home language. In Welsh, and contrary to previous claims, [ɹ] is widespread and more likely to appear in the speech of those from English-speaking homes and in informal contexts.

Discussion and Conclusions

The chapter sought to compare cross-linguistic phonetic interactions and phonological transfer in the speech of Welsh–English bilingual speech. Specifically, we aimed to ascertain to which linguistic background influenced variation in the production of monophthongs in Ammanford and /r/ in Mold. In this section, we discuss the results of these studies in light of the research questions and highlight avenues for future research.

1. Is there evidence for cross-linguistic phonetic interaction in the production of monophthongs and phonological transfer in the production of /r/ in Welsh–English bilingual speech?

We found that 9 out of 11 cross-linguistic vowel pairs were produced identically in the two languages in terms of $F1$ (Bark), $F2$ (Bark), and duration. This provides evidence for stable cross-linguistic phonetic similarities rather than the dynamic influence of speakers' languages on each other. This is surprising in light of previous studies of bilinguals which consider different ways in which speakers acquire two languages and find significant differences. The fact that there were fine-grained differences, however, suggests that there may be phonetic divergence rather than convergence in the realisation of phonologically similar features. This does not appear to affect the whole vowel system but rather the realisation of particular vowels. In particular, the differences between *hwd–hood* vowel pairs merit further investigation. In the case of *hwd–hood*, it is worth noting that back-vowel fronting has been noted in other varieties of English (e.g. Cox and Palethorpe 2001) and it may be possible that more recent changes affecting English are causing divergence between previously identical categories. Further work on older speakers and in different communities would help us to substantiate this claim further.

Evidence was found which suggests phonological transfer in Welsh–English bilingual speech in Mold. Interestingly, this transfer was largely unidirectional and occurred in the Welsh of speakers rather than in their English. The alveolar approximant is a common feature in Mold Welsh speech. The widespread production of the alveolar approximant in Welsh may be seen as surprising as it has been unreported in previous work. Data from older speakers will allow us to ascertain whether the alveolar approximant is increasing in Welsh, leading to convergence with English. Variation in the production of /r/ may be a relatively stable situation (and may indeed have been so for many generations) or undergoing linguistic-internal or contact-induced change.

2. To what extent does linguistic background influence variation with regards to these features?

Linguistic background was not found to influence variation in the realisation of monophthongs. It was significant, however, in the study of /r/ variation in Mold. The data suggest that both home language and style influence variation in Welsh only and that in the trill and tap are more frequent in more formal speech and in the bilingual repertoire of those from Welsh-speaking homes.

The style-shifting towards typically Welsh variants in more careful speech is, perhaps, somewhat predictable in the case of those from English-speaking homes. In cases of second language acquisition, Major (2004: 170) notes that 'the more formal the style, the less L1 transfer and the greater the frequency of target-like forms'. It could be stated, then, that those from English-speaking homes tend to transfer less from English in more formal speech. Having said this, the fact that those from Welsh-speaking homes exhibit the same linguistic behaviour shows that /r/ variation is not confined to those who have acquired Welsh via immersion education.

3. How can the differences the two features be explained in light of community dynamics, long-term language contact, and synchronic Welsh–English bilingualism?

The dynamics of both bilingualism in the wider community and the peer-group dynamics in the bilingual school could be an explanatory factor in the case of the monophthongs. There is extensive evidence from sociolinguistic research which shows that the speech patterns of adolescents are crucially affected by the peer group to which they belong (e.g. Eckert 1988). The town of Ammanford has a Welsh-speaking population of 51.5% (see Communities and Speakers) which means that we can expect a large degree of synchronic contact between the two languages. Similarly, the data on language use suggest that peer groups are not defined by the ability to speak Welsh (as shown in more Welsh-dominant areas, see Morris 2013, 2014) and that pupils from different linguistic backgrounds are part of the same peer groups where English is predominantly used.

The situation is largely similar in Mold although a smaller proportion of the wider population are able to speak Welsh. Here, the peer groups were also not defined by linguistic background, yet this is a significant influence on /r/ variation in Welsh. In this case, we can attribute these differences to differences in the age of acquisition of Welsh (with those from English-speaking homes being *more likely* to produce the approximant) which is also linked to the current use of Welsh. It is apparent from this study and previous work (e.g. Jones 2008; Morris 2014) that differentiating between age of acquisition and current levels of language use is difficult in the Welsh context and the term 'linguistic background' must consider both.

We argue that the similarities between the vowel systems of the two languages and the lack of transfer from Welsh to English in Mold can both be explained in light of history of language contact and shift in the specific communities despite being features which operate independently. It appears that the similarities in the vowel systems may be due to historical contact-induced change which inhibits the cross-linguistic influence which might be expected in the speech of bilinguals (as most categories are identical in both languages). The lack of transfer effects from Welsh to English in the Mold data is also most likely attributable to the history of contact between the two languages in North East Wales, and the dominance of English monolingualism rather than Welsh–English bilingualism. This, we would argue, inhibits transfer from the minority to the majority language in this context regardless of speakers' linguistic backgrounds. It remains to be seen whether this is the case in more Welsh-dominant areas.

The comparison presented in this chapter could suggest that those features which are phonologically similar show little phonetic variation and that phonological transfer can be influenced by extra-linguistic factors. This comparison would be short-sighted, however, as two features were under discussion. More work is needed on more variables and more speech communities across Wales in order to ascertain how both synchronic bilingualism and long-term contact influence variation. In the following section, we make suggestions about how this work could proceed.

Future Work

Looking to future work in the Welsh context, we argue that both experimental and traditional quantitative sociolinguistic approaches to phonetic and phonological variation are needed to address different research questions. The analysis of fine-grained phonetic variation in the production of monophthongs was best served with a tightly controlled experimental approach which allowed us to isolate both the target segments and the extra-linguistic factor (that is to say, linguistic background) under examination in two languages. This can be replicated for other features where the analyst needs to control for phonetic environments between the two languages as far as possible (e.g. Mennen et al. 2015).

The nature of phonological transfer, examined in the Mold study, and phonological variation in general means that data can be elicited and compared more easily from semi-naturalistic or naturalistic speech. Further comparisons with more Welsh home-language communities are needed, as the dynamics of language use may be different. Previous research has shown that home language affects language use in both

English-dominant and Welsh-dominant areas (Musk 2006). Whereas English was the main language of peer interaction in both communities in this chapter, Morris (2014) found that peer groups were largely differentiated by language in a Welsh-dominant community in North West Wales. This may mean that, in some communities at least, the differences between peer groups may be more pronounced which might lead to interesting patterns of variation based on more ethnographic approaches (e.g. Eckert 1988).

Such approaches need not be confined to schools and young speakers, and it is clear that more work on sound change and more comprehensive studies of linguistic background (including those from mixed-language homes and those who have acquired Welsh as a second language) are needed. Indeed, more community-based approaches appear, in our opinion, to be key in analysing variation in the Welsh–English bilingual context where communities are linguistically diverse and the way in which a speaker has acquired Welsh and English may be inherently linked with current language use, language attitudes, and identity.

Appendix

Table 9.11 List of real-word primes used in the study of monophthongs (Ammanford)

Welsh		English	
Target	Real-word primes	Target	Real-word primes
had	wastad, dirnad	had	mad, bad
hâd	boddhad, rhad	hard	lard, starred
hed	ledled, yfed	head	bed, dead
hêd	cred, lled	hared	there, squared
hid	grid, nid	hid	bid, kid
hîd	prid, brîd	heed	deed, feed
hud	astud, barcud	hod	rod, cod
hûd	drud, crud	hoard	bored, lord
hod	parod, hynod	hood	should, could
hôd	bod, dod	who'd	food, mood
hwd	mwgwd, mwd	hud	mud, bud
hŵd	brwd, cnwd	herd	nerd, curd
hyd	hydref, hyd		

References

Aitchison, John, and Harold Carter. 1994. *A geography of the Welsh language 1961–1991*. Cardiff: University of Wales Press.

Alam, Farhana, and Jane Stuart-Smith. 2011. Identity and ethnicity in /t/ in Glasgow-Pakistani high-school girls. *Proceedings of the XVII International Congress of Phonetic Sciences*, 216–219.

Baayen, R. Harald. 2008. *Analyzing linguistic data: A practical introduction to statistics*. Cambridge: Cambridge University Press.

Bates, Douglas, Martin Maechler, Ben Bolker, and Steve Walker. 2015. Fitting linear mixed-effects models using lme4. *Journal of Statistical Software* 67(1): 1–48.

Boersma, Paul and David Weenink. 2015. *Praat: Doing phonetics by computer* (Version 5.4.09). http://www.praat.org/. Accessed 1 June 2015.

Carmarthenshire County Council. 2013. Carmarthenshire county profile (November 2013). http://www.carmarthenshire.gov.uk/English/council/Documents/county%20profile.pdf. Accessed 30 April 2014.

Chand, Vineeta. 2010. Postvocalic (r) in urban Indian English. *English World-wide* 31(1): 1–39.

Core Team, R. 2015. *R: A language and environment for statistical computing*. Vienna: R Foundation for Statistical Computing.

Cox, Felicity, and Sallyanne Palethorpe. 2001. The changing face of Australian English vowels. In *English in Australia*, Varieties of English around the world G26, ed. David Blair, and Peter Collins, 17–44. Amsterdam: John Benjamins.

Davies, Lyn. 1971. Linguistic interference in East Montgomeryshire. *The Montgomeryshire Collections* 62: 183–194.

Eckert, Penelope. 1988. Adolescent social structure and the spread of linguistic change. *Language in Society* 17(2): 183–207.

Elordieta, Gorka, and Nagore Calleja. 2005. Microvariation in accentual alignment in Basque Spanish. *Language and Speech* 48(4): 397–439.

Flege, James Emil. 1995. Second-language speech learning: Theory, findings and problems. In *Speech perception and linguistic experience*, ed. Winifred Strange, 233–277. Timonium: York Press.

Fought, Carmen. 1999. A majority sound change in a minority community: /u/-fronting in Chicano English. *Journal of Sociolinguistics* 3(1): 5–23.

Fowler, Carol A., Valery Sramko, David J. Ostry, Sarah A. Rowland, and Pierre Hallé. 2008. Cross-language phonetic influences on the speech of French-English bilinguals. *Journal of Phonetics* 36: 649–663.

Gathercole, Virginia, and Enlli Môn Thomas. 2009. Bilingual first–language development: Dominant language takeover, threatened minority language take–up. *Bilingualism: Language and Cognition* 12(2): 213–237.

Grosjean, François. 2001. The bilingual's language modes. In *One mind, two languages: Bilingual language processing*, ed. Janet Nicol, 1–22. Oxford: Blackwell.

Guion, Susan G., James Emil Flege, and Jonathan D. Loftin. 2000. The effect of L1 use on pronunciation in Quichua–Spanish bilinguals. *Journal of Phonetics* 28: 27–42.

Holmes, Janet. 1996. Losing voice: Is final /z/ devoicing a feature of Maori English? *World Englishes* 15(2): 193–205.

Jones, Glyn E. 1984. The distinctive vowels and consonants of Welsh. In *Welsh Phonology*, ed. Martin J. Ball, and Glyn E. Jones, 40–65. Cardiff: Cardiff University Press.

Jones, Hywel M. 2008. The changing social context of Welsh: A review of statistical trends. *International journal of bilingual education and bilingualism* 11(5): 541–557.

———. 2012. *A statistical overview of the Welsh language*. Cardiff: Welsh Language Board. http://www.byig–wlb.org.uk/English/publications/Publications/A%20statistical%20overview%20of%20the%20Welsh%20languagef2.pdf. Accessed 17 Feb 2012.

Kehoe, Margaret M., Conxita Lleó, and Martin Rakow. 2004. Voice onset time in bilingual German-Spanish children. *Bilingualism: Language and Cognition* 7: 71–88.

Labov, William. 1972. *Sociolinguistic patterns*. Oxford: Blackwell.

Major, Roy C. 2004. Gender and stylistic variation in second language phonology. *Language Variation and Change* 16: 169–188.

Mayr, Robert, and Hannah Davies. 2011. A cross-dialectal acoustic study of the monophthongs and diphthongs of Welsh. *Journal of the International Phonetic Association* 41: 1–25.

Mayr, Robert, Danna Jones, and Ineke Mennen. 2014. Speech learning in bilinguals: Consonant cluster acquisition. In *Advances in the study of Bilingualism*, ed. Enlli Môn Thomas, and Ineke Mennen, 3–24. Bristol: Multilingual Matters.

Mayr, Robert, Gwennan Howells, and Rhonwen Lewis. 2015a. Asymmetries in phonological development: The case of word-final cluster acquisition in Welsh–English bilingual children. *Journal of Child Language* 42: 146–179.

Mayr, Robert, Jonathan Morris, Ineke Mennen and Daniel Williams. 2015b. Disentangling the effects of long-term language contact and individual bilingualism: The case of monophthongs in Welsh and English. *International*

Journal of Bilingualism. doi: 10.1177/1367006915614921.First published online 26 November 2015.

Mendoza-Denton, Norma. 1996. "Muy Macha": Gender and ideology in gang girls' discourse about makeup. *Ethnos* 61(1–2): 47–63.

Mennen, Ineke. 2004. Bi-directional interference in the intonation of Dutch speakers of Greek. *Journal of Phonetics* 32: 543–563.

Mennen, Ineke, Robert Mayr, and Jonathan Morris. 2015. Influences of language contact and linguistic experience on the production of lexical stress in Welsh and Welsh English. *Proceedings of the 18th International Congress of Phonetic Sciences (ICPhS 2015),* 10–14 August 2015, Glasgow.

Meyerhoff, Miriam. 2009. Replication, transfer and calquing: Using variation as a tool in the study of language contact. *Language Variation and Change* 21: 297–317.

Morris, Jonathan. 2013. Sociolinguistic variation and regional minority language bilingualism: An investigation of Welsh–English bilinguals in North Wales. Ph.D. dissertation, University of Manchester.

———. 2014. The influence of social factors on minority language engagement amongst young people: An investigation of Welsh–English bilinguals in North Wales. *International Journal of the Sociology of Language* 230: 65–89.

Munro, Siân, Martin J. Ball, Nicole Müller, Martin Duckworth, and Fiona Lyddy. 2005. Phonological acquisition in Welsh–English bilingual children. *Journal of Multilingual Communication Disorders* 3(1): 24–49.

Musk, Nigel. 2006. *Performing Bilingualism in Wales with the spotlight on Welsh.* In *A study of the language practices of young people in Bilingual education (=Studies in Language and Culture 8).* Linköping: Linköpings universitet.

Nance, Claire. 2014. Phonetic variation in Scottish Gaelic laterals. *Journal of Phonetics* 47: 1–17.

———. 2015. Intonational variation and change in Scottish Gaelic. *Lingua* 160: 1–19.

Office for National Statistics. 2011a. Area: Ammanford. http://www.neighbourhood.statistics.gov.uk/dissemination/LeadKeyFigures.do?a=7andb=11119995andc=Ammanfordandd=16ande=62andg=6491975andi=1001x1003x1032x1004andm=0andr=1ands=1431249447752andenc=1andnsjs=trueandnsck=falseandnssvg=falseandnswid=1280. Accessed 18 May 2016.

———. 2011b. Area: Mold. http://neighbourhood.statistics.gov.uk/dissemination/LeadTableView.do?a=3andb=800990andc=moldandd=16ande=15andg=414668andi=1001x1003x1004andm=0andr=1ands=1222362554421andenc=1anddsFamilyId=779. Accessed 18 May 2016.

————. 2011c. Welsh Language Skills, 2011 (QS206WA). http://www.neighbourhood.statistics.gov.uk/dissemination/LeadTableView.do?a=5andb=1112
6634andc=Moldandd=16ande=61andg=6490340andi=1001x1003x1032x1
004andm=0andr=1ands=1463587856969andenc=1anddsFamilyId=2499.
Accessed 18 May 2016.

Paradis, Johanne. 2001. Do bilingual two-year-olds have separate phonological systems? *International Journal of Bilingualism* 5: 19–38.

Penhallurick, Robert. 1991. *The Anglo–Welsh dialects of North Wales: A survey of conservative rural spoken English in the counties of Gwynedd and Clwyd.* Frankfurt am Main: Lang.

Piske, Thorsten, Ian R.A. MacKay, and James E. Flege. 2001. Factors affecting degree of foreign accent in an L2: A review. *Journal of Phonetics* 29: 191–215.

Rhys, Mirain, and Enlli Môn Thomas. 2013. Bilingual Welsh–English children's acquisition of vocabulary and reading: Implications for bilingual education. *International Journal of Bilingual Education and Bilingualism* 16(6): 633–656.

Sharma, Devyani, and Lavanya Sankaran. 2011. Cognitive and social forces in dialect shift: Gradual change in London Asian speech. *Language Variation and Change* 23(3): 399–428.

Silva-Corvalán, Carmen. 2000. *Language contact and change.* Oxford: Clarendon Press.

Simon, Ellen. 2010. Phonological transfer of voicing and devoicing rules: Evidence from L1 Dutch and L2 English conversational speech. *Language Sciences* 32: 63–86.

Simonet, Miquel. 2010. Dark and clear laterals in Catalan and Spanish: Interaction of phonetic categories in early bilinguals. *Journal of Phonetics* 38: 663–678.

Sloetjes, Han and Peter Wittenburg. 2008. Annotation by category – ELAN and ISO DCR. *Proceedings of the 6th International Conference on Language Resources and Evaluation (LREC 2008).* http://tla.mpi.nl/tools/tla-tools/elan/

Thomason, Sarah G. 2001. *Language contact: An introduction.* Edinburgh: Edinburgh University Press.

Thomason, Sarah G., and Terrence Kaufman. 1988. *Language contact, creolization, and genetic linguistics.* Berkeley/Los Angeles/London: University of California Press.

Traunmüller, Hartmut. 1990. Analytical expressions for the tonotopic sensory scale. *Journal of the Acoustical Society of America* 88: 97–100.

Treffers-Daller, Jeanine, and Raymond Mougeon. 2005. The role of transfer in language variation and change: Evidence from contact varieties of French. *Bilingualism: Language and cognition* 8(2): 93–98.

Wells, John C. 1982. *Accents of English 2: The British Isles*. Cambridge: Cambridge University Press.

Welsh Assembly Government. 2007. *Defining schools according to Welsh-medium provision (Information document number 023/2007)*. Cardiff: Welsh Assembly Government.

Welsh Government. 2013. *One language for all: Review of Welsh second language at Key Stages 3 and 4*. http://wales.gov.uk/docs/dcells/publications/130926-review-of-welsh-second-lan-en.pdf. Accessed 16 Jan 2014.

Welsh Language Commissioner. 2013. 2011 Census: Results and changes since 2001. http://www.comisiynyddygymraeg.org/English/Assistance/Dataand statisitcs/Pages/2012Censusresultsandchangessince2001.aspx. Accessed 30 April 2014.

Williams, Daniel, and Paola Escudero. 2014. Influences of listeners' native and other dialects on cross-language vowel perception. *Frontiers in Psychology* 5: 1065.

10

'I Heard Lots of Different Languages': Layered Worlds of Separate and Flexible Bilingualism in Cardiff

Frances Rock and Amal Hallak

Mae'r bennod hon yn archwilio amlieithrwydd yn y Gaerdydd gyfoes drwy ddefnyddio dulliau ethnograffeg ieithyddol. Mae'r bennod yn ystyried sut y gallai'r sawl sy'n ymweld â'r Brifddinas gyfeiriadu at yr amgylchedd ieithyddol gyfoethog ac amrywiol mewn ffyrdd gwahanol. Er mwyn gwneud hyn, mae'n tynnu ar syniadau o ddwyieithrwydd 'ar wahân' a dwyieithrwydd 'hyblyg' (Creese and Blackledge 2010) sydd wedi cael eu defnyddio mewn ymchwil i gyd-destunau addysgol ac i leferydd. Drwy gymhwyso'r syniadau hyn at arferion cyfathrebol amlfodd, mae'r bennod yn ystyried (i) i ba raddau mae unigolion yn cydymffurfio â normau sefydliadol ynghylch dewis iaith a (ii) sut y mae normau sefydliadol yn cydfodoli â disgwyliadau ac arferion ieithyddol eraill.

Introduction

Wales's bustling capital, Cardiff, has a population of almost 355,000 (Welsh Government 2016) and, through successive waves of migra-

---

F. Rock (✉) • A. Hallak
Cardiff University, Cardiff, UK

© The Author(s) 2016
M. Durham, J. Morris (eds.), *Sociolinguistics in Wales*,
DOI 10.1057/978-1-137-52897-1_10

tion, has become home to diverse people, languages and semiotic practices. This chapter considers some of this diversity and the way in which languages are used, positioned and oriented to in twenty-first century Cardiff using the concepts of separate and flexible bilingualism. Separate bilingualism is, as the name suggests, a view that languages are separable and separating codes which exhibit and accomplish distinctiveness (Creese and Blackledge 2010). In this view, meaning is made through use of individual languages in a framework where notions of both hierarchy of languages (Bailey 2007: 267) and language practices (García 2009) and correctness of language (Preece 2016: 376) also feature. In contrast, flexible bilingualism is a recognition that languages cannot be neatly distinguished in use and that, as only part of speakers' meaning-making resource, they can combine in ways not adequately captured by the divisive notion of 'language' at all (Creese and Blackledge 2010). The starting point for flexible bilingualism is not the co-occurrence of languages in the form of code-switching but the social actions of speakers through their repertoires of resources and the affordances of those repertoires (García 2009). The notions of separate and flexible bilingualism were developed to describe language pedagogies but the 'ideologies' (Selleck 2012: 26) which underpin them are adaptable to the analysis of institutions and wider social life. Recognising these ways of seeing, experiencing and understanding sense-making, separate and flexible bilingualism, enables analysts to go beyond only considering which languages are used, where, how and why. This allows us to ask questions about the very meaning which speakers attach to language use and their orientations to languages as such. The chapter addresses the following questions: How are multiple languages incorporated into the linguistic landscape? What orientations are brought to bear on multilingual interactions? How do different approaches to bilingualism combine in a small geographical area of a city?

Many works of a wave of 'urban fantasy' literature draw on the idea of two cities coexisting in one place. For example, Neil Gaiman's 'Neverwhere' (1996/2005) sees 'London above', the London of which we are aware, cohabit with 'London below' a city in which Blackfriars is frequented by black-robed monks. Occupants of the parallel cities have different alignments to common things. They see the same sights, streets and activities, but orient, understand and respond differently. So, too, in contemporary

Cardiff, we suggest, different orientations to city life are available to those who see bilingualism as a separation of languages and those who do not. The city, in turn, cues up and provides both separate and flexible bilingualism. This chapter uses linguistic ethnography because of the particular understandings that it permits of 'how social and communicative processes operate in a range of settings and contexts' (Shaw et al. 2015: 1). The chapter draws on examples from naturally occurring encounters, research conversations, field notes, photographs and written texts in order to consider the utility of the notions of separate and flexible bilingualism when they are out of the classroom and on the street by considering the interplay of languages in place alongside social actors' orientations to that interplay. After introducing multilingual cities, we turn to the case of Cardiff and identify a particular ward as the focus of our attention. Following a summary of the methods used in this study, we then consider how the notions of separate and flexible bilingualism map onto this ward and provide ways of considering the language practices there. Finally, we conclude with some reflections on what this examination has revealed.

Introducing the City

Multilingual Cities

'Between 1993 and 2014 the foreign-born population in the UK more than doubled from 3.8 million to around 8.3 million' (Migrant Observatory 2016). It is not by chance then that twenty-first century sociolinguistics has witnessed the development of a wealth of research on urban language contact (e.g. Gregory and Williams 2000; García and Fishman 2002; Block 2006; Simon 2012). Some of this has developed around Vertovec's (2007) term, 'superdiversity', which proposes not only that more migrants are coming to the UK from more places and with more varied backgrounds, but also that they come with a wider variety of statuses, through a wider variety of channels which leads to increasingly diverse patterns of age, gender and work/educational experience. Vertovec (2005) arrived at the idea of superdiversity by comparing the relatively consistent migration patterns to the UK during the 1950s–1970s with those since 1991.

Multilingual cities are only one aspect of the linguistic and communicative life of Wales, yet as multilingual cities go, Wales's capital, Cardiff, offers a distinctive example in the context of the UK. Cardiff has witnessed successive waves of international migration which include the two of which Vertovec speaks alongside the combination of Welsh and English. Those who use the notion of superdiversity are often criticised for missing the fact that urban language contact is nothing new. Cardiff provides a case study in which various old or established diversities (migrants from England and Somalia, for example) meet superdiversity (worldwide new arrivals such as asylum seekers and international students).

In order to begin to understand the two parallel cities of Cardiff proposed here, we draw on the distinction between two constructions of bilingualism, introduced above, which are sometimes known as separate versus flexible bilingualism (Blackledge and Creese 2010: 108–123). Separate bilingualism is akin to Weber's (2014: 3) 'fixed multilingualism' and Canagarajah's (2013: 19–24) 'monolingual orientation' and promotes a view of isolated languages operating in isolation from one another and isolating through their use (Gu 2013: 225; Webber 2014: 9). In institutions, a view of separate bilingualism can establish systems of power and ideological control (Blackledge and Creese 2010: 122). On the other hand, what Creese and Blackledge recognise as 'flexible bilingualism' is a construction which 'normalizes bilingualism without diglossic functional separation' (García 2007: xiii in Creese and Blackledge 2011: 1197). This construction of multilingualism disputes rigid distinctions between different varieties, registers, languages and dialects and instead focuses on the individual with their own usage and resources.

Investigations of the flexible approach often trace their roots to the classrooms of Wales with the work of Cen Williams (1994) on what was originally a pedagogical practice '*trawsieithu*' or 'translanguaging'. Through this practice, input in one language is converted to output in another to facilitate understanding of the transformed information (Lewis et al. 2012: 643–4). The relationship between 'translanguaging' and 'flexible bilingualism' is often left vague and the terms can be seen being used interchangeably. However the concept of translanguaging is usefully taken as a set of practices (García 2009: 45), orientations (Zu Hua 2015: 119) and activities (Sandhu and Higgins 2016:

190) which instantiate the flexible bilingual 'ideology' (Blackledge and Creese 2010: 111).

Translanguaging and flexible/separate bilingualism originally described classroom pedagogies but they can be usefully extended to characterise other social contexts. Additionally they have predominantly been used in the context of spoken language interactions but in this chapter their value for exploring the multimodal cityscape including verbal and visual elements is evidenced. Such extension is underway in the work of Velasco and García (2014), Zhang and Chan (2015) and Sugiharto (2015), for example, and this paper contributes to this expansion. The orientation to either the separate or flexible form of bilingualism is not immovable. It is a matter of norms (Hazel and Mortensen 2013: 8), of expectations about what is appropriate (Garfinkel 1967; Hymes 1972) and is driven by a particular mindset or habitus (Weber 2014: 8). This chapter provides examples of both a separate and flexible mindset in order to explore orientations to the multilingual city. Our claim is not that some people in Cardiff are monolingual and others are not. Neither do we suggest simply that some people have access to particular languages with their different histories and contemporary affordances, whilst others do not, although issues of access and control do feature here. We do not even suggest here that some people use more than one language 'simultaneously' whilst others do not. Rather we consider some of the different ideologies about and orientations to the way that languages can combine and the circumstances and locations of that combination. We suggest that two ideologies coexist, one in which languages are separate and separable and one in which their combination adds to the communications which take place.

Contextualising Cardiff

In the late 1700s, Cardiff, a 'ramshackle, seen-better-days, muddy village on the Taff' was about to undergo a transformation (Mortimer 2014: 22). As Bartholomew (1887) explains, the population rocketed from 1018 in 1801 to 59,494 just 70 years later. This expansion was fuelled by, and fuel to, the coal and iron industries and their infrastructure. By 1901 Cardiff boasted a population of 128,000 (Daunton 1977; in Coop and Thomas 2007: 170) and was made a city four years later. As the population figures suggest, the 'Welsh Metropolis' owed its rise to migration. Cardiff's 1911 census revealed residents drawn from every county of England and Wales as well as 'a cosmopolitan population not rivalled elsewhere in South Wales' (Evans 1985: 352). This latter population included seafarers and labourers who had travelled to Cardiff throughout its boom from places including Somalia, Yemen, West Africa, the West Indies, India, China, Scandinavia, Spain, Greece and Malta (Tweedale 1987: 5) as well as Ireland. Thus, Cardiff has long been a place of arrival and settlement. Yet the city has not always witnessed growth and after the Second World War 'trade went into freefall' and the industries fell away (Mortimer 2014: 36). Despite this, the city has been found to function as a node for contact between peoples of many social classes, places of origin, belief and ethnicity and a wiry combination of extreme racism set against engaged social inclusion (e.g. Threadgold et al. 2008; see also papers in Williams et al. 2015). Cardiff remains a locus for migration as the figures in Table 10.1 indicate.

Table 10.1, showing the origins of Cardiff residents according to three successive censuses, reveals a shift to superdiversity. Through this chapter, we will see how speakers in this transnational context consider how they and others deploy language repertoires, taking Arabic as a case study with attention to Welsh, English and Kurdish too.

Alongside Cardiff's migratory history, questions about Cardiff's Welsh credentials have long been raised. Cardiff has been described as 'a centre for permanent suspicion' elsewhere in Wales, 'regarded as too English, too distant, too flashy, too fast and far to anti-Welsh for many' (Finch 2004: 10) 'geographically part of Wales but culturally Anglicized' (Johnes 2012: 510). Erosion of Welsh occurred during the late fifteenth century (Jones 1981), and particularly in South Wales where Cardiff is situated, during

Table 10.1 Countries of birth of residents of the Cardiff Unitary authority across censuses

Year	Born outside Wales (%)	Born outside the UK (%)
1991	20.9	6
2001	25.1	7.6
2011	31.3	13.3

Table 10.2 Percentage of Cardiff Unitary authority residents who claim knowledge of Welsh

Year	Percentages
1981	5.7
1991	7.2
2001	16.3
2011	15.7

the industrial and post-industrial periods along with language shift to English. Yet through education, public broadcasting and language policy, for example (Holmes 2013: 67–8), Welsh is rallying. Census results from the last 30 years reveal a general increase in the number of people in Cardiff who claim some knowledge of Welsh (as a speaker, listener, reader or writer). This change is summarised in Table 10.2.

Cardiff is emerging as a hub of Welsh learning with the greatest increase in fluent Welsh speakers between 2004–6 and 2013–15 anywhere in Wales, with an increase of almost 7000 between the two periods (Welsh Government and Welsh Language Commissioner 2015: 33) and an increase in the number of people in the city who speak Welsh daily in the same period (ibid. 45).

Thus Cardiff can be seen as a city of 'strangers' and 'aliens' or a city of opportunity to join a multilingual community. Certainly, it is a city that functions. This chapter examines some of the small-scale work on this front in the everyday interactions of multilingual people in Wales. It does so through a focus on just one ward of the city, Cathays.

In the centre of Cardiff, the Unitary Authority Electoral Division of Cathays (Fig. 10.1) spans three main areas, containing different spheres of activity. First, Cathays contains Cardiff's grand civic precincts, in the area known as Cathays Park. This area first welcomed the City Hall, completed in 1904 (Finch 2004: 58). The area's elegant Portland Stone now houses the Museum of Wales, the Welsh Government administrative offices, the Temple of Peace and Health, Cardiff Crown Court and city police station and finally, a focus of this study, many of the buildings of Cardiff University. Welsh and English are visible on signage, around these public buildings but other languages are rarely seen in the public linguistic landscape. A second area of Cathays is a Victorian suburb whose densely terraced streets are frequently dismissed as 'student land'

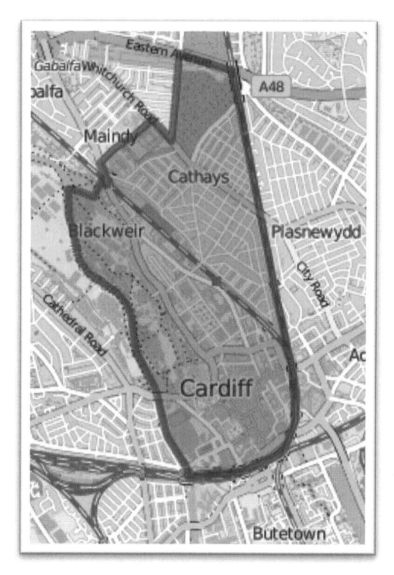

Fig. 10.1 Unitary Authority electoral division of Cathays (Ordnance Survey 2016)

(Finch 2004: 22), seasonal and rapidly changing (Threadgold et al. 2008: 165–6). Here, English, Welsh and other languages can be seen on shops and offices but also in the windows and on doors of houses, in formal and informal advertising, on cars and vans, on walls, railings and any other surface where a mark can be made or a notice pinned, even rubbish bins and pavements themselves. We have chosen to focus on Arabic, in Cathays, because it was the language most frequently claimed as a main language in the 2011 census in Cathays, after English and Welsh. By considering just one ward, in detail, by examining language practices of and surrounding focal individuals, we are able to grasp the city as it is lived.

Methods

This chapter uses an approach to data collection and analysis which fits under what Copland and Creese (2015: 9) and Shaw et al. (2015: 1) describe as the 'umbrella term' of linguistic ethnography. Whilst this term is truly an umbrella, work which takes on this label typically shares some key elements. For Rampton et al. (2015: 15–16), these include: examining patterns through 'telling' rather than 'typical' cases; a focus on providing ways to look, rather than strict guidance on what to see in order to contextualise the selections and idealisations which are inevitable in analysing data and ultimately an understanding that some findings cannot be simply expressed in words. For this chapter, this means that, whilst short fragments of data are presented, along with isolated photographs and interview excerpts, these have been selected for their particular place in the study and the vantage point they give on language in the city. This is 'interpretative' work which considers data from the point of view of social actors (Copland and Creese 2015: 14) some of whom become drawn into the research endeavour itself, selecting and discussing data, as this chapter shows. Thus, as well as considering naturally occurring examples of translingual practice, we also access information about translingual practice by asking speakers about it (see Evas and Cunliffe, this volume).

In considering language locally, we not only examine spoken interactions and participants' talk about them, but also the linguistic landscapes in which the talk and participants are situated. For this, we draw on that body of work which is usually traced back to the activities of Landry and Bourhis (1997) and described as the systematic study of written public texts. We complement this with work from social practices approaches to literacy which see reading and writing as embedded in human activity and social life, not only in classrooms and learning (Barton 1994: 32). This approach provides ways to understand more private texts such as those displayed inside buildings and complement linguistic ethnography as they explicitly address language beyond the spoken interaction.

This chapter is based on work which is part of a large study of language and communication in four superdiverse cities (Cardiff, Birmingham, Leeds and London) around England and Wales (http://bit.do/tlang). The data collection in each city is divided into four phases concerned with observing and analysing the activities of workers in four sectors: business, heritage, sport and law. This chapter is concerned only with the first two of these, business, through a focus on a small shop, and heritage, through a focus on a library. In each site, attention focussed on a Key Participant (KP) who was bilingual.

Data used in this chapter were collected between September 2014 and February 2016 and focussed on two, sixteen-week phases of observation and engagement in each site. This involved attending each site, frequently and for prolonged periods, to take field notes and photographs and to collect audio- and video-recordings of naturally occurring interactions. In each site we also spoke regularly and in-depth with each KP, on whom our attention focussed, but also with others nearby. We also collected data from each KP's home. These close and lengthy periods of observation provide for 'embracing and investigating … complexity' and orient to language as an embedded, ongoing social practice (Swinglehurst 2015: 107). The case study which appears first in this chapter focuses on a librarian, Mrs H, who works in two of the university's libraries, splitting her time between them. Mrs H is from Kurdistan and speaks three languages, Kurdish (Sourani), Arabic and English. She has lived in the UK for 23 years of which 21 have been spent in Cardiff and 18 working for the University Library Service. The case study which is mentioned second, focuses on bilingual shopkeepers, married couple, Mr and Mrs B, and their shop, a mini-market which sold food and food-related items and was just a half mile stroll from Mrs H's workplace. It closed soon after we finished our fieldwork. Mr and Mrs

B are from Iraq and speak both English and Arabic. They came to Britain separately, respectively seventeen and seven years ago. They had run the business jointly since it was founded three years before our study started.

Data Analysis

Separate and Flexible Bilingualism in the University Library

Cardiff University operates under the requirements of the Welsh Language (Wales) Measure 2011 (2014: 102) which means that it provides signage in both Welsh and English (2014: 124). This is proceduralised through the university's Welsh Language Scheme (2014: 8). This is, then, a highly institutionalised form of bilingualism which we might, according to Blackledge and Creese (2010: 113), expect to associate with separate bilingualism. Indeed, whilst Welsh and English are on display around the campus, we suggest that a norm of separate bilingualism is in evidence in the way that those languages are presented. This is illustrated in Fig. 10.2

Fig. 10.2   Signage at Cardiff University

which depicts a sign located at the entrance to the building where the librarian in our university-based case study spends half of her working-life.

The sign in Fig. 10.2 features both and only English and Welsh, in that sequence. It presents extremely closely equivalent information in each language. Similar signage is in place across the university campus and indeed across Cathays Park, the civic centre described above. In the linguistic landscape of this civic and institutional part of Cathays, then, languages are presented as separate codes whose use entails an assumption that identical information is needed in each language, every time it occurs.

Coupland (2012: 11) calls this kind of language display 'parallel text bilingualism' for the way it envisages a straight choice between English and Welsh and frames both languages as parallel and equivalent (2012: 9). Backhaus (2007: 91) refers to such signs as 'homophonic'. This frame of parallel text bilingualism neatly exemplifies separate bilingualism in that it expects each language to operate as if it were a 'homogeneous monolingual variety' (Heller 2002: 48 in Coupland 2012). This 'gives textual form to a standard language ideology which challenges linguistic syncretism' (Coupland 2012: 12). It suppresses variation in each language, through its standard ideologies and suppresses variation in how meaning is created in the two codes and accessed by readers (Coupland 2010: 87). Garrett (2010: 156) reminds us that such display stems from Welsh language legislation and supporting guidance for writers (detailed at the beginning of this section) so these are ideological positionings which individual speakers inevitably orient to. These signs position English and Welsh as alternatives rather than parts of one holistic communicative practice which might draw in both languages in complementary ways. Whilst one may claim that this is not unusual in official, bilingual signs, this breadth is its very potency. Just because such practices are mundane, they are not without power. In this case, we suggest that those visitors to university spaces who have a separate bilingual ideology will be supported in their view of the separate bilingual city. If we think of the idea of two cities living in parallel, such signage can contribute to building a city in which languages are autonomous, independent systems.

As well as separating languages and casting them as isolated and alternative, this signage also ranks them in relation to one another. We can extrapolate from García's observation (2009: 78–9) that translanguaging renders such hierarchies meaningless, that it is reasonable to see them as typical of the separate bilingual ideology. Here, English is vertically prioritised over Welsh which is placed in a 'secondary position' (Tufi 2016: 112). Such display is not chance, but rather 'a planned projection of social values and hierarchies' (Coupland 2012: 2), an ideological decision (Jaworski and Thurlow 2010: 12). This sign presents Welsh but keeps it firmly in place.

This ordering of languages is present on the sign even in the university logo where the normalisation of the visual prioritisation of English over Welsh is cemented and carried across most of the institution. Only the School of Welsh has dispensation to reverse the sequence of languages in the strictly regulated logo (Cardiff University 2014: 8). Such fixing of the sequence of languages through the provision of a hierarchical logo is not unavoidable. Other Welsh universities provide different solutions. To cite just a few examples, those in areas regarded as the Welsh language heartland (Henley and Jones 2001: 5), tend to use the formula illustrated in the logo of Aberystwyth University, shown in Fig. 10.3.

In Fig. 10.3, the Welsh word '*prifysgol*' (university) appears first and the English, 'university' second. This is facilitated through what Coupland (2010: 92) sees as 'creative bilingual entextualisation' which takes advantage of the object–verb order of Welsh which prefers classifier nouns before head nouns, in combination with the verb–object order of English, which prefers the reverse. The Universities of Bangor and Glyndŵr (Wrexham), both to the north, also use this device. Meanwhile, in South Wales, Cardiff is joined by Swansea and the University of South Wales, for example, in visually prioritising English through an upper or left-most position. This sequencing is surely influenced by different orientations to Welsh in the different locations. Gwynedd, for example, where Bangor University is situated, boasts the highest concentration of fluent Welsh speakers in Wales with over 70% of the population claiming to speak Welsh (Welsh

Fig. 10.3 The logo of Aberystwyth University

Government and Welsh Language Commissioner 2015: 115) and where four out of five Welsh speakers are fluent (ibid. 31) and 85% of Welsh speakers speak the language daily (ibid. 45) compared with much lower figures in South Wales. Ceredigion, where Aberystwyth University is based, shows similar strengths. Apart from the predominant norms of language sequence in Cardiff, the university's stated aim, to attract international students, may also be a factor in the situation of English first. 21.9% of students are international (Cardiff University 2016) and the University Language Policy makes specific provision for excluding Welsh when communicating only with those students (2014: 8, 9, 10). Coupland (2010: 92) makes the point that using equivalent wordings, particularly when the Welsh and English words might appear similar can leave such signage open to mockery and 'risks trivialising the value of bilingualism'. On the other hand, using language resources more creatively, as in the Bangor and Aberystwyth examples can be positive for revitalisation, precisely because it entails articulating a diversity of cultural meanings from the range of language resources available. We could extend his argument to suggest that flexible bilingualism, drawing on such features as translanguaging might have implications for language revitalisation.

This normalising of language separation carries over into the work of the institution. This is exemplified in naturally occurring data from the library case study in excerpt 1 where a student, Lucy, is engaged with a service encounter in the university library with Mrs H (all names have been anonymised, throughout).

Excerpt 1 Separate bilingualism in the library

1	Lucy	ur (.) do I have an- any books ur ur due soon or that I must return apart from this
2	Mrs H	okay I'll show you now ur [clicking] okay
3	Lucy	I still get confused
4	Mrs H	yeah I know [laughs] yeah as I said at the moment you have the four books
5	Lucy	yes
6	Mrs H	okay that one is due back on the 26 (.) but I put reservation on it for you
7	Lucy	as- as
8	Mrs H	so you need to return it on the 26th but if somebody else return that copy you might be able to borrow it
9	Lucy	oh yeah sure

10	Mrs H	you understand that
11	Lucy	yeah yeah yeah yeah
12	Mrs H	okay and these three they are all okay until 22nd of November
13	Lucy	oh yeah thank you //very much//
14	Mrs H	// okay // so let me look your reservation you have reserved these but none of them are arrived yet okay so you got four reservation
15	Lucy	and also how- [name of author and book title] ((on reserve))
16	Mrs H	yeah
17	Lucy	ah yeah yeah yeah yeah
18	Mrs H	but it hasn't come yet
19	Lucy	of course
20	Mrs H	okay
21	Lucy	oh right yeah
22	Mrs H	once we receive the book we return it discharge activate the reservation and then you ur you'll be notified by an email
23	Lucy	ah yeah

The interaction itself, in excerpt 1, is entirely in English which is typical. We argue below that the encounter is not only monolingual, but is rooted in an institutional separate bilingual norm. In line 3, we see how this interaction connects exophorically when the student mentions 'still' getting confused, recalling past conversations in English and past experiences mediated through English relating to her library activities. Line 6 sees a reference to putting 'a reservation' on a book, and line 15 to having a book 'on reserve' indicating connections between the actions underway at the computer terminal and other library procedures which will be mediated through English via an electronic infrastructure. In line 14, the speakers refer to past reservations and their results indicating that the English-only world of book administration stretches from the past into the likely future via communications with other students which will also be grounded in separate bilingualism. Finally in line 22 Mrs H discusses an automatically generated email which our wider observations showed would be in English and Welsh but with the separation and linguistic equivalence that we saw on the sign in Fig. 10.2. This is then what Preece would call a 'monolingualised site', typical of UK higher education (2016: 376) as far as routine procedures go, a fact which has consequences for those from more flexible bilingual backgrounds (Preece 2016: 366–368). Whilst Cardiff is not 'monolingualised', the two languages, English and Welsh, take priority in institutional interactions so the exclusion of other languages applies.

Languages other than English and Welsh are also present in the library and a first step towards flexible bilingualism is to orient to this diversity. Thus, we begin to turn to speakers who live in separate-bilingualism-Cardiff but turn a flexible bilingualism eye to the scene. In the excerpt below, one of Mrs H's colleagues, Anna, herself a Welsh speaker, notes the languages which, whilst not obvious at the library service desk, were nonetheless in evidence during her work in the library:

Excerpt 2   Language awareness in the library

278	Anna	I heard lots of different languages (.) yeah I would say (.) do you want do you want to know which ones
279	Amal	//if you could yeah//
280	Frances	// yeah why not //
281	Anna	um (.) I think Portuguese French um (1.3) Spanish (.) Arabic (.) um (1.2) Welsh (.) and probably more I would think yeah (.) Chinese (1.5) yeah yeah it's really nice actually to hear to hear all these different languages being spoken (.) yeah it's exciting

Students who travel to Cardiff for their studies, as elsewhere, bring along their linguistic repertoires which will likely take in English and other languages and will find themselves surrounded by yet more languages, local and otherwise, in university environs (Hazel and Mortensen 2013: 3). Nonetheless in universities, a separate bilingual norm is often present and at odds with staff and students' linguistic diversity (Preece 2011: 122). The norm that has been apparent so far is, therefore, top-down bolstered by the normalisation of English we saw above which is perpetuated by, for example, an encouragement towards but not insistence on Welsh language learning for staff. Speakers observe discrete, separate languages in the physical environment and during institutional encounters. Institutional frameworks which scaffold their activities support this. However Anna's enthusiasm about the languages she hears in the library, in the context of her own use of Welsh, discussed in more detail below, evidence the bottom-up impetus is for more languages to be in play for more of the time and in a greater diversity of ways.

The university's 'Welsh Language Scheme' orients to Welsh as an important component of campus life. It undertakes to 'embed the Welsh language within its culture and working practices' and, maintaining as separate bilingualism ideology, to provide 'the opportunity to study and live your life through the medium of Welsh' (Cardiff University 2014). However the day-to-day reality in the library is that English predominates with Welsh being marked. Yet Welsh was far from absent. Its presence was facilitated by language-related artefacts brought into the work environment by staff, for example. Mrs H's colleagues, Anna mentioned above, explained that she wore a lanyard and a badge which identified her as a Welsh speaker. Anna said that her experience was that people rarely requested to hold library service encounters in Welsh, spontaneously and unprompted, but would sometimes see her language lanyard once interactions were underway and switch to Welsh or initiate an exchange in Welsh opportunistically, as a result (Interview 014). Thus we begin to see flexible bilingualism in the lived reality of the library as interactants soften the 'hard boundaries between languages' (Cenoz and Gorter 2015: 5) through linguistic practices including speech and the wearing of signs.

Mrs H had seen the results of Anna's lanyard and, as a side-effect of our research, had begun to think about how she could diversify her own language practices in the library. Drawing an analogy with Anna's Welsh language badge, she said 'I'm thinking I might suggest with someone I'll- I'll have a badge and- saying speaking Kurdish and Arabic'. She saw this as potentially 'good for the library' and 'helpful for the student' (Interview 010).

These speakers are flexible about language in the space of the library. One might interject that the university is also flexible in that it welcomes both Welsh and English. However, we have suggested that even though there are two languages present, there is a different 'mindset' in operation. The languages are presented as separate, interchangeable and equivalent in Fig. 10.2 and Excerpt 1. They also tend to be offered by appointment and by arrangement, e.g. 'We'll ask you when you register if you prefer to receive your personal correspondence in Welsh or English or bilingually'; 'you can ask for a Welsh-speaking personal tutor', Cardiff University 2014. In these examples we further see that English is the norm here with Welsh, once again, the marked choice. For Anna and Mrs

H, the use of multiple codes is, in contrast, always a potential which can be evoked at any moment. In excerpt 3, Mrs H speaks to students, who she recognised, in both English and Arabic in an exchange which also featured Kurdish (not shown here). Mrs H moved away from the main service desk in order to join the students where they worked (translations from Arabic to English are included in italics, below. A full transcription key appears at the end of the chapter):

Excerpt 3   Flexible bilingualism in the library

1	Mrs H	ur السلام عليكم
		peace be upon you
2	Bahar	السلام عليكم
		and peace be upon you
3	Mrs H	اني تصورت انت كردية قاعدة وياه
		I thought you were Kurdish sitting with him [laughs]
4	Bahar	ah [laughs]
5	Muhammed	the same seminar group
6	Mrs H	I met her yeah I know yeah Bahar
7	Bahar	ايه
		yeah

Here, Mrs H and the two students create a translanguaging space, in other words, one where social spaces with their different norms are integrated by individuals through use of multiple resources to make sense (García and Li Wei 2014: 24–25). This is transformative. It draws together the personal histories of the speakers, expressed through the use of three languages and those languages in combination, with the environment in which they find themselves within a UK institution. Li Wei (2011: 1223) suggests that the key to such translanguaging spaces are creativity (choosing between following and flouting rules and norms) and criticality (using evidence appropriately to question received wisdom). Mrs H's talk, and that of the students, allows them to choose to opt out of the separate bilingualism norm of the library. What is interesting is not simply that they are using more than one language but that they move flexibly between languages making meaning as they move between topics and speech activities. Mrs H made frequent references, during our fieldwork, to the potential of Arabic and Kurdish to be not only 'helpful' to students, as cited above, but also reassuring, even comforting, as they encounter an unfamiliar intellectual environment in a new geographical location. In this instance, Mrs H was able to create a space for a friendly and supportive encounter which went beyond 'business as usual' for a university library, establishing distinctive social arrangements. We have seen the way in which separate bilingualism predominates in the university environment, operating as a norm which offers certain languages in certain ways, specifically a predominance of English at the service desk and a demarcated environment where languages duplicate one another and Welsh and English are presented as mutually exclusive choices. Speakers in those environments can, nonetheless, crease an openness to flexible bilingualism. This openness can manifest in simply noticing and enjoying being in a multilingual environment and being open to engaging in routine tasks across languages. It can, however, extend to translingual practices and seeking out those encounters. Such practices then show that the two Cardiffs coexist in institutional spaces. Separate bilingualism is perpetuated by institutional norms and items in the linguistic landscape and on library users' computers. Flexible bilingualism appears through practices. We now move to a different part of Cathays where a flexible bilingual ideology predominates.

Flexible Bilingualism in the Mini-Market

The shop is, from the moment it is first seen, across the street, a space of flexible bilingualism. Figure 10.4 shows the exterior of the shop with its entrance in the centre.

In the signage outside the mini-market, unlike that outside the university library, there is a lack of equivalence between what is written in English and what is written in its companion language, Arabic, in this case. Instead of giving equivalent information in each language, the signs here provide what was deemed, at the time of their writing, to be appropriate levels of detail for audiences who read in each of the languages used. In English, we see only the name of the shop, 'Zem Zem', transliterated, and the words 'CONTINENTAL FOOD' and 'DAILY FRESH HALAL MEAT'. In Arabic, on the other hand, we see much more detail. For example, in the Arabic text:

Fig. 10.4 The entrance to the mini-market

1. 'CONTINENTAL FOOD' is not mentioned. Instead the food is categorised through a different generalisation. The generalisation chosen is 'Arabic and Oriental' within the first line of text on the main sign:

زمزم. مواد غذائية عربية وشرقية	(Zem Zem. Arabic and oriental food products)

2. The specification of 'DAILY FRESH HALAL MEAT' as it appeared in English is not included in that brief level of detail in Arabic. Instead, the level of detail is deepened through provision of a wealth of information about the range of products available, through the two lines of Arabic above the address and telephone number:

حلويات – لحم بعجين طازج – لحوم حلال طازجة	Sweets/deserts – fresh lahem b'ajeen (lamb pies) – fresh halal meat
تجهيز المناسبات خروف مشوي مع كافة الاكلات العراقية	Catering for events roast lamb with all Iraqi cuisine

The reference to fresh halal meat is also reiterated in both languages in various places. This signage calls to mind Gu's (2013: 225) description of flexible bilingualism entailing the use of languages as 'social resource without clear boundaries' with utterances, after Bakhtin, shaped by 'social, political and historical forces'. In this case, the production of the written text has been guided by social expectations. These include expectations about who will know about what kinds of foods and what languages those individuals might use to access that information, as well as expectations about who will need information on the halal food preparation technique and in what languages. The signage does not simply reproduce information across languages but recognises that different shoppers will bring different forms of experience and knowledge to the shop, as well as different requirements.

Signage which featured a flexible approach to languaging was present inside the shop too. Figures 10.5 and 10.6 illustrate this.

The artefact in Fig. 10.5 is just one of several in the shop on a religious theme. This example features the words 'ما شاء الله / maa shaa Allah' (God willing) in the upper area followed by prayers on Ibrahim which praise Allah and seek blessings on Muhammad and on the family of Muhammad as well as blessings on Ibrahim and the family of Ibrahim.

Like other artefacts in the mini-market, this was purchased during a family trip to London, as the shop was being set up. These artefacts were selected because the shapes and colours were pleasing to the shopkeepers but also *to signify/show that the shop is Arabic* المحل حتى يدل أنو عربي (Home Visit Data: Bus03). During our conversations it emerged that this signification was simultaneously for the benefit of Arabic customers who would find something familiar and to visitors to the shop who were not familiar with such items who would get the 'aura' of something new and, perhaps, enticing (Home Visit Data: Bus03). Thus, whilst this item is in Arabic only, it is not intended only to address customers who can 'read Arabic'. Rather it makes meaning beyond the boundaries of languages and was explicitly intended that way.

There were many signs around the shop in English too, and it emerged during our conversations with the shopkeepers and our observations that the reasons for using particular language choices were com-

Fig. 10.5 Artefacts in the mini-market

Fig. 10.6 Signage in the mini-market

plex and reflected the shop keepers' awareness of and thought about the significance of language use. At other times, decisions were taken automatically as if these choices were obvious and routine. The coloured, star-shaped labels in Fig. 10.6 were just two examples of many similar, prohibitive texts which were displayed around the areas where dates, biscuits and some goods in jars were sold. Mrs B explained that, here, English was the best choice because these are 'easy words'. As she explained, 'ماكو واحد عربي ما يعرف هي المصطلحات' ('there isn't an Arab who wouldn't know those expressions'). It seemed that the signs were also felt to be appropriate for the many customers from mainland Europe who might also welcome 'easy words'. It was perhaps no coincidence that the signage on this point was accessible to as many potential shop visitors as possible. In this instance, it was intended that shoppers would be able to read the text, in order to derive meaning from it and the language choice aimed to maximise that reading. Figures 10.4, 10.5, and 10.6, in combination, indicate that in and around the shop English and Arabic co-exist, serving different purposes for the shopkeepers and different functions for different readers.

Flexible bilingualism was not confined to signage but was also prominent in talk in the shop. In excerpt 4 Mr B serves a number of customers and gets on with stock-taking and ordering between customers:

Excerpt 4 Flexible bilingualism in the shop

1	Male cust. 1	it's quiet today isn't it
2	Mr B	yeah a little bit quiet yeah sometime they come in all together
3	Male cust. 1	[laughs]
4	Mr B	yeah [shop till sounds] thank you (.) عليكم السلام *peace be upon you*
5	Male cust. 2	السلام عليكم *peace be upon you*
6	Mr B	عليكم السلام brother [talking to himself] soup chicken ستة (.) ستة تنين hhh *and also peace be upon you two six (.) six*
7	Male cust. 3	السلام عليكم *peace be upon you*

8	Mr B	عليكم السلام أهلا وسهلا
		and also peace be upon you most welcome
9	Male cust. 3	جالك التمر اللي سألتك عليه يوم الأربع
		have the dates that I asked you about on Wednesday arrived
10	Mr B	التمر الإيراني ولا إياهو
		the Iranian dates or which
11	Male cust. 3	ال الهو الناشف
		the- the dried ones
12	Mr B	الناشف هاد موجود يمك جديد ايه نعم
		the dried ones are there by you they're new (.) oh yeah

Here, languages are deployed as needed and when particular activities, speakers and preferences make them relevant. In turns 1–4 this entails the use of English, initially a language that Male Customer 1 has introduced as he and Mr B make small-talk about the lack of customers and undertake a service encounter. Yet at the end of turn 4, Mr B switches to Arabic, within his turn, offering good wishes as Male customer 1 departs. Male customer 2 too, initiates talk but this time in Arabic. Mr B responds with a greeting in Arabic but an address form in English, 'brother'. The next customer too is familiar to Mr B, Male customer 3, and they too share a greeting in Arabic which they also use for a subsequent stock discussion. Mr B moves fluidly between English and Arabic when speaking to customers such that we start to see them not as separate languages but one holistic repertoire. Even when thinking aloud, more than one language is used, as we see in turn 6. Here, Mr B, talking to himself, moves from English when reading the names of items 'soup chicken' and into Arabic when counting items for his order. In this way, meaning-making becomes 'more than the sum of its parts, in ways that language separation would not allow' (Blackledge and Creese 2010: 114). Specifically, the use of more than one language enables the shopkeeper to identify with shoppers by selecting a code that he knows is familiar to them, to accomplish his work in the way most comfortable to him by naming products in English and counting them in Arabic and to accommodate to shoppers by taking their lead on language choice.

Close

The two worlds of separate and flexible bilingualism are not, then, geographically separated across Cathays with Cathays Park, the home of the university and civic buildings being exclusively a place of separate bilingualism and the residential and shopping areas witnessing only flexible bilingualism. Rather, separate and flexible are layered over one another, across the social space potentially making for a feeling of flexible and separate cities coexisting.

We suggest that there is not a neat cleave between holding an idea of separate bilingualism and one of flexible bilingualism. It might appear that there exists in Cardiff a continuum with separate bilingualism at one extreme, in the middle some speakers, such as those in the library, open to a variety of languages in one space but not actively deploying those languages in concert and at the other end, the flexible bilingualism of shops and streets where languages become one of an array of semiotic means to sell and advertise, show identity and solidarity, get work done and accommodate, but flexible bilingualism is not something that speakers turn off and on. Rather it is an approach to languaging through which language users draw in resources at their disposal and use them creatively, unfettered by restrictions of a separate bilingualism. Through this view, translanguaging not only occurs when speakers are actively code-switching or codemeshing, rather these are just obvious manifestation of flexible bilingualism. However the flexible approach remains even if it is not being obviously spoken at any given moment. In this way, even speakers seen in the separate paradigm as 'monolingual' can in the parallel flexible reality be seen as flexibly bilingual to the extent that they recruit varieties and other resources to accomplish social actions.

This chapter asked three questions which we now revisit.

First, how are multiple languages incorporated into the Linguistic Landscape in Cardiff? Through two case studies, we have seen the presence of a separate and bilingual norm, cohabiting in the same ward, and the different affordances of each. The separate norm suggested, through visual cues such as equivalence and hierarchy, that languages are to be used in isolation from one another with readers either following English or Welsh. In contrast, outside and inside the shop, a flexible norm gave different information in each of English and Arabic with an attempt to make appropriate meanings using the two resources. In making these distinctions, however, we are orienting to something illocutionary in the classification of separate and flexible. It is, of course, possible that an individual speaker will take-up the sign in Fig. 10.2, the university building name, in a flexible way—moving between the languages as they try to work out the meanings of words across both and to evaluate equivalence in each, for example. Whilst the ethnographic approach has enabled us to go beyond only looking at isolated instances of language, we maintain a perspective and cannot encounter every telling case. However we note that because a separate norm is offered, that will not mean that it is taken up. This tension between the dominant norm offered and its take-up is explored in answering our second question, below.

Secondly, we asked what orientations are brought to bear on multilingual interactions. We found speakers who operate in the generally separate bilingual system of the university library stepping outside this system using resources such as lanyards and badges to prompt such movements or simply making them happen through talk in an environment that was otherwise heavily dominated by English. We also found that in shops, where there is no expectation of a separate bilingualism model, communicative practices developed which took in multiple ways of making meaning. We have focussed here on linguistic aspects of this but the examples shown also indicate the significance of other meaning-making resources such as colour, placement and spirituality and it is from a rich semiotic position that the shopkeepers communicated with their customers and potential customers in talk and through the signs and artefacts in and around their shop. Ultimately, speakers did not seem to be constrained by the resources on offer to them and indeed Mrs H's performance in the separate paradigm, in excerpt 1 can be seen as an appropriation of that paradigm to accomplish institutional ends.

Finally we asked how different approaches to bilingualism combine in just one small geographical area of a city. We have seen, within the Cathays ward, places where separate bilingualism predominates, places where separate and flexible bilingualism combine and places where flexible bilingualism seems to be the norm whilst those with a separate mindset could still get by. The metaphor of two realities overlaid across one another, has helped to represent the experience of crossing Cathays and encountering the different forms of bilingualism in their various combinations. It is probably no accident that the metaphor of two cities living in parallel, with residents of each more or less aware of the other, should become a literary trope at this time of superdiversity. This chapter has shown that it would be a crass oversimplification to suggest that different people operate in different worlds, as in the literary representations. However the metaphor lends itself well to the study of linguistic practices where the separate and flexible layer over one another and entwine around one another.

General Transcription Conventions

Underlining	Indicates stress signalled through pitch and volume
(.)	A micropause of 0.9 seconds or less
(1.2)	A pause of 1.0 second or more, duration indicated inside the brackets in seconds
// //	Overlapping talk
hhh	Audible out-breath
=	Latching on
-	Self-correction or speaker breaking off
[ ]	Extra-linguistic features (e.g., [coughs])
(( ))	Unclear speech (double brackets either contain deciphered speech or, where impossible, estimated number of inaudible syllables)
…	Words have been removed, for brevity
?	Rising intonation
'inverted commas'	Reported speech from the crime scene
Italics	Words originally said in Arabic

Acknowledgements We are grateful to the following research staff and students for their invaluable help with this paper: Piotr Węgorowski, Zeen Suad Nafie Al-Rasheed; Bdreah Mubarak F Alswais; Rachel Hu; Zayneb Al-Bundawi. We are also indebted to the editors of this volume for their attentive comments and perseverance. Any remaining errors are our own. The research underpinning this chapter was funded by the Arts and Humanities Research Council, grant no: 29164.

References

Backhaus, Peter. 2007. *Linguistic landscapes: A comparative study of urban multilingualism in Tokyo.* Clevedon: Multilingual Matters.

Bailey, Benjamin. 2007. Heteroglossia and boundaries. In *Bilingualism: A social approach*, ed. Monica Heller, 257–276. Basingstoke: Palgrave.

Bartholomew, John. 1887. *Gazetteer of the British Isles.* Edinburgh: A. and C. Black.

Barton, David. 1994. *Literacy: An introduction to the ecology of written language.* Oxford: Blackwell.

Blackledge, Adrian, and Angela Creese. 2010. *Multilingualism: A critical perspective.* London: Continuum.

Block, David. 2006. *Multilingual identities in a global city: London stories.* Basingstoke: Palgrave Macmillan.

Canagarajah, Suresh. 2013. *Translingual practice: Global Englishes and cosmopolitan relations.* London: Routledge.

Cardiff University. 2014. *Welsh Language scheme.* http://www.cardiff.ac.uk/public-information/corporate-information/welsh-language-scheme. Accessed May 2016.

———. 2016. *Facts and figures.* http://www.cardiff.ac.uk/about/facts-and-figures. Accessed May 2016.

Cenoz, Jasone, and Durk Gorter. 2015. Towards a holistic approach to the study of multilingual education. In *Multilingual education: Between language learning and translanguaging*, ed. Jasone Cenoz, and Durk Gorter, 1–15. Cambridge: Cambridge University Press.

Coop, Simon, and Huw Thomas. 2007. Planning doctrine as an element in planning history: The case of Cardiff. *Planning Perspectives 22*(2): 167–193. doi:10.1080/02665430701213564.

Copland, Fiona, and Angela Creese. 2015. *Linguistic ethnography: Collecting, analysing and presenting data.* London: Sage.

Coupland, Nikolas. 2010. Welsh linguistic landscapes from above and from below. In *Semiotic landscapes: Language, image, space, advances in sociolinguistics*, ed. Adam Jaworski, and Crispin Thurlow, 77–101. London: Continuum.

Coupland, N. 2012. Bilingualism on display: The framing of Welsh and English in Welsh public spaces. *Language in Society* 41(1): 1–27.

Creese, Angela, and Adrian Blackledge. 2010. Translanguaging in the Bilingual classroom: A pedagogy for learning and teaching? *The Modern Language Journal* 94(1): 103–115.

———. 2011. Separate and flexible bilingualism in complementary schools: Multiple language practices in interrelationship. *Journal of Pragmatics* 43(5): 1196–1208.

Daunton, M. 1977. *Coal metropolis: Cardiff 1870–1914*. Leicester: Leicester University Press.

Evans, Neil. 1985. The Welsh Victorian city. *Welsh History Review* 12(3): 350–387.

Finch, Peter. 2004. *Real Cardiff*, 2 edn. Bridgend: Poetry Wales Press.

Gaiman, Neil. 1996. *Neverwhere*. London: Headline Book Publishing.

García, O. 2007. Foreword. In *Disinventing and reconstituting languages*, ed. S. Makoni and A. Pennycook, xi–xv. Clevedon: Multilingual Matters.

García, Ofelia. 2009. *Bilingual education in the 21st century: A global perspective*. Oxford: Wiley-Blackwell.

García, Ofelia, and Joshua Fishman. 2002. *The multilingual apple: Languages in New York City*, 2nd edn. Berlin: Mouton de Gruyter.

García, Ofelia, and Li Wei. 2014. *Translanguaging: Language, bilingualism and education*. Basingstoke: Palgrave.

Garfinkel, Harold. 1967. *Studies in ethnomethodology*. Englewood Cliffs: Prentice-Hall.

Garrett, Peter. 2010. *Attitudes to language*. Cambridge: Cambridge University Press.

Gregory, Eve, and Ann Williams. 2000. *City literacies: Learning to read across generations and cultures*. London: Routledge.

Gu, Michelle. 2013. Language practices and transformation of language ideologies: Mainland Chinese students in a multilingual university in Hong Kong. In *Language alternation, Language choice and language encounter in international tertiary education*, ed. Hartmut Haberland, Dorte Lønsmann, and Bent Preisler, 223–236. Dordrecht: Springer.

Hazel, Spencer, and Janus Mortensen. 2013. Kitchen talk: Exploring linguistic practices in liminal institutional interactions in a multilingual university setting. In *Language alternation, language choice and language encounter in international tertiary education*, ed. Hartmut Haberland, Dorte Lønsmann, and Bent Preisler, 3–30. Dordrecht: Springer.

Heller, M. 2002. Globalization and commodification of bilingualism in Canada. In *Globalization and language teaching*, ed. David Block and Deborah Cameron, 47–64. London: Routledge.

Henley, Andrew, and Rhian Jones. 2001. Cyflog a gallu ieithyddol mewn economi ddwyieithog/Earnings and linguistic ability in a bilingual economy. Research paper no. 2001–18, University of Wales Aberystwyth, School of Management and Business.

Holmes, Janet. 2013. *An introduction to sociolinguistics*, 4 edn. London: Routledge.

Hua, Zu. 2015. Interculturality: Reconceptualising cultural memberships and identities through translanguaging practice. In *Researching identity and interculturality*, ed. Fred Dervin, and Karen Risager, 109–124. London: Routledge.

Hymes, Dell. 1972. On communicative competence. In *Sociolinguistics. Selected readings*, ed. John Pride, and Janet Holmes, 269–293. Harmondsworth: Penguin.

Jaworski, A., and C. Thurlow. 2010. Introducing semiotic landscapes. In *Semiotic landscapes: Language, image, space*, ed. A. Jaworski and C. Thurlow, 1–40. London: Continuum.

Johnes, Martin. 2012. Cardiff: The making and development of the capital city of Wales. *Contemporary British History 9462*(May 2013): 37–41.

Jones, Bedwyr Lewis. 1981. Welsh: linguistic conservatism and shifting bilingualism. In *Minority language today*, ed. Einar Haugen, J. Derrick McClure, and Derick S. Thompson, 40–52. Edinburgh: Edinburgh University Press.

Landry, Rodrigue, and Richard Bourhis. 1997. Linguistic landscape and ethnolinguistic vitality: An empirical study. *Journal of Language and Social Psychology* 16(1): 23–49.

Lewis, Gwyn, Bryn Jones, and Colin Baker. 2012. Translanguaging: Origins and development from school to street and beyond. *Educational Research and Evaluation 18*(7): 641–654.

Mortimer, Dic. 2014. *Cardiff: The biography*. Stroud: Amberley.

O'Leary, P., C. Williams, and N. Evans, eds. 2015. *A tolerant nation? Revisiting ethnic diversity in a devolved Wales*. 2nd ed. Caerdydd/Cardiff: Gwasg Prifysgol Cymru/University of Wales Press.

Ordnance Survey. 2016. Election maps. Available at: https://www.ordnancesurvey.co.uk/election-maps/. Accessed 5 Nov 2016.

Preece, Siân. 2011. Universities in the anglophone centre: Sites of multilingualism. *Applied Linguistics Review* 2: 121–146.

————. 2016. An identity transformation? Social class, language prejudice and the erasure of multilingual capital in higher education. In *The routledge handbook of language and identity*, ed. Siân Preece, 366–381. London: Routledge.

Rampton, Ben, Janet Maybin, and Celia Roberts. 2015. Theory and method in linguistic ethnography. In *Linguistic ethnography: Interdisciplinary explorations*, ed. Julia Snell, Fiona Copland, and Sara Shaw, 14–50. London: Palgrave.

Sandhu, Priti, and Christina Higgins. 2016. Identity in post-colonial contexts. In *The routledge handbook of language and identity*, ed. Siân Preece, 179–194. London: Routledge.

Selleck, Charlotte. 2012. Inclusive policy and exclusionary practice in secondary education in Wales. *International Journal of Bilingual Education and Bilingualism 16*(1): 20–41.

Shaw, Sara, Fiona Copland, and Julia Snell. 2015. An introduction to linguistic ethnography: Interdisciplinary explorations. In *Linguistic ethnography: Interdisciplinary explorations*, ed. Julia Snell, Fiona Copland, and Sara Shaw, 1–13. London: Palgrave.

Simon, Sherry. 2012. *Cities in translation: Intersections of language and memory*. London: Routledge.

Sugiharto, Setiono. 2015. Translingualism in action: Rendering the impossible possible. *The Journal of Asia TEFL* 12(2): 125–154.

Swinglehurst, Deborah. 2015. How linguistic ethnography may enhance our understanding of electronic patient records in health care settings. In *Linguistic ethnography: Interdisciplinary explorations*, ed. Julia Snell, Fiona Copland, and Sara Shaw, 90–109. London: Palgrave.

The Migrant Observatory. 2016. *Migrants in the UK: An overview.* http://migrationobservatory.ox.ac.uk/briefings/migrants-uk-overview. Accessed May 2016.

The Welsh Language (Wales) Measure. 2011. *2014.* Cardiff: National Assembly for Wales.

Threadgold, Terry, Sadie Clifford, Abdi Arwo, Vanessa Powell, Zahera Harb, Xinyi Jiang, and John Jewell. 2008. *Immigration and inclusion in South Wales.* Joseph Rowntree Foundationw. http://www.jrf.org.uk/publications/immigration-and-inclusion-south-wales. Accessed May 2016.

Tufi, S. 2016. Constructing the self in contested spaces: The case of Slovenian-speaking minorities in the area of Trieste. In *Negotiating and contesting identities in linguistic landscapes*, ed. Robert Blackwood, Elizabeth Lanza, and Hirut Woldemariam, 101–116. London: Bloomsbury.

Tweedale, Iain. 1987. From Tiger Bay to the Inner City: A century of black settlement in Butetown. *Radical Wales* Spring: 5–7.

Velasco, Patricia, and Ofelia García. 2014. Translanguaging and the writing of bilingual learners. *Bilingual Research Journal: The Journal of the National Association for Bilingual Education* 37(1): 6–23.

Vertovec, Steven. 2005. Opinion: Super-diversity revealed. *BBC News*, September 20.

———. 2007. Super-diversity and its implications. *Ethnic and Racial Studies* 30(6): 1024–1054.

Weber, Jean-Jacques. 2014. *Flexible multilingual education: Putting children's needs first*. Abingdon: Multilingual Matters.

Wei, Li. 2011. Moment analysis and translanguaging space: Discursive construction of identities by multilingual Chinese youth in Britain. *Journal of Pragmatics* 43(5): 1222–1235.

Welsh Government. 2016. *Population estimates.* https://statswales.wales.gov.uk/Catalogue/Population-and-Migration/Population/Estimates/Local-Authority/populationestimates-by-localauthority-year. Accessed May 2016.

Welsh Government, and Welsh Language Commissioner. 2015. *Welsh language use in Wales 2013–15.* http://gov.wales/docs/statistics/2016/160301-welsh-language-use-in-wales-2013-15-en.pdf. Accessed May 2016.

Williams, Cen. 1994. *Arfarniad o ddulliau dysgu ac addysgu yng nghyd-destun addysg uwchradd ddwyieithog* [An evaluation of teaching and learning methods in the context of bilingual secondary education] (Unpublished PhD thesis). University of Wales, Bangor, UK.

Zhang, Hong, and Brian Hok-Shing Chan. 2015. Translanguaging in multimodal Macao posters: Flexible versus separate multilingualism. *International Journal of Bilingualism*: 1–23 doi: 10.1177/1367006915594691.

Index

Note: Page number followed by 'n' refers to notes

© The Author(s) 2016

M. Durham, J. Morris (eds.), *Sociolinguistics in Wales*,
DOI 10.1057/978-1-137-52897-1